ALERTA

A Multicultural, Bilingual Approach to Teaching Young Children

**Leslie R. Williams and Yvonne De Gaetano
with the ALERTA Staff**

Institute for Urban and Minority Education
Teachers College, Columbia University

Addison-Wesley Publishing Company
Menlo Park, California   Reading, Massachusetts
London   Amsterdam   Don Mills, Ontario   Sydney

Acknowledgments

ALERTA's developers wish to give special acknowledgment to the staff and parents of the Manhattan, Dewitt, and Trabajamos Head Start Centers who provided invaluable assistance from 1976 to 1980 in the design and refinement of the ALERTA program.

We also wish to thank the many other people who helped us prepare this source book. Recognition is due to George A. Coleman, Carol Camarillo, and Myrtle Gaynor for the time they generously gave to the project. We gratefully acknowledge Donna Marie Chandler for her help in the creation of learning materials from photographs, Carmen A. Jiménez for her analysis and testing of training designs, Beryle Banfield for her helpful and perceptive reading of an early version of the manuscript, Judith Lesch for her synthesis of research on the psychomotor development of young children, and Lillian Carino and Orelda Hicks for their diligence in the typing of the manuscript.

Particular thanks are given to Soledad Arenas, of the United States Administration for Children, Youth and Families, without whose wisdom and foresight this project would not have been initiated. Thanks also go to Edmund W. Gordon for creating the environment within which the project was created, the Institute for Urban and Minority Education at Teachers College, Columbia University.

The ALERTA Multicultural Bilingual Preschool Curriculum Development Project at the Institute for Urban and Minority Education at Teachers College, Columbia University was funded from 1976–1979 through the Administration for Children, Youth and Families' Contract No. 005-76-1164, and from 1979–1980 through the same agency's Contract No. 005-79-1024 as part of the Head Start Strategy for Spanish-Speaking Children (Soledad Arenas, Project Officer). Since the autumn of 1980, the curriculum has continued to be revised and refined through the work of some of the original curriculum developers at Teachers College.

This book is published by the Addison-Wesley INNOVATIVE DIVISION.

Design by Victoria Ann Philp

Illustrations by Jane McCreary

ISBN 0-201-20092-9

ABCDEFGHIJKL-ML-8987654

The ALERTA Project Staff

Institute for Urban and Minority Education
Teachers College, Columbia University

Directors

Charles C. Harrington and Leslie R. Williams (Co-Directors), 1976–1979
Leslie R. Williams (Executive Director) 1979–1980
Yvonne De Gaetano and Leila R. Arjona (Co-Directors) 1979–1980

Associate Director

Iris R. Sutherland, 1976–78

Curriculum Specialist

Harriet K. Cuffaro, 1976–77

Project Associates

Ada Anglada, 1976–77
Regina de Assís, 1976–78
Carmen Iris Garcia Crosby, 1976–79
Deborah Allen, 1977–78
Leila R. Arjona, 1978–79
Yvonne De Gaetano, 1978–79
Norma Sinnette, 1978–79

Sociolinguists/Program Evaluators

William G. Milán, 1976–77
Gerald Murray, 1977–79
Sonia Orrico, 1978–79

Illustrator

Karen Heller, 1976–80

Editor

Georganne Chapin, 1977–79

Translator

Carlos Dominicci, 1978–79

To

Nino De Gaetano

YDG

and

David H. Williams

LRW

CONTENTS

FOREWORD

Recently in the United States, multicultural education and bilingual education have assumed a new importance in the minds of some educators searching for ways to provide educational programs of quality appropriate for all segments of the population. Presumably you are reading this book now because you too are looking for ways of strengthening your own program, making it work to the best advantage of the children in it. We welcome you to the rank of seekers!

In ALERTA, you will find one approach to a multicultural bilingual curriculum for young children. ALERTA is designed for use by Head Start and day-care staff and parents, private nursery-school teachers and parents, public school prekindergarten or kindergarten teachers and parents, or any other group involved in the teaching of young children. As the curriculum is more than a collection of learning activities, a certain amount of explanation must be given in order to make clear how this source book may be used. We urge you, therefore, to read Chapters One and Two and think about that introductory material before you turn to the sections on the rationale for, and implementation of, each part of the program.

It is the purpose of this source book to present you with a way of designing a program to reflect and use as vehicles for learning the collected experiences of the children within it. The overall aim of our effort and yours is to build upon the knowledge and skills the children bring to school so that they can continue to learn with joy and a genuine feeling of self-worth.

The curriculum presented here was developed through the interaction of a team of teachers, parents, early childhood educators, anthropologists, sociolinguists, and curriculum specialists with three- and four-year-old children in preexisting Head Start centers operating in communities across the United States. When the ALERTA curriculum project was founded in 1976, the developers did not have a preconceived idea of the final product. Instead of working from already established program plans, they spent three years visiting cooperating Head Start Centers, observing the children at work, meeting with the teachers and parents of those children, walking in the communities where the centers were located, and noting the thousands of details that make up people's day-to-day lives.

During this period, the developers reviewed existing early childhood programs, examined the child development literature, looked closely at recent anthropological descriptions of the culturally diverse populations the project would serve, and gathered extensive samples of the language of adults and children in the participating communities. Implications drawn from study and reflection were regularly supplemented by direct contact with members of the community who had insights of their own to add to the curriculum design.

A unique feature of the curriculum development process was that each person working on the developer team was recognized to have a perspective stemming from past training and present sensitivities. For that reason, not everyone was involved in the same tasks, but everyone's contribution was considered equally important. For example, one of the anthropology students associated with the project elected to have a haircut in a barbershop near one of the participating Head Start Centers. He listened carefully to the conversations around him; when one of the other customers mentioned his family, the student asked whether any children of that family were enrolled in the nearby Head Start program. That question brought an enthusiastic response and a spontaneous evaluation of the Head Start Center's success in promoting children's early learning. Comments from others present revealed perspectives that the student could see had a direct bearing on the design of the preschool curriculum—a view of early childhood as a time when memories were made that could influence a person's attitudes and actions for the rest of his or her life. At a subsequent staff meeting, the student offered that perception as one of the possible deep structures that could influence eventual choice of content for the curriculum.

Such insights accumulated through careful observation of the actual workings of communities were coupled with extended contact with children and frequent meetings with the children's teachers and parents. At one such meeting, the developers raised the notion of early memories; parents and teachers alike began to recollect games, songs, stories, and rhymes from their childhoods that had powerful, positive associations for them. They explored the relationship of use of such activities to the learning goals they wished to attain with the children and found that many of the traditional games and songs were excellent avenues for teaching and learning. The result of their discussion was the beginning of an activities file for the project, a collection of resources drawn directly from the children's cultures that could be used in designing learning activities.

The process used to develop ALERTA highlights the definition of *curriculum* that the developers brought to the project. In the past when teachers and educators have talked about curriculum, many have made the assumption that what goes on in school can be separated from the remainder of a child's life and made narrow in focus (concentrating only on academic skills, for example), without any effect on the quality or rate of a child's total learning. ALERTA's developers questioned that assumption. Young children generally spend less than one-third of their waking hours in a school setting. The remainder of their time is spent at home or in the larger community, where they are constantly learning and growing in capability. If the school does not recognize that important experience, it runs the risk of being disconnected from the business of life in the children's minds and therefore having a very limited impact.

The ALERTA developers saw that, in the larger sense, a curriculum is everything that goes on in a child's life. Such a definition implies that a curriculum cannot be put once and for all into one specific set of activities but must be the continuing creation of teachers, parents, and community members who observe, draw from, and build upon the children's actual world. This notion underlies the approach taken in this source book.

The children and families who participated in the first years of ALERTA's development presently live in New York City and come from varying backgrounds. The original group of families to use the program included people from the Dominican Republic, Puerto Rico, Ecuador, Honduras, the United States (southern rural and northern urban African-American), the English-speaking Caribbean, and West Africa. Examples used in this text largely reflect elements of the cultures and languages (English and Spanish) of those populations. It is important to understand, however, that the examples could just as easily come from any other cultural or linguistic group. ALERTA can be used in any part of the world with any group of people. It works equally well in North America, for example, with Cambodian children, Russian Jewish immigrants, French-Canadians, Vietnamese children, New Englanders, Native Americans, and children of German-American parentage living in the rural Midwest of the United States. In fact, the essence of ALERTA is that the curriculum content is derived from observations of children in the context of their cultures and communities. At present ALERTA is being used by urban populations and by rural groups, from northern Maine to Florida, throughout the Midwest, in the Southwest, and in California and Alaska.

For full development of a second language in English-speaking as well as non-English-speaking children, it is recommended that 50 percent or more of the children be speakers of a language other than English and that from 30 to 50 percent speak English as their first language. The bilingual component of ALERTA can, however, be used without specific percentages of children being present. English-speaking children in those circumstances will not be expected to become fully bilingual. The curriculum may also be used simply as a multicultural approach, without the bilingual component.

It should be noted that the recent idea of multicultural, bilingual programs in schools for young children has brought with it some misunderstandings about how such programs are developed. In workshops or other meetings one frequently hears discussions that seem to imply that a translation of any existing program into a second language will meet the need for bilingualism; in visits to many existing "multicultural" programs, you can see evidence of a simple "icing-on-the-cake" approach in which ethnically oriented cooking experiences or dances particular to the cultures represented are attached to an already existing program. Such an approach ignores the complexity of the issues that must be addressed in genuine attempts at multicultural, bilingual early childhood education.

The program described in this book rejects the notion that bilingual perspectives or perspectives that are multicultural are simple additions to a preconceived program. Instead, it maintains that the development of such perspectives pervades the total process of human growth and development. This being so, multiculturalism and bilingualism must be interwoven with the entire structure of the program in order to have real meaning for the persons—children or adults—participating in it.

CHAPTER ONE

An Introduction to the ALERTA Program

Early one morning a visitor walked into an early childhood center located in the heart of a large city on the eastern seaboard of the United States. Signs on the door in English and in Spanish made use of children's art to direct him to the office of the program administrators and to invite him to visit the classrooms. As he walked down the hall, his eyes were drawn to three large collage murals that appeared to have been made by adults in the center. One depicted the neighborhood where the center was located and was bright with storefronts, advertising, and vehicles of all kinds. The center stood out as an active and important point of reference among the other buildings. Another mural appeared to illustrate a neighborhood in a tropical climate. Here the dominant impression was one of low buildings, trees, grass, and flowers. People moved among the vibrant plants toward beaches or through a marketplace where they bought fruits and vegetables. The third mural looked like a suburban community. Houses of several types lined a curved drive leading to a shopping mall.

The visitor turned a corner and walked past a room with an open door. A quick glance into the room showed that women and men were using it to work on projects of some kind. Two people in one corner were cutting out shapes that appeared to be puzzles. Several people were meeting around a table covered with lengths and pieces of cloth. Now and then they referred to patterns tacked on the wall in front of them. The room as a whole was cheerful. Posters representing several countries were on the walls, and comfortable chairs were grouped around a library corner where materials for both children and adults were displayed on shelves.

Continuing down the hall, the visitor passed two classrooms. In one, young children were selecting materials from various areas of the room to work with on their own. A small group was gathered on a rug around one of the teachers, who was conversing with the children about materials for the construction of kites. Each area of the room appeared to be clearly defined and was decorated with the children's productions, photographs of the neighborhood, and other illustrations related to the work of that section. Each area also contained items representative of unique characteristics of the cultural groups present. In the second classroom, most of the children were gathered in a circle and were moving with their teachers through the steps of a game. A chorus of "Matarile, Rile, Ron" followed the visitor as he reached the director's office, knocked, and went in.

On the same morning in the rural Midwest, two women walked up the steps of a community building located at the edge of a small town. Standing on the porch, they could look back at an almost limitless stretch of plains, rolling gently into purples and lavenders in the distance. Here and there the expanse was broken by a butte or a small collection of ranch buildings. The community building contained an early childhood center, and the two women were nutritionists from the extension service who were visiting at the invitation of the parents of the children attending the program.

The parent coordinator came out to meet them and ushered them toward the meeting hall where they would be doing their presentation. On the way, they also passed classrooms filled with busy young children. They caught a glimpse of children in one area constructing a large cattle ranch out of blocks and wooden "people-pieces." In another area, an elderly visitor sat with four children on a *couch. She was singing an old Native American song and illustrating its meaning through motion. The children were watching closely and following her movements. On a low table at one end of the room, a half-finished model of the town was drying in the sun; and in a nearby corner, five children worked with their teacher to sort the collection of leaves, sticks, and seeds they had gathered on a recent walk. The children spoke easily as they worked, describing the groups they were forming and the basis for their selection of materials for each group.*

Staff and parents at both of these early childhood centers were using the ALERTA Program, a multicultural, bilingual approach to the education of young children. *Alerta* is a Spanish word that can be understood to mean "heightened awareness." It is also an acronym for the phrase *A Learning Environment Responsive to All.* The acronym expresses the fundamental idea behind the program's approach; namely, that education will have its greatest effect if it is designed to make use of the knowledge, skills, and accumulated experience that each child brings to the classroom. ALERTA is a process for acknowledging and integrating both the developmental characteristics and the cultural/environmental backgrounds of children into all aspects of their early learning so that new capabilities will be built upon old. A primary concern of the program is continuity of experience. The developers of ALERTA are convinced that movement from the known to the unknown is always the most effective way to teach. Moreover, the developers believe that respect for and constructive use of the cultural diversity that has always been a hallmark of the United States can lead to increased cooperation among the various groups that make up our society. Understanding often leads to appreciation and appreciation to mutual help. Through the exchange, everyone involved grows and becomes richer in spirit, as individuals and as a people.

What Is the ALERTA Process?

Teachers wishing to use ALERTA should begin with a fundamental understanding of the most basic characteristics of the curriculum process. ALERTA is first and foremost a *child-centered* curriculum, grounded in a firm understanding of child development and respect for the individual. With deep awareness of the fact that every individual belongs to a group with a heritage and past, ALERTA draws from and builds upon the traditions that the child brings to the center as well as upon the individual's current experience in the community where he or she lives. Another basic characteristic of the program, therefore, is that it is *multicultural* in approach.

For areas of the country where there is a large percentage of people who speak a language other than English, ALERTA also advocates a *bilingual* approach to learning. In such a circumstance, bilingualism is encouraged for *all* children (including native speakers of English), through the continued development of the first language as a foundation for systematic acquisition of the second.

ALERTA encourages teachers to form partnerships with parents of the children they serve, with other teachers, with administrators, with community resources, and with the children themselves in order to identify and make use of the children's capabilities in the introduction of new learning activities. Through such partnerships, teachers first collect information on the developmental characteristics and cultural/environmental experience of the children and then select and arrange materials in their learning spaces (classrooms, hallways, offices, and kitchens) to reflect the present cultures of all the children enrolled in their center. In order to furnish their center with appropriate materials, teachers carefully review commercially available books, table toys, games, and accessories to identify those that accurately represent aspects of the collected experience of their children. When commerical materials do not accurately illustrate aspects of the cultures of the families, teachers draw upon community resources to construct the materials needed.

As the total center comes more and more to reflect the populations it serves, teachers observe the children's use of the materials and equipment and subsequently note the interests, knowledge, and skills the children display. The teachers then use their observations as the foundations for designing new learning activities for children, always building the introduction of new concepts on those that the children have already acquired. In each new activity, teachers make a conscious attempt to use materials representing aspects of the cultures of individual children and/or the neighborhoods where they live.

Some of these learning activities may be conducted in large groups, particularly if they involve music or games. Most of the learning activities, however, are done in small clusters (four to six children). They may be carried out in any area of the room or outside of the classroom, if that is appropriate to the intent of an activity. According to teachers' observations of individual children, the learning activities may be designed for linguistic, cognitive, psychomotor, or socioemotional growth, or some combination of these. Sometimes the activities are done under the direction of a teacher; at other times, children pursue the activities independently.

Teachers using the bilingual component of ALERTA employ teaching strategies to aid the children in second language acquisition. All ALERTA teachers use strategies that foster language development in general, as continued growth in the use of language is understood to be closely connected to the children's development in other domains.

The process described here is a continuous one. Teachers using ALERTA soon discover that each step they take to put the program in place leads naturally to another one, just as they find that it also has implications for steps already accomplished. For example, a teacher who has observed a child's fascination with trailer trucks may design a small group activity in which the children construct their versions of "rigs" at the woodworking table. The children's trucks may then be placed in the block area, where their presence may require the addition of such accessories as road-building materials. Children's play with the trucks may lead to their wanting to look at books about trucks, dress up as truck drivers, or produce goods for the trucks to carry. As the teacher adds such materials to the classroom environment, additional opportunities are created for the children to reveal more about their interests and developmental levels, and the teacher has more material to use in designing new learning activities.

What Does ALERTA Expect to Accomplish?

ALERTA has four primary goals. It is expected that use of the curriculum will:

1. Promote each child's appreciation of herself or himself as a person capable of a wide variety of intellectual and physical activities.

2. Encourage the children's positive recognition of the ways people from various groups are the same as well as the ways they are different from one another.

3. Foster an active curiosity in young children about the events that make up their lives so that they are led by their interest to engage with and successfully solve problems.

4. Develop in the children specific attitudes and skills that will help them deal successfully with school in today's culturally plural society.

Teachers using the bilingual component of ALERTA have two additional goals. For them, use of the curriculum will:

5. Promote the continued development of the children's first language in all aspects of their learning.

6. Effect the acquisition of a second language in all the children participating in the program.

The processes through which teachers develop specific methods for attaining each of the previously mentioned goals are described in detail in subsequent chapters of this source book. For the purposes of this introduction, however, persons wanting to use the curriculum should think about the circumstances that contribute to meeting ALERTA's goals.

The ALERTA Curriculum Model can be used in private nursery schools, public school kindergartens, day-care centers, Head Start programs, or any other type of early childhood program. The process that ALERTA represents can in fact be used at any educational level. When the model is adopted by a Head Start Center, two assumptions are made regarding the centers in which its adoption is desired.

First, it is assumed that the basic premises and goals of Head Start are accepted. Second, it is assumed that the center is implementing the performance standards for Head Start programs set out by the Administration for Children, Youth and Families. The basic premises underlying Head Start's approach for early learning are now held in common by many early childhood programs throughout the country. They are:

–All children share certain needs and can benefit from a comprehensive, interdisciplinary program that will both foster development and remedy problems through a broad range of services. Within this comprehensive program, careful planning should be done to meet the individual differences and needs of the children.

–The child's entire family as well as the community should be involved as direct participants in the program. Such involvement is seen as necessary in order to maximize the strengths and make use of the unique experiences of each child in learning.

–Parents should be assisted to increase their knowledge, understanding, and skills in child development.

–The program should meet the special needs of handicapped children admitted to it.

–Program activities should be carried out in a manner to avoid sex-role stereotyping as well as racial and ethnic stereotyping.[1]

From these underlying premises have come eight Head Start Program Goals.

1. Create a comprehensive, interdisciplinary program to foster development.

2. Involve family and community.

3. Establish a greater degree of social competence in young children; i.e., "the child's everyday effectiveness in dealing with both present environment and later responsibilities in school and life." In considering social competence, there is to be an "interrelatedness of physical and mental health and attention to nutritional needs."

4. Encourage self-confidence, spontaneity, curiosity, and self-discipline, which will assist in social and emotional health.

5. Enhance mental processes and skills with particular attention given to conceptual and communication skills.

6. Establish patterns and expectations of success for the child and create a climate of confidence for the present and the future.

7. Increase the ability of child and family to relate to each other and to other persons.

8. Enhance a sense of dignity and the self-worth of child and family.[2]

ALERTA is an expansion of those premises and goals into a particular approach in the actual operation of an early childhood program with a strong multicultural, bilingual focus. To get the maximum benefit from use of ALERTA, it is expected that persons choosing it will be implementing the Head Start Program Performance Standards in their center, or if the center is not a Head Start program, is operating at a level consistent with the expectations of the performance standards.

[1]*Head Start Program Performance Standards,* OCD Notice N-30-364-4 (July 1975), pp. 1–3. Washington, D.C.: U.S. Government Printing Office.

In addition, ALERTA makes the following recommendations.

1. The parent group and the sponsoring board of the center should agree with and support the program, as shown by their active participation in its adoption.

2. The center staff at all levels should agree with and support the program, as shown by their active community involvement and participation in its adoption.

3. Staff and parents should show interest in and sensitivity toward the various cultures found in their community.

4. Staff and parents should be willing to learn about cultures, including their own, through a series of special workshops or other types of training.

5. When using ALERTA's bilingual component, at least 50 percent of the classroom staff must be fluently bilingual (Spanish/English).[3] This 50 percent must be proficient in reading, writing, understanding, and speaking Spanish[4] and English.

6. For full use of the bilingual component, at least 50 percent of the children in the classroom must be bilingual or monolingual in a language other than English. If the stated percentage of such children does not exist at the center, then the aim of bilingual development for all the children at the center will have to be modified to reflect a more realistic goal.

[2]*Ibid.*
[3]Or in English and another language spoken by 50 percent of the children.
[4]Or the other language spoken by 50 percent of the children.

How to Use This Source Book

For the convenience of persons using ALERTA, the process of implementing the curriculum has been divided into nine levels.

Level 1   Developing Partnerships in the Use of ALERTA

Level 2   Discovering the Cultures in Your Classroom

Level 3   Identifying and Using Community Resources

Level 4   Preparing a Multicultural, Bilingual Learning Environment for Young Children

Level 5   Observing Children's Interests, Developmental Levels, and Language Use

Level 6   Planning for Learning across All Domains

Level 7   Integrating Strategies for Language Learning throughout the Program

Level 8   Designing Opportunities for Learning

Level 9   Assessing Your Progress in the Use of ALERTA

Movement through one level at a time enables staff systematically and logically to put into place the different parts of the total program. Each level of implementation is presented in the chapters that follow, with explanation of its rationale and the materials involved in carrying that level out.

In each section there is also a series of exercises to help teachers and others become skilled in the use of the various levels. Many of the exercises have accompanying worksheets, charts, or forms to use in practicing the skill addressed. Samples of the forms are included in the text. The full-sized versions are placed at the end of the book, with perforations for easy removal when each exercise is being done. By working through the exercises, staff and interested parents will see how the nine levels build on one another and how the curriculum that results is adapted to the experiences of the children in their own community. Before exploring the nine levels, however, it is important to take a closer look at the three basic characteristics of ALERTA and how they are woven throughout the program.

CHAPTER TWO

ALERTA: A Child-Centered, Multicultural, Bilingual Approach to Early Learning

ALERTA's approach to early learning is a process that builds on a foundation of knowledge about the young child. That knowledge has three aspects: awareness of the interests and developmental patterns characteristic of young children; awareness of the specific knowledge that the children have already acquired through membership in a particular family, cultural group, and community; and awareness of young children's growing capacity to use language to describe and relate to their world. Persons using ALERTA need to be clear about each of those aspects, understanding what the terms *child-centered, multicultural,* and *bilingual* mean from the ALERTA point of view, and understanding how awareness of these three aspects of the program affects all that the teacher does in the course of a typical day. This chapter of the source book explains each term and gives examples of its application in ALERTA.

What is Child-Centered Teaching in ALERTA?

Because early childhood teachers care deeply about young children, most tend to believe that they are child-centered in orientation. In fact, however, their training may not have had a child-centered point of view, and consequently, their teaching style is not child-centered.

Over the years, there have been many programs to prepare teachers of young children. The most common approach to preparation has been to present the prospective teachers with methods courses, focusing on activities for children in the areas of, perhaps, language arts, mathematics, science, art, and music. Sometimes student teachers have been introduced to a series of units, sets of learning experiences already planned and developed for young children. The teacher's role in using the materials has been to follow the specified plan. In both these approaches to teacher preparation, the *teacher* is seen as the focus of activity in the classroom. It is the teacher who decides far in advance of meeting the children exactly what will be taught in the preschool, what the content will be, what activities will be used, and what sequence will be followed in the presentation. Classrooms such as these might be described as *teacher-centered.*

Other teacher educators and students of the development of young children, however, feel that young children learn more effectively if planning for them is based on observations of the children's skills. Those teacher educators present the principles of child development to their students and introduce them to techniques of child observation. They teach the prospective teachers to plan carefully for children's new learning by taking into account that which the children in their classroom already know. This type of planning encourages individualization, the designing of different activities for small groups of children with characteristics in common. It also encourages children to learn at their own pace instead of always working as part of a large group. Teachers who regularly use observations of the children's skills as a basis for planning oversee one type of child-centered program.

The term *child-centered* has also been understood to mean that teachers do not do any "real" planning at all. Instead, it is thought, teachers simply set out materials in the classroom, and the children spend the whole day in free play. The teacher does not teach but acts as a parent figure or a facilitator of the children's activity. This interpretation is exactly the opposite of a teacher-centered orientation. Here, the children make the decisions, and the teacher at all times follows the children's lead.

In ALERTA's approach to early learning a balance is sought between these two extremes. The adults in the classroom do plan very carefully. They set up the learning environment for the children, change that environment frequently enough to keep it stimulating, design specific learning activities for small clusters of children and for large groups as well, and interact with the children in deliberate ways to introduce them to new concepts or strengthen concepts already present. They do all of this, however, on the basis of frequent observations of both the children's interests and developmental levels (present skills).

Activities always reflect the life of the children themselves. In planning, the active learning characteristics of young children, their ways of processing information, their current interests, and the cultural traditions of their parents are all essential considerations. This is why ALERTA does not use a set of preplanned activities for teaching children. Instead, ALERTA prepares teachers to be child-centered in their thinking so that all their planning revolves around recognition of the strengths and dispositions children bring with them to the learning situation in the context of their multicultural environments.

**Types of
Child-Centered Classrooms**

ALERTA

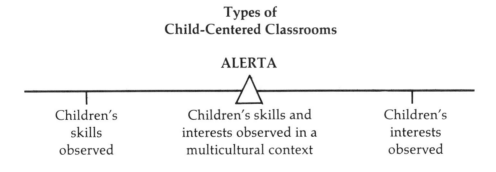

| Children's skills observed | Children's skills and interests observed in a multicultural context | Children's interests observed |

Child-Centered Planning

Child-centered planning in ALERTA thus has two dimensions. The first is that children's *interests* become a source of themes or topics that are used to help children connect sets of learning experiences. The second dimension is that teachers and parents need to be keenly aware of the *developmental levels* of the children so that activities and experiences can be designed for the children's present ways of understanding their world. It is crucial for teacher and parents to be tuned in to the children's world—their emotional world, their world of thinking, and their physical world. The interests that the children show become the keys to unlock these worlds.

Using Children's Interests

Before adults in the classroom can use the children's interest well, they have to find out what those interests really are. The best way to do that is to pay careful attention to what the children are saying and doing as they move from area to area during both child-initiated and adult-directed portions of the day. Frequently children will make spontaneous comments about something that has captured their imagination. For example, a child in the family corner who is reenacting the arrival of a new brother or sister at home might remark that "the baby looks funny, because it has no teeth." If other observations on the characteristics of babies follow from that child or from other children working in the area, it is a clue to observant adults that a set of experiences on the likenesses and differences between babies, children, and adults would be a good way of furthering the children's learning. The subject would be likely to hold the children's interest, and interest leads to a desire to find out more, to learn more, and to do more.

Children also make important and revealing comments when participating in activities that are being directed by adults. In one center, the teacher was introducing children to different ways that pineapple can be used in cooking. Just as the pineapple was put onto the table, one child said, "Ooo . . . Prickles! How do you peel a pineapple?" As the activity developed, the child had a chance first to guess how and then try out some of her suggestions.

In an activity the following week the teacher remembered the question the child had asked and designed other activities with materials that needed to be peeled or prepared before being used. The children once again had the chance to experiment with possible answers by trying different ways to solve the problem.

In both instances noted, present interests were used to bring about new learning. Using children's interests is also closely tied to creating a program that is multicultural in orientation. A later section of this chapter will illustrate how children's interests and culture are partners in ALERTA's approach. But first, consideration must be given to the characteristics of young children.

Understanding the Children's World

ALERTA accepts the evidence that young children have special ways of understanding the world around them and their relationship to it. Built into the foundations of ALERTA are two general ideas—first, that growth occurs as each child becomes more competent and therefore has the urge to think, feel, and act in more complex ways; and second, that the environment (including home, family, and community as well as the classroom setting) has a very strong influence on that process of growth. Because the environment is considered so important in a child's development, there is an emphasis on maintaining a close relationship between home and school. Continuity in a young child's experience is important for a smooth transition to the school setting and for the best possible growth and development of the individual. A look at the worlds of the child shows the strong role the environment plays in all aspects of children's development and learning.

The World of Feelings: Socioemotional Development

The world of feelings is very closely connected to a child's openness to new learning. Susan Isaacs, a British educator who designed programs based on child observations, has pointed out that an essential element in learning at any level is interest. People are most likely to be interested in their surroundings when they feel comfortable and unafraid, when given warm support, and when they regard themselves as capable and worthy beings. For young children, such a sense of well-being depends upon the feelings generated from their parents or caregivers in their homes. Continuity between the home and the school experience thus becomes crucial to effective learning and a path to healthy socioemotional development.

Moving from the safe world of the familiar to new experiences requires the extension of the trust one has for one's parents or caregivers to new people and new situations. Such trust tends to be generated when children enter a classroom where kindness, helpfulness, generosity, and respect for others are displayed. Young children learn in part through observation of the behavior of others and through imitation. In classrooms where such positive traits are consistently present, children will be likely to show the same traits, growing in understanding of themselves and of others.

The way one is treated by others can affect one's self-image. Both children and adults consider themselves worthy and capable when their cultural origins and family backgrounds are shown respect and when their contributions to society are recognized. A positive self-image leads children to attempt new or complex activities, with the result that they are likely to become increasingly competent.

The ALERTA program accepts the idea presented by Erik Erikson that children tend to go through a sequence of stages in their socioemotional development. In each stage, the child must face a problem to be resolved. In the first stage, for example, children must decide to trust or not trust others. The conclusion they come to depends on how others treat them. In the next stage, trusting children move to practice new skills on their own. (Teachers of two- to three-year-olds often hear them say, "I want to do it by myself!") The third stage centers on children's willingness to try new activities, even at the risk of not being able to master the new activity right away. Children at this stage who are successfully dealing with the problem initiate or select new activities to do on their own and stay with the work long enough to practice the new skills involved. They also spontaneously express interest in many facets of the world around them. This is the stage of development typical of most preschool children.

It can be seen that socioemotional development in young children has many sides (self-respect, belief in oneself as capable, willingness to try, and so on) that are related to each other and other areas of a child's growth. Development in the socioemotional domain is considered in ALERTA to be an important foundation that the children bring with them to school. It is also an outcome of the curriculum in the sense that existing feelings and ways of behaving may be expanded and built upon. Healthy socioemotional growth is at the heart of the educational effort.

Adults in ALERTA classrooms use their knowledge of general patterns in the socioemotional development of young children to provide a learning environment that encourages children to trust others, provide new skills, and initiate new activities. The adults know that their own behavior will be carefully observed and imitated by the children, so they interact with the children and with each other in ways that illustrate trust and respect. They plan activities that will encourage children to work both on their own and in groups, and they set aside portions of each day for activities that are child-initiated; that is, chosen and carried out by the children themselves. Throughout all of this activity, the adults remain aware that their roles are active ones as planners of learning experiences, as interactors with the children, and as observers and supporters of the children's rapid progress.

The World of Thinking:
Cognitive/Linguistic Development

By the time children reach preschool age, cognitive growth and language acquisition are so closely linked that separation of the two is virtually impossible. The development of both thinking and language skills appears to occur in an ordered way, with simpler skills forming the foundation for more complex ones. The way children see their world, experience it, and understand it may be different from the way adults do. Jean Piaget has suggested, for example, that young children tend to pay attention to only one aspect of an activity at a time. They may group objects by color or shape, for instance, but will not do both at the same time. They have trouble seeing someone else's point of view, being convinced that the world revolves around themselves. They may have difficulty in sorting out time sequences and cause/effect relationships. In addition, their thinking is strongly influenced by what they *see,* even if what they see is an illusion.

Most observers of the development of thinking and language skills in young children agree that the growth of intelligence is an active process. It depends not only on potentials inherited from the children's parents but also on the opportunities the children have to interact with a variety of things, people, and events in the first six years of their lives. It is important to understand that children do not simply receive impressions from the outside world. Instead their minds act upon the information they take in, organizing it to fit the existing structures of their minds, or, if that is not possible, creating new structures in their minds to contain the new information. More crucial than the information itself are the ways that children organize it, forming relationships between concepts and arranging them into more and more complex patterns in their minds.

Children follow many different processes as they continue to organize what they are learning. To name just a few, they distinguish and begin recognizing the different characteristics of objects through experimenting with them, grouping objects in different ways, and associating events with one another. In each case, ideas are most clearly formed

when children have a chance to handle the objects being explored or physically take part in an activity. Young children learn with their whole bodies—by touching, smelling, and tasting as well as by seeing, hearing, and moving in ways that let them discover the possibilities of the object or the event. It is very important in teaching young children that they be presented with as many opportunities as possible for active exploration in their total learning environment. This concept ought to remind adults who teach that all activities should be taught by moving from simple forms to more complex ones, from gross distinctions to finer ones, and from the concrete (real objects) to the abstract (pictures and words).

Children's understanding and acquisition of language is also directly affected by their experimentation with real objects and participation in events. It is much easier to recognize and talk about a mango after having seen, handled, and tasted a real mango. A picture of something that has never been experienced does not provide a complete idea of what the object is all about. Many young children appear to learn more easily when they are presented with real objects before they see pictures of them or have a discussion about them.

Awareness of the characteristics of young children's thinking is evident in ALERTA classrooms in the kinds of manipulative materials present and in the content of all learning activities. Each classroom contains a range of manipulative materials so that children can work at their own levels, where they will not become either frustrated or bored. In setting out materials for use in cluster work, the teaching adults pay careful attention to providing the right amount of cognitive discrepancy for individuals, presenting activities that are neither too simple nor too complex for the children. The materials present also encourage the children to practice many different kinds of thinking skills. Not only are there materials for sorting and for making constructions of various types but there are also materials for arranging in sequences; illustrating cause and effect relationships; and allowing the children to experiment with physical, mathematical, and aesthetic relationships.

Adults in the classroom also closely attend to the characteristics of young children's thinking in their choice of content for learning activities. They know that children will attend most closely to activities that reflect aspects of the children's lives. Objects and events that the children have experienced or observed in the context of the traditions of their families or community environments are incorporated into as many activities as possible. ALERTA teachers understand that use of familiar objects and events may favorably influence the extent to which young children reveal and exercise their emerging cognitive skills. In ALERTA classrooms, therefore, adults do not perform an activity while the children simply watch. Nor do adults use cultural content that most of the children have not directly or indirectly experienced. Instead children are actively engaged in all activities, extending their skills and concepts through interaction with a familiar world.

Finally, adults who teach in ALERTA classrooms recognize the distinctive features of young children's thought by linking language development with all other dimensions of the children's work. Language is never taught separately from other activities. Use of language by both children and adults becomes a living part of whatever activity is underway, whether it is in the block or art area, in a group activity, outdoors, or inside the classroom. Language is also regarded in ALERTA as an important aspect of a child's identity, a view that connects language with all areas of an individual's growth and development. More is said about this linkage in the discussion of ALERTA's bilingual approach to learning.

The World of Doing: Psychomotor Development

As children mature they form a relationship with space—the physical world in which they find themselves. One of the first tasks faced by very young children is that of separating themselves from their environment; that is, determining where their bodies end and the rest of the world begins. By the time children reach preschool, the formation of the concept of self in space is well underway but not necessarily complete. Three-and four-year-olds may still experience some difficulty in orienting themselves in various activities, integrating their movements into a whole, and defining a personal space—a space where they can work without interfering with the work of others.

It is common for early childhood programs to attend to the children's emerging capacities in this area by designing different activities to encourage "large motor" and "small motor" development. Particular attention is paid to exercise of the fine muscles in the hands in order to prepare the children for the tasks they will encounter in the first grade. Although this approach is useful in many ways, it is possible to make finer distinctions in observation of the ways young children relate to the space around them.

The psychomotor development of preschool children can be regarded, for example, as the growing capacity to control the use of one's entire body and the independent use of one's limbs *in relation to the physical environment.* Several categories of activities can be derived from these processes: use of the body as a whole while staying within a defined space, use of the body as a whole while moving through space, independent use of the limbs while staying in a defined space, and independent use of the limbs while moving the body through space. There may also be the category of controlling the body while the *space* around one is moving.

Examples make these distinctions clear. The first type of activity, using the body as a whole while staying within a defined space, can be illustrated by a child's riding a tricycle within a specified area. The child's total body—feet, limbs, hands—is engaged in operating the tricycle. Because so much concentration is going into making the tricycle work, the child sometimes has difficulty staying on course. Before the wanderer learns to control her vehicle she may interfere with the activities of other children in the area. Staying within bounds takes practice.

Use of the body as a whole while moving through space is seen in the chasing games loved by young children. It is also seen in such activities as carrying a pitcher of juice to the snack table. The child has to keep control over some circumstance such as avoiding obstacles or not spilling the juice while moving from place to place. The frequency of falls and accidents in these and similar situations shows the importance of opportunities for practice.

The third category, independent use of the limbs while staying in a defined space, covers the many table activities common to early childhood education centers. Older, more mature children are able to stay seated at tables at an activity for relatively long periods of time. Young children, however, may have energy flows that make sustained sitting difficult, even for a very interesting activity. Sometimes adults interpret the restlessness they see as due to "short attention spans." There may be more to it than that, however. The muscles of young children may not yet be fully enough developed to allow for long periods of controlled immobility. Also, the concentration required for fine motor activities may build a tension in the children that needs release.

Independent use of the limbs while moving the body through space is seen in children's imitation of such sports as soccer and basketball. In those sports, players must "shoot" accurately while running or jumping. Young children are often not yet coordinated enough to accurately replicate the movements of the game, but that does not

stop their attempts to reproduce what they have seen. With activities that encourage such movements, their skill increases.

The final category, controlling the body while the space around one is moving, is well illustrated in children's attempts to stand upright in a moving bus. It is also the skill needed to ride a horse, hang onto a playground merry-go-round, or balance on a seesaw.

In practice, each described category of psychomotor development is tied to both the cognitive/linguistic and socioemotional development of children. The way children use their bodies in games or other activities requiring physical skill does in many instances reflect exercise of their thinking skills. The body is also frequently used to express meaning or emotional response through culturally determined gestures. Children come to the learning situation with whole repertories of possible facial expressions, hand movements, and bodily stances that vary in meaning across cultures. Such expressions and gestures are so powerful as to almost constitute languages in themselves, and they offer additional keys to past and present cultural influences on the children.

ALERTA classrooms are responsive to the psychomotor needs of young children in their arrangement; in the scheduling and range of activities offered; and in the use of culturally appropriate games, dances, and other forms of play. Typically, an ALERTA classroom is arranged into well-defined interest areas such as the block building area, housekeeping area, and art area. Clear demarcation of the areas through placement of furniture and shelves or child-sized room dividers encourages the children to identify particular spaces with particular types of activity. Although the children do move freely from area to area, as they work they come to absorb the meaning of defined space and learn to regulate their own activity so that they do not encroach upon that of other people.

Adults who teach in ALERTA classrooms arrange their daily schedules to alternate quiet periods with active ones. They also insure that the activities they plan for the quiet periods last no longer than appropriate for the children's tolerance of constraint. ALERTA teachers also do not leave all outdoor or gym activities to the children's own devising but regularly plan games that require responses across the various categories of movement discussed previously. As much as possible, ALERTA children are encouraged to maintain their learning environment themselves. Through serving their own food, cleaning the classroom areas, caring for plants and animals, and arranging the works they produce, they have additional opportunities to refine their psychomotor skills.

Finally, ALERTA teachers are sensitive to the variation in body movements used to convey meaning. Whenever appropriate they incorporate such expressions and gestures into their strategies for teaching. Through observation of their teachers, the children come to develop multiple body language repertoires that they can apply according to the circumstance of their use.

These brief overviews of child-development principles used in ALERTA illustrate some of the foundations that make this curriculum child-centered. You will have many opportunities to practice the use of these concepts in the chapters to follow. Equally important for understanding ALERTA's overall approach is its definition of education that is multicultural. The next section explores the meaning of that term to show its close connections with a child-centered perspective.

A Multicultural Perspective on Early Education

A program with a multicultural perspective recognizes that children bring with them to the learning situation more than the developmental characteristics discussed briefly in the previous section. They also bring specific knowledge and skills they have acquired through membership in a particular group of people. The collected knowledge and skills of the group to which the children belong is the culture of that group.

All groups, and consequently, all children, have a culture. One way to define culture is to say that it is everything that makes up the life of a people—the objects they use in daily life, the ways they conduct their lives (that is, their customs), and the deep-seated and often unconscious reasons they do things in a certain way (their values). Culture is the memory of a group of people—their history and the traditions rooted in their past. But just as importantly, culture is also all the detail that makes up their present lives.

Cultures change. They do not stay frozen in time. Throughout history the cultures of all peoples have been changing to respond to whatever new circumstances arise from generation to generation. The fact that cultures are dynamic, they they change over time, is often not well understood by persons attempting to incorporate culture into an educational program. Those educators tend to focus on the objects people used to use in their daily lives and on the colorful customs of an earlier age in the characterization of "the Japanese," "the Irish," "the Greeks," "the Sioux," "Vietnamese," "Chicanos," "Puerto Ricans," or "Black Americans." Although this view does have a certain usefulness in pointing out that various groups have developed different sets of customs to meet the common demands of life, it leaves out the rich textures of variation of custom within groups of people and the continuing creation of custom as an act of living.

This view also leaves out recognition of the fact that environment profoundly influences the direction in which cultures grow. When people leave the place of their origin and settle in another land, their customs do not necessarily develop in the same ways as do those of the people who remained in the homeland. The culture of Portuguese people in Lisbon today, for example, is not the same as the culture of Portuguese people who emigrated to Rhode Island. The two cultures have a common origin, but they are no longer one and the same.

In times past, many groups of people lived in relative isolation from other cultural groups. Lack of contact with other people resulted in members of particular groups having only one culture—the one into which they were born and which served to regulate the business of their lives. In today's complex world, however, most groups live side-by-side with people of other cultures and are influenced by that contact.

Almost all children in the United States today come into direct contact with members of cultures different from those of their parents, and many children have more than one culture represented in their immediate families. The result of this circumstance is that the children are likely to learn more than one culture and, with practice, can change their responses and behaviors to suit the deep-seated expectations of those cultures.

Even when different cultures do not appear to be represented in a single family, its members often find differences between generations in customs and expectations for behavior. Children also respond to these variations by developing sets of behaviors that can be situationally applied. For example, children may speak and act one way in the presence of their grandparents and another way when playing with other children. If this ability to adapt is nurtured, it stays with us into adulthood.

In brief, then, most of us are faced with the fact that, in different aspects of our lives, different demands are placed upon us. Interactions at home often require a set of behaviors different from those required in interactions at work. Children can learn at an early age to respond to cultural expectations. They can learn that their parents (or, for that matter, by each parent) and their peers expect different behaviors. Adaptation to different social relationships and situations may constitute part of the process of an individual's cultural learning.

Preschool programs that focus on the positive, adaptive value of multiculturalism will incorporate the richness of experience brought by the individual children, thereby enabling all the children to increase their vision of and ability to adapt to this complex world. The opportunity to continue to develop flexibility of thought and understanding of the ways of others is a gift that a multicultural preschool can offer its participants.

How Do ALERTA Teachers Make Use of Cultures?

In planning for a program (or classroom) that is multicultural, ALERTA teachers begin by accepting each child as an individual who is also a member of one or more cultural groups. ALERTA teachers encourage children and assure them (through their behavior) that the children's cultural backgrounds are respected and valued.

Recognition of many cultures in a preschool classroom calls for planning so that every child in every classroom will have a healthy acceptance of self and a positive awareness of others. Teaching adults must make sure, however, that in enhancing and encouraging the children's self-identity, self-acceptance, and cultural diversity, opportunities are also provided for the children to discover and discuss the many ways in which all people are alike. It is important that teachers and parents do not neglect to provide a balance by highlighting the important similarities in human cultures and the relationships among groups.

The role that staff members are called upon to carry out in multicultural classrooms is a formidable one and must be enacted well if the purposes of the program are to be met. Pivotal to the total climate, the feeling, and the flavor of the learning environment are the staff's attitudes and values. Teachers and participating parents need to come to grips first with their personal feelings and beliefs about their own culture(s), their self-identity and level of self-esteem, and then with their feelings and beliefs about the cultures of other people. Self-examination is important, because for good or ill, young children see their teachers not only as representative of the adult world but, in many cases, as models or mirrors through which they see themselves.

After self-examination, ALERTA teachers develop keen observational skills that allow them to look at the children, their families, and the community without the cultural and racial stereotyping that so often characterizes how we unintentionally "see." It is very important to realize that we all grow up inadvertently picking up a variety of attitudes and ideas that are negative to groups different from the one to which we belong and that we often learn negative feelings about our own group as well. The reasons for this are complex and have to do with the social, economic, and political realities with which we live. The point here is that once we as teachers realize that in order to carry out a program that is multicultural we must begin by accepting our own culture and the cultures around us, we become truly free to enjoy the beauty, excitement, and joy that all cultures possess.

The information that ALERTA teachers glean from observations of the community in which their school or center is located and from guided study of the specific detail of the cultures represented in their classroom is subsequently used in a variety of ways. Culture—past and present—will be reflected in the classrooms and throughout the entire center or school in displays of attractive and fresh pictures, bulletin boards, exhibits, wall hangings, and other decoration. Not only will reflections of the children's cultures permeate the total learning environment but they will also be embedded in learning materials and activities. ALERTA teachers extract the cultural content they have observed to excite the children's interest and incorporate it into materials they design and create. They also select developmentally appropriate aspects of the cultures to use in activities that do not rely on manipulative materials, such as storytelling, role plays, games, and songs. The important thing to understand is that culture is never taught separately in an ALERTA classroom. There is no "culture time" or "culture corner." Cultural content is interwoven into the tapestry of living and learning so that children and adults in the program see it as it is—variations in the expression of human life.

As a person who wishes to use ALERTA's approach, you will be presented with exercises designed to promote self-examination of your attitudes toward and understanding of the cultures with which you have contact. Your engagement with such experiences, whether you are working singly or in a group, will be fundamental to successful use of ALERTA. The succeeding chapters suggest a variety of ways for you to acquire and use as a vehicle for teaching specific information on the cultures of the children you teach. There will also be opportunities for you to explore more fully the cultures that you yourself represent, to heighten your own awareness of the impact of culture on learning.

Part of any culture is its language. In some parts of the United States, languages other than English are spoken and remain a vital part of the identity of various groups.

ALERTA's understanding of the phenomena of language development and bilingualism and their implications for ALERTA's teaching strategies are discussed next.

Language Development and Bilingualism

The development of language (or languages) does not occur in isolation, without connection to other aspects of a person's life, but is part of the total cultural experience of the individual. Language learning is a social phenomenon that develops in the context of community life. It is shaped by culturally defined rules for using it and by the specific social situations in which it is applied. Language is intimately bound with the cognitive and socioemotional development of children. They must learn to deal at the same time with the underlying rules of language and the different ways language can be used according to the social setting. As has been mentioned, language is also tied to children's physical development in the sense that people communicate nonverbally through culturally specific sets of motions.

Language is the medium through which a person communicates his or her joys, doubts, successes, and sorrows. The source of these intimate emotions is most frequently the home, and consequently, the language of the home comes to have powerful affective associations for the individual. The child's first definition of self comes to him or her through the home and through the language used there. If children are pressured to abandon the language of their home, it is likely that their self-image will suffer—a situation that may have long-range impact on their learning power.

If, on the other hand, the home language is respected and nurtured in educational settings, there is a greater chance that the child will remain receptive to learning. The home language will be available for use as a foundation for continued concept development and will provide an avenue for learning a second language that may be needed for the child's access to the larger society.

A substantial number of the world's children today are raised bilingually, because their societies recognize that communication among nations is critical for their economic and political survival. Only in a few outposts of the world have the advantages of bilingualism been ignored. In the United States it continues to be essential for children of linguistic minorities to learn English so that they can enter the work force. Minority group members have traditionally understood that facility in English has direct bearing on their children's social and occupational advancement. Only recently, however, many North Americans who are native speakers of English have also come to appreciate the advantages of fluency in a second language. These English speakers might be traveling more than they did previously or receiving foreign visitors in the United States, or they may be more aware of the variety of languages represented in their own neighborhoods and feel that they will be able to participate more in the life of their community if they become bilingual. Such people are now receptive to encouraging bilingualism in their children.

There are many different degrees of bilingualism, ranging from complete fluency in both languages to dominant use of one language and very limited use of the other. The ALERTA curriculum is designed to promote fluency in two languages for *all* of the children (English-speaking and non-English-speaking) in the program. The conditions that must be present for successful use of ALERTA's bilingual component are discussed in detail in later chapters. But first, teachers must consider the issue of regional variations in language and their attitudes toward use of such variations in the classroom.

Regional Variations in Language

All languages develop regional variations, which may be a result of the circumstances of particular environments in which people live. For example, a group of people may develop descriptive phrases for weather conditions found only in their part of the country or invent distinctive names for indigenous plants. Variations also result from contact of one linguistic group with another, a process that has been going on since the beginning of history.

The fact of language variation historically has caused some confusion in the minds of teachers and parents. There are widespread notions concerning "purity" and correctness in language that can take the exaggerated form of dismissing some regional variations as incorrect or "impure." It is frequently stated, for example, that the Spanish spoken by Puerto Rican and other Caribbean Hispanics is "not really Spanish," or is an inferior type of Spanish. If this is to be accepted, then by the same token the language spoken by North Americans is not really English or is an inferior type of English. We know that these statements are not true.

Linguists tell us that all people speak their language according to the region where they live. In the Hispanic Caribbean, in Mexico, and throughout Latin America and Spain, varieties of Spanish are spoken. Different accents and different vocabulary words can be heard, but it is all Spanish. The same can be said of the varieties of English spoken throughout the fifty states of the United States, England, Australia, and the English-speaking Caribbean. One will detect strikingly different accents and different words used, but the language is still English. Again it must be stressed that *every* language has local variants and that it is usually a matter of political and historical accident which form of the language is thought to be the "correct" one.

Languages that have been in daily contact over a number of years borrow from one another. Often the borrowed words become incorporated into the borrowing language. This was the case with the Spanish words *azucar* (sugar) and *tambor* (drum), among others, which were derived from Arabic words during the long period when Arabic speakers occupied Spain. Similar examples of language-borrowing in words that have been incorporated into English are *restaurant* and *pork*, both of which come from French. The Spanish spoken in the United States by some people of second or third generation may incorporate words that have been borrowed from the English language. Many Spanish words have become part of the English language, too. Examples are *rodeo, patio, corral*, and *hacienda*. These examples, of course, represent only a miniscule fraction of incorporated linguistic features in Spanish and English. What is important to realize is that the borrowing occurs most strongly on the level of simple vocabulary. There are substantially fewer borrowings in the basic sound system or grammatical structure of the language.

There are, however, instances where some linguists now believe that borrowings of basic sound systems and grammatical structures have occurred. Such an instance is found in the languages developed by African-Americans and Caribbean people of African descent. When Africans were forcibly transported to the New World, they were harshly stripped of the visible signs of their cultures. Preservation of a sense of self under these extreme conditions required retention at a deeper level of some aspects of their language as well as of nonvisible aspects of their cultures (their value systems).

The likelihood of their retaining certain deep structures of their languages was increased by two circumstances. First, although they came from many different nations or peoples and in the Americas did not have an African language in common, the majority of them came from West Africa, an area where many languages had developed from the same linguistic origins. (Just as most European languages developed from an ancient Indo-European root, most West African languages developed from a common origin.) Therefore, the Africans who were brought to the Americas did share certain linguistic characteristics. Second, most of the Africans were not formally taught the new languages that they were expected to speak (English, Spanish, Portuguese, French, or Dutch). As their exposure to the new tongues was for a long time deliberately limited, any rich expression of their inner lives required that they draw upon reserves from their heritage and meld old structures into the new languages. The development of language variations among people of African descent in the Americas has led some linguists to regard these variations as separate languages and to think of children who speak one of these languages as well as English, Spanish, Portuguese, or French as truly bilingual.

How Do ALERTA Teachers Promote Bilingualism?

As with their acquisition of a multicultural perspective, the first step ALERTA teachers must take is to examine their own attitudes toward language variation in the children they teach. Some teachers are comfortable in viewing language variation as an expression of cultural difference, but others reject this view in favor of characterizing the children's language as "deficient." An attitude such as this quickly communicates itself to the children in the same way that racial or ethnic bias does. The result is likely to be diminished performance on the children's part—another example of young children's tendency to view their teacher as a mirror to the self.

ALERTA teachers accept the variation of language that children bring to the classroom. They do not tell the children that their manner of speaking is "wrong" or "incorrect." They themselves model the most widely used variation of the language in question so that the children will have the opportunity to recognize and use the alternative vocabulary structures while they retain their own.

Because language learning, especially for young children, is tied to the contexts in which language is used, language is never taught separately from other activities. Instead it is embedded in all activities that the adults design for the children and is used by adults to reinforce newly learned concepts during child-initiated portions of the day.

In order to provide them with as much individual attention as possible, the children are divided into clusters that work intensively on an activity with a teacher for a short period each day. All new concepts are introduced to the children in their first language. Subsequent cluster activities are later used to reintroduce the concept in the second language.

ALERTA teachers do not code-switch or mingle two languages in the same sentence. When they are carrying out an activity in a first language cluster, they continue to speak the children's first language for the duration of the activity. Conversely, when they are conducting a cluster in the children's second language, they stay with that language as much as possible, acting out any meanings that are not immediately clear to the children. This technique allows the children to associate new vocabulary and grammatical structures with the context in which they are working and reduces the potential for confusion.

Exactly how the activity clusters are formed and what strategies ALERTA teachers use to promote first language development and second language acquisition is explained in detail in subsequent chapters. Once again you will have opportunities to examine your own attitudes toward language teaching and learning, and a variety of exercises will be presented to practice the skills necessary for using ALERTA's bilingual approach to early learning.

Now it's time to begin the process of actual use of ALERTA. In the chapter to come you will begin the exploration of the partnerships that form the foundation of "A Learning Environment Responsive to All."

CHAPTER THREE

Level 1: Developing Partnerships in the Use of ALERTA

A parent entered the kindergarten class of an urban public school. She saw three adults involved in various activities in the room. One woman was weaving with three children. A young woman was listening to a small group of children plan a trip in the neighborhood. The third adult was helping children measure balsa wood strips for kite making. These three adults had carefully planned the activities for that day together. Each had an active role in carrying out that plan. Who was the teacher?

In an early childhood program a woman dressed in a white uniform sat talking intently with two other women. At times laughter was heard coming from the group—then seriousness followed. The women were talking about food—recipes and the food likes and dislikes each person had as a child. The woman in white was the cook for a Head Start program in Connecticut, and the other two persons were the teacher and assistant for the three- and four-year-olds' classroom. They had come together to solve a problem: How to get the children in the program to eat the large shipment of spinach that had been delivered to the cook on that very day. Experience told the cook that the children, who were from various Hispanic backgrounds, did not eat spinach when she cooked it. So she had decided to talk with the two Hispanic adults of one classroom in order to find out how spinach was prepared in Hispanic households. By remembering and sharing recipes, the teachers were able to give the cook several ideas. That afternoon the cook combined the ingredients of a popular Hispanic Caribbean dish with the spinach to make a spicy, tasty casserole. The result was extremely well received by the children and adults at the center. In this instance, who was the cook?

At the heart of ALERTA is the child, but at its foundation is the collaborative approach. ALERTA was developed through the collaboration of a team of professional and nonprofessional people. Every voice was heard in that effort, every thought respected. So too in the process of implementing ALERTA we ask adults to form partnerships to insure that the program will be supported at all levels and that the people involved will work together in a variety of ways for the total development of children. In Head Start Centers and in many other early childhood settings with small staffs, everyone—teacher, administrators, parents, nutrition and social service workers—is seen as an equal participant in the development of the philosophy and principles of ALERTA. In a public-school setting the partnership may be formed among parents, teachers, and guidance counselor, or parents, teachers, and principal. But no matter who the partners are, people are asked to begin to work together in closer and perhaps new ways.

The developers of ALERTA are aware that almost all schools and early-learning centers have an inherent hierarchy. Salaries are not equal, responsibilities are not equal, and the titles of "teacher" and "assistant" have different power connotations. There are, however, very real and positive results that are obtained from sharing responsibilities and from planning and working together to create an atmosphere of respect for all, where growth is promoted for both children and adults. People using ALERTA need to consciously put aside the traditional roles and titles under which they have worked and begin to see themselves as part of a team working toward the implementation of a program in which everyone has an important role. Such collaboration brings out a whole new view of teaching and learning.

What a partnership or team means in a Head Start setting may need to be redefined when thinking of its operation in a public school. In many educational settings teachers work in self-contained classrooms. There, a team approach may take a different form; but in these settings, too, partnerships are possible. ALERTA teachers are asked to understand and embrace the notion that children's first teachers are their parents. Teachers and parents can and do work together to produce effective, exciting results. Teachers can also incorporate members of the community into the classroom environment as teachers, friends, and members of the children's everyday culture. In this way, children are helped to see the connections among home, school, and community in very concrete ways. Such collaboration enables creativity, knowledge, and growth for all.

The following exercises have been designed to help those implementing ALERTA begin to form partnerships. Some exercises are intended for use in groups (staff, parents, and community people). Others may be done by a teacher or teacher and aide alone. The exercises have been organized into two categories: (1) activities to promote self-awareness, and (2) suggestions of practical ways for adults in the program to work together. The former were selected for their potential in helping participants to know each other at deeper levels at the same time as they become aware of their own cultures. The latter exercises were selected to offer concrete steps toward the formation of partnerships in the use of ALERTA. It should be noted that some of the activities require a "leader" who organizes the workshop materials and initiates the action. That leader could be you or one of your partners. You might enjoy alternating the leadership role among members of your group.

Self-awareness

We begin establishing partnerships by focusing on the interpersonal relationships among those with whom we will work closely. In any organizational setting, human relationships are complex in nature. The complexities stem from a variety of factors, including variation in cultural and ethnic backgrounds, educational levels, working experiences, and personalities. In addition, teachers differ from each other in their teaching styles. Human relations exercises that examine these variations often result in increased understanding among individuals, so that working toward a common goal for children can become a reality.

EXERCISE 1

Posters

For this activity the group will need an assortment of posters depicting scenes from several different environments. Depending on who will be participating in the exercise, you may choose to include urban scenes, rural landscapes, northern environments, tropical vegetation and architecture, quiet or busy scenes, celebrations, funny or serious events, or any other illustration evocative of parts of the world members of the group may have experienced.

There should be more posters than there are numbers of participants. The posters should be spread out in an area where each one is visible to everyone in the group. The floor is ideal for this, because the participants can walk around each poster to look at it closely. After looking at each poster, the participants should each choose one poster that they feel most expresses something important about themselves or that represents "who they are." Then, sitting in a circle with their posters in front of them, one-by-one the people will share with the group the reasons why they chose the particular poster they did.

The posters will serve as a medium through which all group members can reveal something about themselves so that they will begin to see different dimensions of each other as human beings.

EXERCISE 2

Introductions

Everyone writes his or her name on a slip of paper. The papers are then folded and mixed together. Without first looking at the name, each participant chooses one paper and thinks of the qualities of the person whose name appears on it. People should think of the unique traits that make that person who he or she is. After the group has been given time to think, someone volunteers to begin. Each participant talks about the qualities of the person whose name he or she has or about special events they recall involving that person. At the end of the telling, the person's name is revealed.

Ideally this activity should be experienced with people who know each other well or who have worked together for a time. The "introductions" serve to highlight people's special talents or capabilities that familiarity may have made easy to overlook. They also may bring up special aspects of people's personalities or experiences that will be of benefit to the group in later use of the program.

EXERCISE 3

Collages

This activity serves a twofold purpose: It enables persons to talk about themselves on a personal level through something they have made, and it enables people to explore how their culture (values, traditions, and present environment) affects who they are.

In preparation for this exercise a variety of "scrounge" materials such as cloth scraps, buttons, yarn, colored tissue, styrofoam pieces, and aluminum foil should be collected. There should also be enough basic materials (scissors, glue, oaktag, and construction paper) for everyone to use.

All materials should be attractively set out on a table at the time of the meeting. Other tables should be ready for the participants to use as work spaces. To begin, people are invited to take any of the materials they wish to use in making a collage that depicts their feelings or recollections about their childhood and their present life.

It is important for everyone to understand that it is not the purpose of this exercise to make a pretty picture. The purpose is to think about and express what has been important to you in the past and what is important to you today. The participants should work on their collages by themselves. Everyone should have enough time to enjoy making and finishing his or her collage. The initiator of this exercise should also be sure to make a collage.

When everyone has finished, the people assemble into a circle where they can see each other's finished work and share with each other the thoughts, feelings, and information about themselves that making the collage brought to consciousness. People who have taken part in this exercise have reported that it has allowed them to see their colleagues in a new light, as it reveals unexpected dimensions of their lives.

EXERCISE 4

Photographs[1]

Everyone sits in a circle for this exercise. People are asked to take from their pockets or purses an imaginary photograph. The "photograph" captures a significant custom, event, or person from childhood. One-by-one, people volunteer to talk about the "photograph" and share recollections of a special time or person from childhood.

EXERCISE 5

Team Work

The participants are asked to choose an art medium with which they will work as a group. Blocks, clay, or other building materials would be especially appropriate for the activity. There should be enough of the material chosen so that each participant can take an active part in the work. If there are more than four or five persons involved in the activity, they should divide themselves into two or more teams or groups (three to five people each). Each team will make or construct something its members decide upon as a group. The teams should work in different areas of a room. After enough time has been given for the construction (thirty to forty-five minutes), the groups will then connect their various constructions in any way they want. Finally the groups come together and then decide on what the united construction represents.

The teams end the exercise by discussing the following.

–how they began working
–how they made their plan
–how they negotiated for space, materials, etc.
–how leadership developed in the activity
–how they decided on what to build
–how they felt when they had to unite the various structures

---

[1] Sandy Fiddler contributed this exercise during a session for the training of ALERTA workshop leaders.

Chapter Three

These are some of the considerations that arise when working in collaboration with others. The exercise offers an opportunity for such considerations to be discussed in a nonthreatening manner and provides a bridge to the activities that follow.

Practical Suggestions for Working Together

The kinds of self-awareness and self-sharing exercises presented previously are very important in building the paths of communication needed for effective partnership. They alone will not yield long-term results, however, unless they are followed by activities that enable people to see how that self-awareness and awareness of the capabilities of others can be put to use in their immediate working situation. The final section of this chapter is devoted to practical ways that people can begin to discover ways of working together to achieve a common goal—the implementation of ALERTA in their classroom or center.

Job titles and job descriptions help in the carrying out of one's work. They make clear just what is to be done so that work responsibilities can be efficiently addressed and carried out. They can also be limiting when you are asked to begin to work in new ways by forming partnerships with others. How can the nonclassroom staff of a school setting be involved in the implementation of ALERTA? How can personal talents and interests of individuals become an organic part of a program? How can we begin to leave the defined area to which we were assigned so that work becomes a more creative act? The following activities begin to explore some of these questions.

EXERCISE 6

ALERTA Puzzle[2]

In preparation for the activity a parent or teacher makes a large (at least 20″ × 15″, but the larger the better) cardboard or foamboard puzzle incorporating the word *ALERTA* and a heart-shaped piece at the puzzle's center. (The puzzlemaker may use the pattern shown in this book or devise one of his or her own.) No one of the group who will be putting the puzzle together should see it ahead of time.

At the time of the workshop each participant is given one or two pieces of the puzzle and asked to work with the others in a group to construct the puzzle. As the puzzle pieces are put into place,

participants will begin to see that the word *ALERTA* is being formed. The heart-shaped puzzle piece in the middle should be kept by the puzzlemaker to be supplied at the very end of the activity, when the rest of the puzzle has been reconstructed. As the final piece is put into place, the puzzlemaker should remind the group that, "At the heart of ALERTA is the child...."

Discussion of the experience should stress that the ALERTA puzzle could not be completed without everyone's help and that, in a similar fashion, use of the program is most complete when undertaken as a joint effort. This activity could

---

[2] For this exercise we are indebted to Batsheva Fenster, an ALERTA workshop leader.

be an effective prelude to a discussion of job responsibilities or the nature of parent contributions to the program.

EXERCISE 7

Role Play of
Community Discussion

This exercise should be preceded by a review of the process and concepts underlying the ALERTA program (see Chapters One and Two). It will be most effective if people have already familiarized themselves with the introductory material and use the activity to articulate what they have understood about the program's philosophy and practice.

To begin the role play, participants divide into two groups. One group will represent parents and/or community members, and the other group will represent ALERTA staff implementing the program. The "parents or community people" will ask many questions regarding the content and process of the curriculum. The ALERTA staff will present: (1) the philosophy and characteristics of the program, (2) the workings of ALERTA in a school setting or in a classroom, and (3) answers to the parents'/community members' questions. At least one-half hour should be allowed for the preparation of the role play. The role descriptions that follow may be distributed as deemed appropriate. Other role descriptions should be prepared if those included do not reflect the community.

The result of this exchange is likely

to be refinement of the school or center staff's position about why they want to use ALERTA and clarification of the issues that may be raised in a real community or parent-teacher meeting. The exercise affords specific preparation to staff members for public presentation of their views.

Roles for Community Discussion

1. You are a Vietnamese woman who has been married for five years. Your only child is three years old and attending the Head Start Center. You don't know anything about bilingual education. You ask many questions.

2. You are an African-American father. You are very concerned about your children's education. Your two children go to the Head Start Center. You want them to learn to read quickly.

3. You are a Cuban mother. Your oldest child is four and is in Head Start. You speak very little English and you are anxious for your children to learn English.

4. You are an elderly Chicana grandmother. Your granddaughter is in Head Start. You take care of her while her parents work. You don't really know too much about the existing program at the center.

5. You are a Jewish father. You have four children. Your two middle children now attend Head Start. Your oldest is in a public school bilingual program. You are very dissatisfied with the public school program.

6. You are an African-American woman who has three children. Your young son attends the Head Start Center. You are very concerned that all your children have a good education and grow up with a positive self-image. You are interested in many issues.

7. You are a Dominican father. You have been here for less than a year. Your son and daughter attend Head Start. You are pleased with what they are learning, but you are interested in helping the children maintain their Spanish.

8. You are a Puerto Rican grandmother. You believe school is a place for traditional learning. You are upset when your grandchildren come home with paint on their clothes. You want more discipline in the schools. You speak no English.

9. You are a Puerto Rican mother who was born and raised in New York. You speak very little Spanish, but you would like to relearn it. You want your children to learn Spanish at an early age.

10. You are a Mexican-American mother. Your husband is from Honduras. Your two younger children are in Head Start. Your oldest boy in public school is ashamed of being Hispanic and refuses to speak Spanish. You are concerned.

11. You are an Irish-American mother. Your family has lived in the neighborhood for four generations. Your little boy is in Head Start. You are concerned with the fact that the neighborhood has changed. You don't understand many of the customs of the new people. You speak up in meetings.

12. You are a Puerto Rican father. Your boy attends the Head Start program and you are interested in what the new program is about. You ask many questions about the nature of the bilingual program, strategies, studies, etc.

13. You are an ALERTA staff member. You firmly believe in bilingualism's being fostered at an early age. You believe that children should be taught from their interests and developmental levels. You know the importance of children's growing up with knowledge and pride in their family, ethnic or racial groups, and in themselves. You believe teaching is creative work that grows from the child. You always work from people's strengths. You have chosen to use ALERTA because the model represents these beliefs.

EXERCISE 8

Perceptions of Roles[3]

Each participant should have paper and pencil. The people pair themselves off and write on the top of their papers the job title of the person with whom they are doing the activity. Each person then writes down five responsibilities that he or she believes go with that job title.

After everyone has finished writing, each participant shares with his or her partner the perceptions of the work the other performs. After each team of two speaks together, the group meets as a whole again to share what participants have learned of each other's work.

EXERCISE 9

Questionnaire on Preferences and Capabilities

This exercise may be used as a natural follow-up to the preceding activity. The questionnaire is distributed to each participant with instructions to answer each question quickly. When everyone has finished, the results are shared with the whole group or with individuals who plan to work together in specific ways.

After the initial sharing, participants are asked to volunteer what new information was learned about the talents, interests, and aspirations of people in the group. These are listed on a newsprint wall chart. The group then lists on another wall chart five types of work that cut across role categories in use of ALERTA: (1) coordination of parent input into the program; (2) design/con-struction of learning materials and decoration for the classroom; (3) provision of learning activities, particularly those requiring special talents (such as the ability to play an instrument, demonstrate a dance, or tell a story in a way that captures children's attention); (4) coordination of community resources for the children's use; and (5) planning/management of ongoing staff development work as the program proceeds. Finally, participants match interests and talents of individuals with the various types of work. Note should be made of these special preferences, talents, and abilities so that they can be drawn upon at each level of ALERTA's use.

---

[3] Exercises 8 and 9 are variations of ones contributed to the ALERTA program by Dr. Robert E. Daniels in his work as staff developer with Head Start staff in New York.

Questionnaire on Preferences and Capabilities

Directions: Answer each of the questions below quickly, using the first thoughts that come to mind as you read each one.

1. People who know me think I am _____

   _____

   _____

2. I love to 1. _____

   2. _____

   3. _____

3. I can _____ very well.

4. At my job I don't like to _____ ,

5. and I like to _____ .

6. Professionally in the future I would like to _____

   _____

   _____

7. Personally in the future I would like to _____

   _____

   _____

EXERCISE 10

Childhood Memories in Stories, Songs, and Games

The purpose of this activity is to encourage sharing of knowledge of the details that make up the program participants' cultures by drawing upon positive childhood memories. In this instance the group works together to recollect children's songs, games, rhymes, and stories that are particular to the cultures in which they were raised.

People in the group are first asked to remember their favorite childhood games and recall any songs or rhymes that were associated with them. They are also asked to remember stories (traditional stories or family histories) that their grandparents or other relatives may have told them. As the discussion proceeds, volunteers are asked to tell the story or demonstrate the game for the rest of the group.

While each volunteer is speaking, another person acting as a recorder quickly jots down on an index card the gist of each recollection so that it can be used at another time with children in the classroom. Those persons who seem particularly comfortable sharing with the group can be asked to come into the classroom on a subsequent day to do their song, story, game, or rhyme with the children. At the conclusion of the workshop, participants may wish to discuss the similarities of stories and games across cultural groups and the underlying values presented in story/game form.

One person should take the responsibility for organizing the index cards into a resource file for the center, school, or classroom. The file can be organized according to the cultural groups represented at the center and the particular songs, games, rhymes, or stories that originated with each. As time goes on, the file can be expanded as other parents and staff add their recollections. Teachers and parents can draw upon the file to select material that reflects their children's cultures and/or current interests and refine it into learning activities appropriate for the children's developmental levels.

At the end of this chapter are examples of such childhood memories that have been transformed by teachers into activities for three- to five-year-old children. Some of these may be useful in starting with your group the kind of discussion in this exercise.

Recipe Sharing and Cooking Together

Frequently both parents and teachers enjoy remembering their favorite simple recipes that were characteristic of the cultural group(s) in which they were raised. Another workshop that encourages sharing is one centered around recipe exchange and variation in food preparation across cultures.

Participants are asked ahead of time to identify a recipe coming from their cultural tradition that they think could be used successfully with young children in the classroom, or one they think other adults in the program would enjoy knowing. On the day of the workshop, each participant may bring the ingredients necessary, or the person organizing the workshop may decide ahead of time on two or three recipes and have the ingredients of those brought in. The contributor of each recipe will demonstrate how to cook it. At the conclusion of the meeting all the participants can sit down together to enjoy the results of their work.

On subsequent days parents or teachers who demonstrated recipes suitable for use with young children can be asked to cook with a group of children in the classroom. Large recipe charts may be kept in the classroom with the name and picture of the person who donated the recipe and/or cooked with the children. Parents and staff can also make books of more elaborate recipes to be shared among the adults.

The examples of possible activities found at the end of this chapter contain a sample of recipes collected from parents and teachers who participated in such a workshop.

Multicultural Perspectives on Health Care[4]

Health-care practices can be as revealing of cultural similarities and differences as are oral traditions and nutritional preferences. This area can also be tapped as an avenue for forming closer ties of understanding among program participants. To begin the exercise, parents and teachers note on individual slips of paper customs or rituals related to maintaining health or home remedies (along with identification of the illness they were meant to cure) that they remember seeing their grandparents or parents follow. (It is not necessary for participants to put their names on the papers.)

All the slips of paper are then shaken together in a paper bag and redistributed randomly to the participants. Volunteers are asked to read aloud the slip they have received and to comment on whether the custom described is similar to or different from one they have experienced. In each case, all of the other participants are invited to add any information about or insight they have into the practice. This part of the exercise usually moves quickly into an informal exchange of recollections and allows exploration of ob-

---

[4] This exercise is a variation of one designed by M. Patricia Carlton for an ALERTA staff development workshop.

served behaviors in the community that participants may have found puzzling. The conversation may also point out that some customs followed only a generation or two ago may no longer be a part of the culture of a group, whereas other customs continue to be followed to the present day.

A General Comment on Level 1

The exercises described in this chapter have been presented with the specific goal of enabling people to work collaboratively in the implementation of the ALERTA Program. Partnership commitment does not end here, however. As you will see in the following chapters, each implementation level builds on the notion of partnerships. Everyone using ALERTA becomes involved to a different degree at different times. At each level of implementation the involvement of the group will be deepened and strengthened. As you move into the exercises to come, you may want to return periodically to this chapter to select ice breakers for group meetings. You are welcome to adapt or change any of the activities included here to suit your purpose better or develop your own exercises for team building. For the time being, though, you are invited to use insights from Level 1 to "see" the cultures represented by the children in your classroom.

To Illustrate Uses of Information Gathered Through Exercises 10 and 11 of ALERTA's Level 1

The activities presented on the following pages have been designed to illustrate how information volunteered by parents in workshops on oral traditions or in cooking/nutrition workshops can be transformed into learning activities for three- to five-year-old children. This collection represents only a small sample of such activities. You can use the collection as a launching point if your program serves children of the cultural traditions represented in the sample, but it should quickly be expanded or replaced by activities suggested by the workshops *you* have had with parents and other teachers. If you are working with cultural groups different from those drawn upon here, you may wish to use the collection simply to review how to make learning activities appropriate for young children. It is vital to understand that the resources for activity design that come to you through the parents' recollections, commercial activity files, and other sources often need to be simplified or otherwise adapted in order to become accessible to preschoolers' ways of understanding the world.

Equally important, you should realize that you would use these activities in your own way based on what you have previously observed as appropriate to your children's interests and levels of development. You would change the procedure to suit the goal and objective you have selected for the children you were working with on a given day, and you would vary your language of presentation according to whether you were working toward first language development or second language acquisition in the children. (Use of goals and objectives in ALERTA is discussed in Chapter Eight of this source book. Information on use of activities for first language development or second language acquisition is found in Chapter Nine.)

Many additional activity suggestions can be found in the books and other materials listed in the appendix of this book. Ideas taken from such sources would also be transformed according to your observations of the children in your classroom and the purposes you want to achieve with each learning experience presented to the children.

Game/Dance Songs

Cultures all over the world have a "childlore," game and dance songs that are passed from generation to generation of children. The songs here come from the Caribbean, South America, and North America. Many others from around the world can be found in collections of children's songs. You or people you know may be familiar with the tunes that go with each game. If you are not, there have been a number of recordings made of the songs. All the following songs appear on the Folkways recording #FC 7830 entitled *ALERTA SINGS.*

"Brinca la tablita"

"Brinca la tablita" is commonly heard in both the Hispanic Caribbean and South America. Originally children said these verses as they jumped back and forth across a wooden beam. Nowadays, the jumping is done over a jump rope, held taut and slightly above the ground by two of the children playing the game.

Brinca la tablita	Dos y dos son cuatro	y ocho veinticuatro
que yo la brinqué	cuatro y dos son seis	y ocho treintaidós
bríncala tu ahora	seis y dos son ocho	anima bendita
que yo me cansé	y ocho diez y seis	me arrodilla yo

Once the children have learned a stanza they can sing it while one child performs the designated action. Two children may hold a rope for one child to jump over several times. The children may take turns jumping and holding the rope.

"Dis Long Time Gal"[5]

The song "Dis Long Time Gal" is a Jamaican folk song and is written in Jamaican dialect. Years ago, these songs were popular in the villages, but as time went on they became less well known. Such folk songs are now being revived and are done at festival time or for other special gatherings. The children usually wear traditional clothing when doing the dance. The John Crow is a large bird with a bald head ("peel head") and is a scavenger. It is found all over the island.

To begin the actions, the children stand in two rows facing a partner. When the chorus is played, the girls curtsy and the boys bow. The children in both rows place their hands on their hips.

Song	**Actions**
(1) Dis long time gal 　　a neva see you	Children step left once and then step right.
Come mek me hol' you han'	Each child stretches right hand out and shakes partner's right hand.
Dis long time gal 　　a neva see you	Repeat the actions.
Come mek me hol' you han'	
Chorus[6] 　Peel head John Crow 　　si dun' pon tree top 　　pick off de blossom	Children in one line place right foot forward and pirouette twice while their partners place fingers of hand lightly on pirouetting child's head.
Mek me hol' you han' gal, 　　mek me hol' you han'.	At the word *blossom*, partners face each other and bend knees.

---

[5] "Dis Long Time Gal" is taken from the *Four Year Old Manuals* of the curriculum designed by faculty at the University of the West Indies School of Education. It is reprinted with permission of D.R.B. Grant, Director of the Centre for Early Childhood Education, at the University of the West Indies, Kingston, Jamaica.

[6] The last three lines of the chorus change to reflect the last line of the preceding verse each time the chorus is sung.

(2) Dis long time gal
    a neva see you

Come mek we walk
    an' talk

Dis long time gal
    a neva see you

Come mek we walk
    an' talk.

(3) Dis long time gal
    a neva see you

Come mek we wheel
    an' tun

Dis long time gal
    a neva see you

Come mek we wheel
    an' tun.

Coda

Mek we wheel an'
    tun till we tumble dun'

Mek me hol' you han'
    gal

Mek we wheel an'
    tun till we tumble dun'

Mek me hol' you han' gal.

Actions as in the first stanza, but instead of shaking hands partners take hands and walk to the left at the words *Come mek we walk and talk.*

Repeat the above actions, but children now walk to the right at the words *Come mek we walk and talk.*

Actions for chorus are repeated as chorus is sung.

Repeat the action for first stanza, except that partners hold hands and make one turn to the left.

Repeat the action of first stanza, this time making one turn to the right.

Do two double turns; i.e., both partners holding two hands and turning together with arms above heads.

Note: To help the children do the actions correctly, use two children for demonstration while the others watch.

"Willoughby"

"Willoughby" originated on Willoughby Street in Brooklyn, New York. The game is played by two lines of children facing each other. The two children at the head of the line "strut" down the "alley" using any motions they like as they go along. It is sung to the tune of "Shortnin' Bread."

(1) This is the way you Willoughby, Willoughby, Willoughby
This is the way you Willoughby all day long.

(2) Oh, strutting down the alley, alley, alley
Strutting down the alley all day long.

(3) Oh, here comes another one, just like the other one
Here comes another one all day long.

"Matarile"

"Matarile" is a very popular game in many Latin American countries. The child who faces the line of players is able to choose which occupation he or she would like to have. In the recorded version of the song, the girl rejects occupations traditionally held by women to select one more akin to her interests.

(1) Ambos a dos, matarile, rile, rile.
Ambos a dos, matarile, rile, ron.

(2) ¿Qué quiere usted? matarile, rile, rile.
¿Qué quiere usted? matarile, rile, ron.

(3) Yo quiero un paje, matarile, rile, rile.
Yo quiero un paje, matarile, rile, ron.

(4) Escójalo usted, matarile, rile, rile.
Escójalo usted, matarile, rile, ron.

(5) Yo escojo a María, matarile, rile, rile.
Yo escojo a María, matarile, rile, ron.

(6) ¿Qué oficio le va a poner? matarile, rile, rile.
¿Qué oficio le va a poner? matarile, rile, ron.

(7) Le pondremos, costurera (o sastre) (maestra/o, lavandero/o,
doctor/a, escritor/a, ingeniero/a, pelotero/a, secretaria/o, etc.)
matarile, rile, rile.
Le pondremos, costurera (o sastre) matarile, rile, ron.

(8) Ella (o el) dice que sí (no) le gusta, matarile, rile, rile.
Ella (o el) dice que sí (no) le gusta, matarile, rile, ron.

(9) Celebremos todos juntos, matarile, rile, rile.
Celebremos todos juntos, matarile, rile, ron.

A child faces a line of players. The child walks toward the line, then back as he or she sings verses 1, 3, 5, and 7. The children in the line walk toward the child and back as they sing verses 2, 4, 6, and 8. All the children sing verse 9 as they form a circle and skip around. After the third verse, the child chooses one child on the opposite line by name. If this child accepts the occupation offered in verse 7, she or he joins the child to form a new line. If not, verse 7 is repeated and another occupation is offered. When the last child is left on the first line, the game may be repeated and new occupations offered.

"Head to Shoulders"

"Head to Shoulders" appears to have taken its present form in African-American communities of the southern United States. Today it can be heard in many neighborhoods throughout the country.

The song moves through each verse suggesting movements that can easily be done by the children. In the last verse, all the preceding lines are repeated in the correct order.

(1) Head to shoulders, baby, 1, 2, 3
Head to shoulders, baby, 1, 2, 3
Head to shoulders
Head to shoulders
Head to shoulders
Head to shoulders
Head to shoulders, baby, 1, 2, 3

(2) Knee to ankle, baby, 1, 2, 3
Knee to ankle, baby, 1, 2, 3
Knee to ankle
Knee to ankle
Knee to ankle
Knee to ankle
Knee to ankle, baby, 1, 2, 3

(3) Push the buggy, baby, 1, 2, 3, etc.

(4) Round the world, baby, 1, 2, 3, etc.

(5) That's all baby, 1, 2, 3, etc.

(6) Head to shoulders,
Knee to ankle,
Push the buggy,
Round the world,
That's all, baby, 1, 2, 3.

"San Serení"

"San Serení" is a place name, and the song reflects the activity of the town. Names of other occupations may be substituted for "lavanderos" and "carpinteros."

San Serení de la buena, buena vida
hacen así, así, los lavanderos,
así, así, así . . . así me gusta a mi.

The verses are repeated, using different occupations (e.g., los carpinteros, los médicos, los maestros, etc.), for as long as the children's interest is sustained. This activity could be used as a culminating or follow-up activity after walks in the neighborhood and discussions about the workers they have observed. Three to four pairs of children (six to eight children) make a circle and sing "San Serení." As each occupation is named in the song, the children act it out. On the last "así" of each verse, the children clap their hands in unison, turn toward their partners, link right arms, and swing around once.

"Little David"[7]

"Little David" is an adaptation of an African-American spiritual from the southern United States, which became popular in the English-speaking Caribbean. In this version the words are changed to reflect the use of instruments made by the children.

(1) Little David, play on your harp
Hallelu, Hallelu
Little David, play on your harp
Hallelu.

(2) Little Tommy, play on your drum
Hallelu, Hallelu
Little Tommy, play on your drum
Hallelu.

[7] "Little David" is taken from the *Four Year Old Manuals* of the curriculum designed by faculty at the University of the West Indies School of Education. It is reprinted with permission of D.R.B. Grant, Director of the Centre for Early Childhood Education, at the University of the West Indies, Kingston, Jamaica.

(3) Little Mary, play on your jingles
　　　Hallelu, Hallelu
　　Little Mary, play on your jingles
　　　Hallelu.

(4) Little Johnny, shake your maracas
　　　Hallelu, Hallelu
　　Little Johnny, shake your maracas
　　　Hallelu.

"Tengo una muñeca"

"Tengo una muñeca" has many variations that are heard throughout Latin America. It can be used as a lullaby or bedtime song or in role plays in the housekeeping area.

(1) Tengo una muñeca
　　vestida de azul
　　con zapatos blancos
　　y el velo de tul.

(2) La saqué a paseo
　　y se me enfermó
　　la tengo en la cama
　　con mucho dolor.

(3) Esta mañanita
　　me dijo el doctor
　　que le dé jarabe
　　con un tenedor.

Chanting Rhymes/Fingerplays

Other aspects of childlore are rhymes and various forms of fingerplays. These are also usually done as part of a game but do not have a tune that is sung. Instead the children chant the words, using the cadence they have learned in their community.

Jump Rope Rhymes

In the past, many children learned jump rope rhymes that they repeated and passed on to younger children as part of their play. The handing down of such rhymes and games has been part of the African-American tradition and can be found among other cultural groups as well. In many areas of the country today rhymes are still passed on from child to child. Sometimes parents remember rhymes that children do not seem to be saying as much at present. Many parents enjoy hearing the rhymes again, and the children enjoy learning them too. Two examples of jump rope rhymes are:

"Room for Rent"

Room for Rent
　Apply within

When I run out
　You run in!

(Children take turns skipping while two children turn the rope. One person skips for the duration of the rhyme. At "You run in" another person begins to skip.)

"Cinderella"

Cinderella, Cinderella dressed in yellow.
　　Went downtown to meet her fellow.

How many kisses did she get?
　　1, 2, 3, 4, etc.

(Children keep counting as the person skips. Whenever a child steps on the rope, he or she is out.)

Fingerplays/Action Songs

The short rhymes that follow are used in many Spanish-speaking countries to encourage young children. "Andando" encourages toddlers to walk. "Tortitas" is done with a clapping motion, as if the child were actually making tortitas. (Tortitas are similar to

Mexican tortillas.) "Sana, sana" is a rhyme used to smooth away the pain of a small injury a child has received. "Pon, pon" is a fingerplay in which a child uses the index finger of one hand in the cupped fist of the other to show the action of a mortar and pestle.

"Andando"

Andando
Andando
Que mamita te va ayudando.

Andando
Andando
Que papito te va ayundando.

"Sana, sana"

Sana, sana
colita de rana
si no se sana hoy
¡se sana mañana!

"Tortitas"

Tortitas, tortitas
tortitas de manteca
para mamita
para mamita
para mamita
que besa y besa.

"Pon, pon"

Pon, pon
pon, pon
el dedito en el pilón
acetón a la macetita
¡Ay, ay, ay
mi cabecita!

Oral Histories and Traditional Stories

The bibliography at the end of this source book contains a number of resources on traditional stories from different parts of the world. Parents and teachers may recollect stories told to them by their grandparents or other relatives at family gatherings. Some of these stories may have already been specially prepared for young children, but most of them are probably meant for older children or even for adults. Teachers using such stories with young children must take care to make the story both interesting and understandable to the children they teach.

There are three questions you should ask yourself each time you adapt a traditional story for use with young children.

1. Is the content of the story the type to which young children can relate?

2. Does the length of the story permit it to be told in one sitting?

3. Has the story been adapted into language appropriate for young children (including use of the language variation, vocabulary , etc., most familiar to the children)?

The most successful technique in adapting a story is not to *read* it to the children, but simply to *tell* it in a conversational way. You can show the children illustrations from the book in which you found the story as you tell it, or better yet, you can act out the story while telling it. Another suggestion for making the story appealing to young children is to use teacher- or parent-made flannelboard story pieces or puppets to illustrate the action of the story as you go along. These flannelboard pieces or puppets can later be placed in the library area for children to use during child-initiated portions of the day.

On the following pages is a traditional Vietnamese story that has been adapted from its original form to one suitable for use with four- and five-year-old children. Even in its adapted form, you may want to tell it in two sittings instead of one, because of its length. Suggestions for flannelboard story pieces are found at the end of the story.

This story has been included as an *example* of ways traditional tales can be made appropriate for use in early childhood settings. It is important to remember that stories from *all* the cultural traditions that your children represent should be adapted in this way. Workshops for parents and teachers should be held periodically to identify the stories, simplify them, and to create the puppets or story pieces to accompany their use.

Little Finger of the Watermelon Patch*

Once a long time ago in a country now called Vietnam a little girl was born. Her mother and father were very poor. They lived in a little house in the forest, where her father cut wood to earn money for the family. The mother and father were very happy with their little girl. They thought she was wonderful—smart and good-looking, too. There was just one thing that was different about their little girl, and that was that she was a **very** *little girl. In fact, she was only as big as your little finger! That's why her parents named her Nàng Út (nahng ŏop), which means "Miss Little Finger" in Vietnamese.*

Nàng Út's parents loved her very much. Whenever they went into the forest to work, they carried Nàng Út with them, letting her ride in the cloth her father wrapped around his head as a hat. One day, when the family was working in the woods, Nàng Út's parents spotted a watermelon patch in a clearing in the forest. "Let's stop here for lunch," her mother said, and so they did. All of them ate a lot of the delicious watermelon for lunch. Then Nàng Út's mother and father curled up to take a short nap before going back to work. But Nàng Út wanted to play. She walked away from her parents and began to climb up on the watermelons and slide down the sides.

After a while, Nàng Út became very tired, too. She crawled into a hollow piece of bamboo to take a short nap where it was cool and shady. While she was sleeping, her parents woke up. Not seeing her, they thought she was lost. They called and called her name, but Nàng Út didn't hear them because she was fast asleep. Her parents looked and looked for her, but they didn't find her. Sadly, they started home, hoping that they would find her on the way.

When Nàng Út woke up, she found she was all alone. She was very scared. She wanted her mother. She wanted her father. She knew that they loved her and that they would be very worried about her. She looked and looked, but she couldn't find them. She decided she had better stay in the watermelon patch where at least there was plenty of food. There was also the hollow bamboo that she could use as a tiny house. Nàng Út stayed in the watermelon patch for many years. She grew up there, even though she never really became very big. When she was grown up, she still was only as big as an ear of corn!

One day, in a city far away from the watermelon patch, the king of Vietnam called his three sons to his room.

"I am going to choose one of you to be the king after me," he said. "I have to find which one of you will be the best king. I am going to test you to see which of you I should choose. I want each of you to go out into the country today and pick a wife worthy of being a queen. Whichever one of you picks the best wife will be king after me."

The three sons set out on horseback to find their wives. Soon they came to a crossroads.

---

* This story was adapted from the tale of the same name found in *The Brocaded Slipper and Other Vietnamese Tales* by Lynette Dyer Vuong (Addison-Wesley Publishing Company, 1982)

"Why don't you go to the left?" said the older brothers to the youngest one. "We will go to the right. We'll do better if we don't all go the same way."

The older brothers said that because they thought the youngest brother wasn't very smart, and they wanted to get rid of him. The youngest brother didn't care. He rode off to the left. After a long time, he came to a wonderful watermelon patch right in the middle of the forest.

"What beautiful watermelons!" he said. "I think I'll stop here to have my lunch." He dismounted and cut up a watermelon to eat.

As he began to eat, he was startled to hear a voice that said "Stop it! Those are my watermelons!" The young man looked around and was amazed to see a very small young woman, no bigger than an ear of corn, standing in front of him.

"Who are you?" the young man asked.

"I am Nàng Út," replied the beautiful young woman, and she told him her sad story. The young man was sad, too, as he listened to Nàng Út's story.

"I know what!" he exclaimed. "I'll take you back to my father's palace and maybe there we will be able to find someone who knows your mother and father." So Nàng Út rode back to the palace in the hand of the kind young man.

When the youngest son arrived home, he was surprised to see that his older brothers were there ahead of him, each with a beautiful young woman to marry. The king was very happy to think that all his sons had found brides, and he was not ready to listen to his youngest son's story about Nàng Út. The king insisted that the weddings be held right away; and almost before she knew it Nàng Út found herself married to the king's youngest son. Nàng Út hadn't expected to be married, but she was happy because she liked the kind young man.

"Now," said the King, "each of my new daughters must prepare a meal for me to eat tomorrow morning. I will pick the most tasty meal, and the husband of that clever daughter will become king."

"Oh, no!" thought the youngest son. "How can my tiny wife cook a big meal?"

The next morning, however, when he woke up, the youngest son found a beautiful tray of food waiting to be carried to the king. There was delicious roast duck, special fried rice and a wonderful asparagus soup. The young man ran with the tray to his father, the king, who was tasting the food prepared by the other two wives. The king picked up a piece of the roast duck with his chopsticks and ate it.

"How delicious!" he exclaimed. Then he tasted the rice. "Wonderful!" he said. Finally he sipped soup from his china spoon. "This is the best soup I ever ate. My youngest son and Nàng Út will become king and queen!"

"Wait, father!" cried the other two sons. "Give us another chance. It is not fair to judge everything on cooking." "Well perhaps you are right," said the king. "Here is what you must do. Tomorrow morning each of you must bring a silk robe that your wife has made. Whoever brings the best robe will become king!"

"Oh, no!" thought the youngest son. "How can my tiny wife make a big silk robe?"

But the next morning, when he woke up, he found a beautiful silk robe lying on the bed waiting to be taken to his father. "Hurry!" said Nàng Út. "Don't be late!" The young man ran to his father's room with the robe. His father, the king, was already trying on the other robes.

"These are nice," he said. Then he tried on the robe Nàng Út had made. "What a comfortable robe!" he said. "I've never worn such a finely made robe before. You and Nàng Út will become king and queen."

"Wait!" said the older brothers. "That's not fair. Everything should not be judged on cooking and sewing. We need another chance to show how smart and talented our wives are. They can do any kind of work needed to run the kingdom with us. Give us another chance!" "Well," said the king, "perhaps you are right. Tomorrow morning each of you must come to my room with your wives, and show me how much you know about being king and queen."

"Oh, no!" thought the youngest son. "How can my tiny wife show how smart she is? She is too small to be heard!"

But the next morning, when he woke up, the young man was amazed to see that his tiny wife Nàng Út was gone. In her place stood a beautiful young woman who was as tall as he was. It was Nàng Út.

"I am a fairy woman," said Nàng Út. "When I was born to human parents, I had to spend my years as a tiny person. Two days ago, my fairy powers finally began to come to me, and I was able to cook the fine meal and sew the beautiful robe. Now I will go with you to your father, the king. We will show him how smart we are."

And they did. The king was so pleased to see Nàng Út as a woman as tall as his son, and he was so happy to hear how much she knew that he said once more, "My son and his wife, Nàng Út, will be king and queen after me!"

And so it was. Nàng Út became queen, and her husband, the new king, sent out messengers to find her parents. When her parents had been found, they were brought to the palace where they spent many happy years with their daughter and son-in-law.

Story Pieces   Little Finger of the Watermelon Patch

The two parents	Watermelons and vines
Nàng Út as tiny person	Hollow bamboo scaled to Nàng Út's size
King's youngest son	Tray with Nàng Út's foods for king
Two older brothers	Silk robe for king
The king	Nàng Út, the same height as youngest son

Cooking Activities

Recipes contributed by parents and staff in workshops have usually been designed for adults and therefore may need simplification before they can be used easily with young children. In ALERTA, cooking in the classroom is most often done with small clusters of children (as described in Chapters Eight and Nine). The children themselves do as much of the work as possible, under their teacher's guidance. For that reason, ALERTA recommends the use of a recipe chart on which the ingredients and the steps involved in preparation of the dish are presented to the children in the form of illustrations. As much as possible, the following examples of recipes have been arranged in order from those that are simple to those requiring a higher level of skill. Your assessment of the children's developmental levels would, of course, be very important in your determination of how much a recipe should be simplified. All recipes using hot oil must be done only under the strictest supervision.

Applesauce*
(Scottish-American origin)

5 apples
1 lemon
1 tablespoon sugar
cinnamon
water

1. Wash the apples.

2. Cut apples into quarters and remove seeds. (You may pare the quarters or not, as you prefer.)

3. Cut the quarters into small pieces.

4. Squeeze the juice out of the lemon into a bowl or cup.

5. Cover the apple pieces with water, and boil.

6. Add the lemon juice and sugar, and sprinkle with cinnamon.

7. Stir often as the applesauce is cooking.

8. Cook for about 20 minutes.

Pizza*
(Italian-American origin)

English muffins
tomato sauce
oregano
mozzarella cheese
ground black pepper

1. Separate each muffin, and toast lightly.

2. Spoon on tomato sauce to cover muffin half.

3. Add one slice of cheese to each muffin half.

4. Sprinkle on oregano and pepper.

5. Broil muffin halves for about 5 minutes, or until cheese melts and bubbles.

Wheat Germ Honey Banana Snack*
(A new recipe originating in California)

bananas
honey
wheat germ

1. Cut each banana into four pieces.

2. Roll each piece in honey.

3. Then roll each piece in wheat germ.

4. Place all pieces flat on a plate or cookie sheet.

5. Place in refrigerator.

6. Eat when fruit is chilled.

* All recipes marked with an asterisk were contributed by parents and staff of the Educational Alliance Head Start Center in New York City.

Corn Bread*
(Originated in the southern United States)

1 cup corn meal
1 cup flour (can be whole wheat)
¼ cup sugar (or honey)
3 teaspoons baking powder

½ teaspoon salt
1 egg
1 cup milk
¼ cup oil

1. Mix all dry ingredients together in a big bowl.

2. Mix all wet ingredients together in another bowl.

3. Add the wet ingredients to the dry ingredients and stir until mixed.

4. Grease baking pan.

5. Pour batter into pan and bake for 30 to 35 minutes in a 375-degree oven. Bread is done when top is golden brown.

Rice Pudding*
(Version of an old favorite
originating in the Hispanic Caribbean)

2 8-ounce cans of cream of coconut
2 13-ounce cans of evaporated milk
2 cups uncooked rice
2 tablespoons sweet butter
3 tablespoons sugar
1 teaspoon vanilla

2 tablespoons raisins
ginger
cinnamon
salt
cloves

1. Put all the ingredients except the rice in a large, heavy-bottomed saucepan.

2. When mixture boils, add the rice.

3. Simmer until rice is tender, stirring often so that rice does not stick.

4. Cool pudding and then refrigerate it.

5. Serve pudding lightly sprinkled with cinnamon.

Gok Chai (fried wonton skins with peanuts)*
(Chinese-American origin)

½ pound roasted, shelled peanuts
2 teaspoons white sugar
2 eggs
1 packet of wonton skins
oil for frying

1. Grind peanuts by rolling over them with a rolling pin.

2. Add the sugar to the ground peanuts.

3. Beat the eggs, and add them to peanut mixture.

4. Put a spoonful of the mixture in the middle of each piece of wonton skin.

5. Pinch each skin tightly closed.

6. Fry on both sides in hot oil until golden brown.

Potato Latkes (pancakes)*

(Eastern European-Jewish dish, which is
traditionally eaten during Chanukah)

5 potatoes
2 eggs
¼ onion
matzoh meal (could substitute flour)
salt
oil for frying

1. Wash, peel, and grate the potatoes.

2. Crack the eggs and add them to the grated potatoes.

3. Chop the onion.

4. Add the chopped onion, matzoh meal, and a dash of salt to the grated potatoes. (Add enough matzoh meal to thicken the batter.)

5. Mix well.

6. Form into flat, small patties.

7. Fry patties in hot oil until golden brown.

8. Drain fried patties on paper towels.

9. Eat with sour cream and/or apple-sauce.

Tostones

(Originated in the Hispanic Caribbean)

green plantains
salt
water
pepper
oil for frying

1. Peel the plantains.

2. Slice the plantains in oval slices.

3. Place slices in salt water and let them remain there for at least ½ hour. Remove them from the water and pat dry with paper towel.

4. Fry the plantain slices in hot oil for about 30 seconds on each side.

5. Take slices out of frying pan and mash each one by pressing on it with a folded brown paper bag.

6. Put individual flattened slices back into frying pan to fry until golden brown.

7. Sprinkle with salt and pepper before eating.

Beef Patties

(Originated in the English-speaking Caribbean)

Beef patties are a popular food among Jamaicans. They are nutritious and, if served with milk or some other drink, constitute lunch or snack for many people. These Jamaican patties are sometimes very "hot" as a result of use of red pepper (hot pepper); but if they are made for children unused to hot food, only a small quantity of black pepper should be used. *Teachers* should prepare the pastry *two days in advance* of the appointed day.

For Pastry (Done by teacher alone)

5 ounces suet
½ teaspoon salt
2 cups flour
⅓ cup ice
whites of two eggs
cold water

1. Start the pastry by trimming all the skin and fatty membrane from suet.

2. Set the suet overnight in a freezer.

3. The next day, with a very sharp knife, shave suet as finely as possible.

4. Combine salt and flour, and then work in suet as you would shortening in plain pastry, cutting it in with two knives.

5. Add enough iced water so that dough can be rolled out.

6. Form into a ball and pat gently with a rolling pin.

7. Turn the dough over once or twice so that it will hold together.

8. Wrap in waxed paper and set in freezer overnight.

9. Defrost the pastry the morning that you take it to your classroom.

For Filling (Done with children)

1 pound ground beef (with fat in it)
1 teaspoon ground thyme or
    4 sprigs fresh or dried thyme in leaf
annatto seeds or paprika for coloring
1 ounce scallion
½ teaspoon salt
½ teaspoon black pepper
¼ loaf of French-style bread

1. Grind the scallion in a meat grinder.

2. Add the ground scallion and ½ teaspoon salt to the ground meat.

3. Place the meat in a saucepan and add half of the thyme.

4. Cook the meat mixture on a hot plate without adding water or oil until the broth is dried out and only oil from the meat remains.

5. Pour the excess oil off and add the annatto seeds. Later, when the oil on the annatto seeds has turned red, it should be strained and used to color the meat. (Children should *not* do this step.)

6. While the meat is being cooked, place the bread in a saucepan and pour enough cold water over it to cover it.

7. Let the bread soak for a few minutes and then squeeze it dry, saving the water.

8. Pass the bread through a meat grinder; then return the ground bread to the water.

9. Add the rest of the thyme to the bread and let it cook until the bread is dry.

10. Combine meat and cooked bread.

11. Add either the oil from the annatto seeds or the paprika to color the meat.

12. Cook for another 20 minutes and remove from the hot plate.

13. Let the mixture cool for filling the pastry circles.

14. Pull off small pieces of the pastry dough. These pieces should be large enough to roll into a circle six inches in diameter. Dip dough in flour before rolling.

15. Use rolling pins to roll the dough thin and a round-shaped cookie cutter about six inches in diameter to cut the shape for filling with meat.

16. In the center of each circle place approximately one tablespoon of meat.

17. Fold the dough over to form a crescent shape.

18. Seal edges either by brushing on egg white or by crimping edge and folding dough slightly under. Do not prick the pastry.

19. Bake in ungreased baking tin for 35 minutes at a temperature of 300 degrees. If smaller patties are required, use a smaller pastry cutter.

CHAPTER FOUR

Level 2: Discovering the Cultures in Your Classroom

One of the resources that you tapped in forming partnerships during Level 1 was your understanding of what makes up a culture—whether your own or that of the children you teach. This chapter encourages you to think even more deeply about culture and its effect on what we think, what we feel, how we learn, and how we teach.

Everyone has a culture. Culture is everything that makes up the way of life of a people, so it is not possible for someone to be "cultureless." Some of the ways that cultures are distinctive were pointed out in Chapter Two. We know, for example, that cultures are constantly changing, because they are formed from the combined experience of our past (the history and traditions of our people) and our present, everyday lives (including the place we live, with all its influences upon us). We also know that any one cultural group can have a great number of individual variations within it. This fact becomes clear in the following two descriptions.

José was born in Jayuya, Puerto Rico. His small cement house is located in a rural barrio of Jayuya where José's mother and father were born. Once, José's father went to Pennsylvania to work for six months. Every morning José can be seen walking to the local school on a paved road surrounded by tall green panapén and mango trees. He wears his green and white uniform.

Mario was born in Boston, Massachusetts. He lives in Chelsea, a community adjacent to Boston. Mario's mother was born in Carolina, Puerto Rico, and Mario's father was born in Rio Grande, Puerto Rico. Every morning Mario's mother accompanies him to school, which is three blocks away from his house. On the way to school Mario and his mother go past grocery stores, a pizza shop, a pharmacy, and a police precinct.

Both of the boys described are of Puerto Rican parentage. They speak Spanish at home, observe Puerto Rican customs and traditions, and eat the same or similar foods; however, their present environment and lives are quite different. The boys are constantly being bombarded with stimuli and experiences that affect them and make them very different from each other. Both have a culture, and each of the cultures is equally valuable.

Sometimes people whose ancestors came to the United States four or more generations ago from northern Europe and the British Isles tend to think of themselves as not having a culture anymore. It is not uncommon to hear people holding this belief to say, "I'm not anything particular, just plain American, I guess." Because people with northern European and British ancestry have been part of the majority in the United States, they have tended to lose sight of their own distinctive characteristics. It is easier to recognize cultural patterns that are different from one's own than those patterns that characterize the larger society in the United States. It is important for *all* people to realize that they are the transmitters of a valuable culture and that that culture can be used to increase their knowledge and understanding both of themselves and of others.

The purpose of ALERTA's Level 2 is to enable you first to become more aware of the elements of your own culture; second, to identify the cultures that are actually represented in your classroom; third, to acquire specific information on those cultures; and finally to use that information to extend the children's present knowledge and skills. As you begin this process, you may start to appreciate how each level of program implementation is connected at a deep level to both the preceding and succeeding ones. It may become evident to you, for example, that insights and information you gained from doing the exercises in Level 1 will be useful to you in your work in Level 2.

Your Own Culture

Before we can begin to understand and appreciate the culture of those different from ourselves, we must first understand and appreciate our own culture and background. All of us, no matter how many generations of "Americans" we have behind us, still carry within ourselves certain traditions, values, and customs that are part of our individual or family culture. The following exercises may be used to sensitize adults to their own cultures. Several of them may be done before you look at the cultures of the children you teach, or they may be done at intervals throughout the school year. Once again, you may wish to do some of these activities with partners. You can also do them alone.

EXERCISE 1

A Multicultural Nation

The purpose of this activity is to underscore the many groups that make up the United States. Chart your family members by writing down where each person was born. Refer to the sample chart (squares are used to symbolize males and circles to represent females). When you are working in a group, share with your partners the names of the different states or countries represented on your chart. As you share, someone should write the names of the places on large sheets of paper. You may be surprised at the diversity that appears. The activity may be extended by discussing which of these countries were included in your course of study as you were growing up. Some countries will have been mentioned more than others, yet all groups have made positive contributions to the United States.

Chart of Family Origins

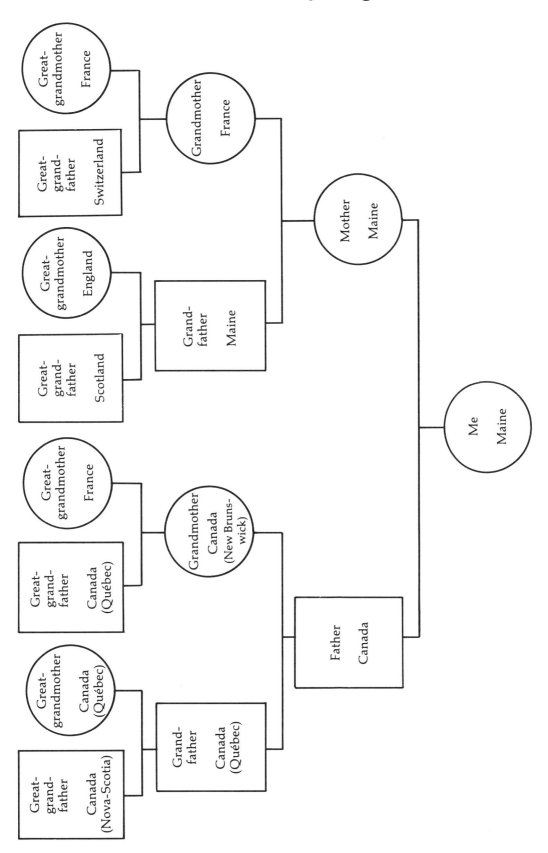

Three Levels of Culture

Identification of the places of birth or upbringing of the persons in your family over several generations yields only a certain kind of information. It can give you clues to the origins of some of the customs or traditions that are part of your family today, but it does not tell you much about the distinctive features of your culture(s). This exercise is designed to illustrate that every culture is made up of many elements and that these elements can be sorted into at least three important categories.

To start the activity, list everything you can think of that makes up a culture in general (not a specific culture this time), such as music, food, concepts of beauty, celebration of holidays, clothing styles, child-rearing practices, religion, and so forth. (For this exercise, several heads really are better than one!) When you have listed as many elements as you

Cultural Group: _____

What?	How?	Why?

can think of, try to sort what you have written into three groups: (1) things (*what* objects or visible signs are part of the culture); (2) traditions/customs (*how* members of the group conduct their lives); and (3) values (*why* members of the group do what they do). Your new chart might look something like this:

What ?	How ?	Why ?
Music Food Clothing etc.	Child-rearing practices Celebration of holidays etc.	Concepts of beauty Religion etc.

Now take a culture with which you have had direct experience, and write examples for each of the areas that you noted in the first part of the exercise. If you have difficulty thinking of specific instances, you may want to look at the example of such a chart (see "Cultural Group: North Dakota Chippewa"). You will notice how in the example the past and present have been combined into a single cultural portrait.

When you have completed your chart, ask some of your colleagues or supervisors to review it with you for accuracy and for avoidance of unconscious stereotyping. Even better, discussion will come from doing this exercise in small groups of teachers and parents and then sharing perceptions about each other's charts. In an atmosphere of mutual learning and exchange of information, views of the specific elements of various cultures can be refined, and misconceptions that appear can be dispelled.

One important outcome of the activity should be an awareness that there are different levels of culture. The first level (objects, music, art, and so on) is the surface level of the culture. It is that which can be seen or heard separate from the people who are its creators. The second level is deeper. It is customs, or ways of carrying out the business of everyday life. The second level is an activity instead of an object and is seen through someone who knows and does the activity. The third level—values—is the deepest of all. It is so imbedded in people that often it is very hard for an "outsider" to see it directly or accurately. Instead, values are displayed indirectly by the way people act in various situations, by gestures and tone of voice in response to the behavior of others, and by what activities in their lives people choose to emphasize. Both customs and values can also be influenced by individual preferences. This fact accounts for the great amount of individual variation that is found in any one cultural group.

Reflecting on these differences may lead you as a teacher to think about how cultures can be represented in a classroom for young children. Clearly the surface level is easier to incorporate than the other two levels, but attention to the surface level alone will not make an educational setting truly multicultural. More is said about use of culture in the classroom later in this chapter.

Cultural Group: North Dakota Chippewa[1]

What?	How?	Why?
Food	*Lifestyle*	*Religion*
Gullette	Close connection	Native (old)
Bangs	with parents,	Burial customs (old)
Bullets	grandparents, children	Catholic faith
Juneberries	Rural life	
Chokecherries		*Laws*
Fish	*Recreation*	Chief's law (old)
Pemmican (old)	Pow wows	Tribal law (new)
Jerky	Rodeo	State and federal law (new)
Tacos (new)	Bowling	
Hamburgers (new)	Basketball	*Education*
Le-zur-ro-oni	Softball/baseball	Elders as teachers
Rub-a-boo	Horseback riding	(old tradition)
Lee-grotoon	Bingo	Learning by doing
Bull-lo-ro	All-night fiddle parties	(verbally and visually)
Putchen		Boarding schools
	Customs	Mission schools
Dance	Sharing lots of food	Federal and state
Pow wow (sun dance,	for celebration	cooperative schools
war dance)	Smoking peace pipes (old)	Cultural studies
Modern dance	Name-giving ceremony	
Jig	Weddings	*Attitudes and Values*
Square dance	Funerals (wakes)	Cooperative action
Bush dances		Value of children
	Construction of Homes	Respect for adults
Music	Tepees (for camping	All resources were made
Guitar	at Pow wows)	use of (old)
Local bands	Wigwams (old)	
Drum	Log houses	
Fiddle	Sod houses (old)	
Country-western	Modern houses	
Clothing	*Medicine*	
Buckskin (old)	Use of plants	
Beadwork (old)		
Blue jeans	*Holidays*	
Boots	Metchief Day	
Western-style	New Year's Eve and Day	
clothing	(kissing tradition)	
Chooks (toque)	Christmas Eve and Day	
	St. Ann's Day	
Art		
Floral design in beadwork	*Language*	
and appliqués	Metis or Metchief	
Frequent use of red,	English	
pink, yellow	French	
Meaning of certain	Cree	
colors		
Willow baskets		
Wood carving		
Hooked rugs		
Quilting		

[1] This chart was compiled by the staff of the Turtle Mountain Head Start Program, Belcourt, North Dakota.

EXERCISE 3

Reflections in Finger Paint

An art activity is sometimes a useful device for reflecting or bringing to consciousness different levels of your culture. This is another exercise that is more effective if it is done in a group. Each participant fingerpaints a memory from his or her childhood or present life. There is no time limit on this activity nor any specifications on what colors or techniques should be used. Your skill as an artist is not important. What *is* important is your working in a relaxed atmosphere, at your own pace, to recollect a scene or happening that in some way was typical of your childhood or present life.

When everyone has finished painting, volunteers can explain their painting to the others in the group. Together the group can look for evidence of each of the three levels of culture introduced in Exercise 2. The discussion will bring out additional details that you may not have thought about previously as part of culture.

This exercise is very similar to the collage exercise suggested for Level 1. The major difference is not the materials used but the degree of specificity you are now able to achieve in the discussion as you become more aware of the elements that make up a person's culture.

EXERCISE 4

Evocative Objects

A variation on the previous exercise is to ask your partners to bring together objects from their past or present lives that hold a special meaning for them. The group sits in a circle so that everyone can see each other's objects clearly. Individuals show their objects and talk about the significance of each in their lives. After everyone has had a chance to speak, the group discusses how what was said presents examples of each of the three levels of culture.

Identifying Children's Cultures

Becoming sensitive to one's own culture is an important step toward identifying the cultures that are represented by the children in your classroom. The process readies you to think about what you should know about the children's cumulative experiences and frames of reference. Even though the children in your program are very young, they already have a working knowledge of the sights and sounds of their own neighborhood, they anticipate family customs they have enjoyed, and they have strong attachments to the people who are significant in their lives. If they have frequently traveled with their families back to the homes of grandparents or other relatives, they may have another whole set of associations that are equally powerful for them. In addition, they are the inheritors of the traditions that are part of their families' identification with one or another cultural group. All of these aspects of children's lives can become rich sources to tap in the design of learning activities. The next three exercises suggest ways you might begin to collect and represent information about the culture of the children your program serves.

EXERCISE 5

Survey of Children's Culture

It may be in your initial collection of information of the children's cultures that partnerships first come fully into play. Social service workers, teachers, and parents can all contribute to the gathering of pertinent information. If parents are well informed about the program, they are likely to be willing to share their experiences and other information with the staff. Such sharing can also become a way of involving them more intimately in the program.

Gathering Information from Parents/Caregivers

1. _____ was born in _____
   Child's name   City/place of birth

*2. _____ was born in _____
    Mother's name   City/place of birth

*3. _____ was born in _____
    Father's name   City/place of birth

*4. _____ was born in _____
    Caregiver   City/place of birth

5. The family lives at: _____

   _____

6. They have lived there for _____
                                          Length of time

7. There are _____ family members living together.

8. The family members living together are: (List and give relationship to child)

   _____

   _____

   _____

   _____

   _____

   _____

   _____

*Omit if not applicable.

---

9. _____ has traveled to (List city/cities, country)
   _{Child's name}

   _____

   _____

   _____

   _____

10. by (Means of transportation) _____

   _____

   _____

   _____

11. At home _____ is/are spoken.
   _{Language(s)}

12. _____ usually plays (Location; e.g., playground, home, etc.)
   _{Child's name}

   _____

   _____

   _____

The survey of the children's cultures should be a natural continuation of the type of partnership exercises introduced in Chapter Three. This time around, however, you will be focusing on learning more about the family origins and experiences of individual children in your program.

Here is a form posing several questions that will help you to start the survey. It is *not* intended that you ask parents to fill out the form. Instead, it is recommended that you work the questions into informal conversations or meetings with parents and then make notes when you are alone so that you will remember the information. You may think of additional questions that you would like to include in this first compilation as well.

Mapping Family Origins

As you begin to collect specific information from families, you will want to represent that information in some way that has meaning for both the adults and children in the program. This exercise is intended for parents and teachers—not for children. (See Exercise 7 for suggestions for direct work with children.)

Prior to one of your scheduled staff and/or parent meetings, the people who will be participating should bring small photographs of themselves. The person coordinating the meeting should provide two wall maps—one of the world and one of the United States—as well as scissors, tape, and yarn. At the meeting itself, participants arrange their photographs around the maps and, using the yarn, link each photo with the country or state of origin of their parents (or grandparents). The result will look something like the example shown.

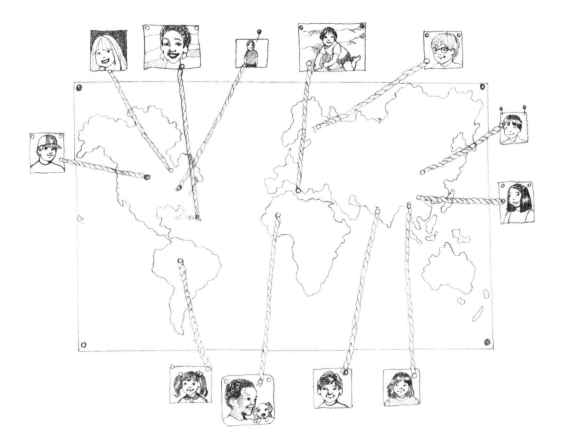

The finished product may be used in the parents' or teachers' room or in the halls of the school as a way of introducing visitors to the program.

EXERCISE 7

Child Charts

Map displays of the sort previously described have no meaning for young children. As you begin to represent in your classroom information on the children's family origins, you will want to devise some other types of displays the children can "read" themselves.

One suggestion is to ask the parents to bring in photographs of the children that may be used to create child charts. During child-initiated portions of the day, work with each child to create a portion of a language-experience chart that incorporates (1) the child's photograph, (2) a photograph or drawing of the child's present home, (3) a drawing of a type of transportation that has been important in the child's life, and (4) a representation of the place to or from which the child has traveled. An illustration of such a chart is found in this exercise.

You might want to include other kinds of information on the chart instead of what has been suggested. The one thing to keep in mind is that the chart should be simple enough for the children to be able to decode, even though they do not yet know how to read. A variation of this exercise is to work with each child to make an "All About Me" book that the children could take home as a gift to their parents.

Sample Child Chart (for class)

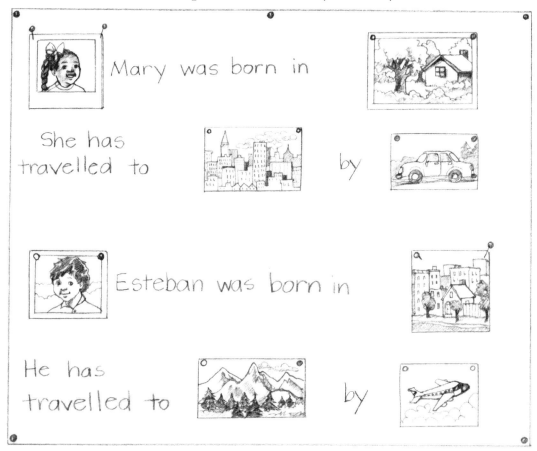

"All About Me" Book or Individual Child Chart

All About Me

I am _____.

I live here. My address is 344 Eighth Avenue.

My daddy takes me to school on the bus.

I went to the Dominican Republic with my mother.

We went in an airplane.

Acquiring Specific Information on the Culture in Your Classroom

The next step after you have noted what cultural groups are actually represented in your classroom is for you to start thinking about the specific elements that make up each of those cultures. When you are very familiar with a particular group, you can list specifics for that culture in the same way you did in Exercise 2. You must remember, however, that not every family in the group will follow the same customs.

When you are only superficially familiar with the culture of a group, you must be on your guard to avoid generalizations. Your knowledge of the group must become increasingly specific and detailed for it to be helpful in your eventual design of learning activities for the children. For example, although there is a common tendency to apply a single label to a language or racial group, (such as "Hispanic," "Asian," "Black," etc.), it is most important that as an ALERTA teacher you understand that many of the assumptions underlying these designations are too broad to be useful and often inaccurate as well. It is not enough to know that you teach Black children. Blacks may come from many areas of the United States or from different countries. They bring with them different backgrounds and experiences.

Similarly, it is not enough to know that a group of children are native speakers of a language other than English. Throughout the various regions of the Caribbean, for example, there are distinct differences in history and customs, even though Spanish is the common language of Cuba, the Dominican Republic, and Puerto Rico. In addition, although these three islands share certain characteristics, they are different from one another in significant respects and are undergoing constant change. The information available (in books or through interviews with community members) concerning traditional cultural values may therefore be limited, skewed, or otherwise unreliable. This caution should be kept in mind when using resources to learn about any group with which you are unfamiliar.

One way of acquiring specific information is to plan a series of workshops for parents, staff, and community members who would like to contribute toward the formulation of the program. The exercises that follow are examples of such workshops.

EXERCISE 8

Lifestyles as Reflections of the Environment

This exercise is designed to clarify ways in which environment can affect lifestyles of groups of people. Have various materials available for use at the workshop site. These can include cardboard boxes, egg cartons, colored cloth, and poster paint as well as large rolls of brown wrapping paper. The workshop participants divide themselves into two groups. One group will create a model of the neighborhood in which they live in the United States. The other group will create a neighborhood from which they

came or one that reflects a lifestyle in the area from which they came. Each group can construct and paint on a large piece of brown paper. After everyone has finished, a discussion can take place regarding the outcomes of the two models. Someone may list the physical differences shown. The many adjustments that must be made in order for people to adapt to an environment and lifestyle different from those in which they were raised should be discussed and carefully noted.

EXERCISE 9

Names and Origins of Typical Foods

One way to highlight differences among groups that are in some ways similar to one another is to consider foods. Blacks from the rural South have different food habits from Haitians or from urban northerners. Many of us are familiar with the wide variations in how the Chinese from different regions prepare foods. The activity presented here draws upon the Hispanic Caribbean for its examples. Other areas could be used equally well. In addition to identifying foods particu-

lar to the island cultures, this exercise points out that those cultures have been shaped by at least three prior influences.

Bring in or have your partners bring in different types of fruits and vegetables eaten in the Hispanic Caribbean. These should include yautía, corn, ñame, bananas, plantains, and if possible guavas, mangoes, or any other tropical fruits. Display these on a large table where there are three stand-up cards with the words *Taino, African,* and *Spanish* written on them. Ask volunteers to classify where each group of foods came from originally. The following is an example of such a classification.

Taino	Spanish	African
Yautía	Lemons	Bananas
Corn	Oranges	Plantains
Mangoes	Coffee	Coconuts
Guavas	Grapes	Yams
Tobacco		

Ask participants to name other tropical foods that are associated with the Hispanic Caribbean, and have the group as a whole classify them as well. At the end of the activity participants can be asked to write recipes of how some of these foods are prepared.

To show some of the differences that can appear even in something as "simple" as food, a list can be made of the various names in Spanish for the same foods on the three islands. For example:

Cuba	Puerto Rico	Dominican Republic
Mamoncillo	Quenepa	Limoncillo
Fu-fu	Mofongo	Mangu
Fruta bomba	Papaya (lechoza)	Lechoza
Arroz con frijoles	Arroz con habichuelas	Arroz con frijoles
Naranja	China	Naranja (china)
Flauta	Bollo de pan	Telera
Cangrejo	Jueyes	Jaiba

EXERCISE 10

Types and Origins of Musical Forms

Gathering information on the musical traditions and instruments typical of a cultural group is another possible point of departure for a parent/staff workshop. To show lines of continuity among various elements of a culture we will once again use the Hispanic Caribbean as an illustration of the process.

The workshop begins with a display of the instruments traditionally played in the islands. (The instruments should be collected ahead of time from members of the community who still use them, if possible.) The workshop participants should know that, like the foods named in the previous exercise, these instruments have different origins. The maracas and güiro, for instance, are instruments that have been inherited from the Taino culture. The tamborine and guitar are Spanish in origin, and the tambor and bongo are African in origin.

Next, the workshop coordinator should play recordings of music of the islands and call attention to the different rhythms and sounds produced from the same instruments. The *merengue* from the Dominican Republic can be contrasted with the *seis* from Puerto Rico and the *guaguanco* from Cuba. Some participants may be able to describe how the lyrics in these types of music served as a form of dissemination of news or gossip from various areas or towns. A different style of music can then be heard by playing a Puerto Rican *danza* and a Cuban *danzón*. Comments should be invited from the participants. The exercise can end by having several people play the instruments for the group. If at all possible, the musicians should be people from the community.

As you participate in workshops of this sort, it will be extremely helpful for you to continue adding to the resource file that you began to create during Level 1 of the program. (See Chapter Three.) When several teachers and parents work together on the file over a period of time, the result will be a continually expanding resource that can be shared among partners for both workshop planning and the creation of learning activities for the children. Notes on what people said in the workshops, drawings or photographs of culturally specific objects or activities, and descriptions of how such materials are used in daily life all might be included in your collection. The following is an example of the kind of notes that could result from the Exercise 10 workshop.

Notes on Dance and Music in the Hispanic Caribbean

At the time Spain was establishing its colonies in the New World, its folklore consisted of many heterogenous elements. Eclectic in nature, that folklore was able to incorporate new components easily, especially those surrounding religious rituals. The colonial period of the Hispanic Caribbean transformed the music and dance of Spain, giving it characteristics that reflected the indigenous cultural influences.

During the period of slavery in the Hispanic Caribbean, African rhythms were introduced into the music and dance of the islands. The degree of African influence on the dance and music of the Spanish colonies depended on the concentration of the African populations throughout the colonies. Although the Indian population was largely destroyed in the Caribbean, the influence of this cultural group is still felt, particularly in the mountain regions. The African rhythms, however, are more dominant and can readily be noted.

As one-by-one the colonies were established, their ruling elite began importing the formal court fashions of Europe. Although danzas, contradanzas, quadrillas, and valses *assumed regional characteristics, they were largely an imitation of the formality of the restored European courts. These dances were normally done in formal ballrooms. The ballroom dances, however, were eventually so influenced by African rhythms and instruments that they became recognized as comprising a distinct form of dance and music. An example of the unique configuration of instruments, rhythms, and customs can be seen in such dances as the* guaracha, danzón, mambo, *and* cha-cha-cha.

The guaracha is an old Cuban dance said to be based on the tango as well as on African rhythms. It was used as part of the program in most dance events. The guaracha was widely used in the theatre and therefore was easily transported by theatre groups to the other islands of the Hispanic Caribbean.

The danzón is another Cuban dance said to have been fully developed by 1877. It is attributed to Miguel Failde. Its origin can be traced to an earlier dance known as the contradanza, which was in fact a country dance of English origin dating back to the sixteenth century. It was introduced into France in the late seventeenth century, where it acquired unique characteristics of that period and place. From there, it was transported to the Dominican Republic (then a French colony), where it was further shaped by the unique lifestyle of that nation. During the slave rebellions of 1791, many "French Dominicans" fled to Cuba, particularly to the province of Oriente, taking with them the dances of the time—including the contradanza. In Cuba, the dance underwent further changes and eventually evolved into a distinct pattern known as the danzón.

In the Dominican Republic the merengue emerged from the particular music and dance forms being combined there. The exact origin of the merengue is not well known, but it is viewed as yet another expression of that unique mosaic of cultures characteristic of the Hispanic Caribbean. The merengue is recognized as a major folk dance of the Dominican Republic, but its rhythm is also utilized by contemporary musicians as inspiration for many new compositions. One influence upon the merengue was certainly the Spanish paso-doble. The two forms are very similar in the positions and movements of the dance partners.

The rhythms that emerged in Puerto Rico from contact of the different cultures resulted in dances such as bombas, plenas, and danzas. Some of the bombas are known as cunyá, yubá, cuembé, and holandés. It is interesting to note that the bombas have some French elements. The French influence was brought to Puerto Rico by slaves who were first captives in the French colonies. The bombas, however, are primarily of African origin and developed in the coastal regions of Puerto Rico, where many people of African descent were living. First for the slaves and later for their descendants, the bomba represented a major form of recreation. It was often performed on Saturday nights and on other festive occasions such as the end of the zafra (time for sugarcane cutting).

The plena is a later dance form that is also of African origin. It is said to have been first seen in Ponce, but it soon became known in other parts of the island such as Caguas, Loiza, Santurce, and San Juan. Eventually it became popular all over. A rhyme from the island goes:

*La plena que yo conozco
no es de la China ni del Japón
porque la plena viene de Ponce
y es del Barrio de San Antón.*

One characteristic of the plena is its use of social themes. In this respect, it has been compared to the Spanish romance, also known for its social commentary.

The danza of Puerto Rico is clearly of Spanish origin. Its beginnings date back to the sixteenth century, but it did not develop fully until the nineteenth century. Another popular dance of Spanish origin is the seis, which is also a form of music having many variations and is recognized as the backbone of Puerto Rican music. The seis is the most popular form of dance and music in Puerto Rico today.

Instruments Commonly Used in the Hispanic Caribbean

The Taino, Spanish, and African cultural influences woven through the cultures of the Hispanic Caribbean can also be seen in instruments used on the three islands.

Both maracas and the güiro were used by the Tainos, who occupied the islands before Columbus arrived. The Indians used the dried fruit of the higüera tree for the maraca globes and a thick-skinned member of the cucumber family for güiros. When shaken, the maracas produce a sound from the movement of small pebbles sealed inside the globes. A wire comb is stroked against shallow grooves on one side of the güiro in order to produce a rasping sound. Maracas and güiros are used to accent rhythms underlying the melodies played on other instruments.

Several varieties of stringed instruments were adapted from the Spanish guitar. The cuatro (with four strings) and the tiple (like a small guitar but often having only five strings) are direct descendants of that instrument. The pandereta (a type of tamborine) also originated in Spain.

The African influence can be seen in the tambor and bongoes as well as in the marimbola, a large, boxlike instrument played by plucking flexible steel slats laid across an opening on one side.

Other percussion instruments of indeterminate origin are used in parts of the Hispanic Caribbean. The clave *(cencerro) is played by covering openings on the bottom of the tube with the palm of the hand and striking the top with a solid wooden rod. A resonant "tocking" sound results.*

Using Culturally Specific Information to Extend the Children's Knowledge and Skills

The point has been made throughout this chapter that children bring with them experiences that are inextricable from themselves and their cultures. These experiences are rich sources that can be tapped as the basis for preparation of the classroom environment, creation of learning materials, and design of activities for the children.

One aspect of the preparation of the classroom environment—the display of information on the children's family origins—has already been discussed in Exercise 7. Selecting materials that avoid stereotyping and project positive images of the groups represented by the children in your program is another way to prepare the environment. When you cannot locate commercial materials that accurately reflect the ethnicity, racial characteristics, and cultural experiences of the children, it is possible for you (and your partners) to construct the learning materials needed. Each area of the classroom should eventually be well stocked with materials that present the children with positive reflections of themselves. Finally, you can plan activities that incorporate elements of the three levels of culture in ways that are appropriate for children's developmental levels. Each of these three uses of culturally specific information is discussed in the following exercises.

EXERCISE 11

Avoidance of Stereotyping in Classroom Learning Materials

One of the most immediate ways that you can apply your growing knowledge of the children's cultures is in critical review of the learning materials that you presently have in your classroom. Your aims in this exercise are first to identify any materials that are oriented toward a particular racial or ethnic group represented in your classroom, and second to ask yourself some important questions about *how* a certain cultural or racial group is depicted. Those questions cover two broad areas: racism and sexism. It is an unfortunate fact that many materials intended to portray diversity actually present stereotypes; that is, overly sim-

ple, inaccurate, or negative images of what people from a given group are like. ALERTA teachers and parents need to be very sensitive to the possible presence of stereotypes and to remove materials that contain them from their classrooms. If you are going to use materials to extend the children's knowledge and skills, you want to do so in positive rather than negative ways.

To begin, you and your partners should take examples of various types of learning materials from each area of your classroom. If you are working in a group, display the materials on a broad surface so that they are visible to everyone. Discuss the materials one at a time, using the questions on the following pages to guide your exploration. You may find it easiest to begin with the children's books, as they contain most of the elements you need to consider; but you should also look closely at puppets and manipula- tives such as puzzles and lotto games. You may wish to formulate additional questions to ask yourself as you work. Those materials that successfully "pass the test" can be placed back in your classrooms. Any that you find to contain stereotypes should be eliminated.

Questions to Ask Yourself When Examining Learning Materials for Evidence of Stereotypes

Portrayal of Racial/Ethnic/Cultural Groups

1. Do the materials contain negative messages about a particular group?

2. Are illustrations of the physical characteristics of characters in the ma- terials unreal or unnatural (for example, Asians portrayed as yellow, Blacks hav- ing "white" facial features, Native Americans having red skin)?

3. In books, is there evidence of condescension in the treatment of a minority group character?

4. Are the lifestyles of minority group members depicted as inferior to the life- style of the majority group?

5. Do particular words used to describe a minority group present negative images of the group?

Portrayal of Women

1. Are women appearing in the mate- rials always portrayed in traditional sex roles (for example, teacher, nurse, secre- tary, housewife)?

2. In books, do women have passive roles and men have active roles in the story?

3. Are high-status occupations (such as being a doctor or holding a decision- making position) associated only with men in the story?

4. Are women depicted as defenseless and/or dependent?

5. Is the success of a woman based on her good looks and physical attributes or on her initiative and intelligence?

Selecting/Creating Learning Materials That Reflect Elements of Specific Cultures

The next step in applying your knowledge is to add learning materials that accurately reflect the physical characteristics and combined experiences of the children in your classroom. Each area of your room should have a selection of such materials available to the children for periods of the day when they choose their own work. The materials should also be well integrated into the short cluster activities that you do with the children each day.

Sometimes you will be able to locate commercial materials that meet the requirements set out in Exercise 11. At other times you will be creating materials especially tailored to the children's frame of reference.

In making such materials, you need to know very specifically about the objects that are significant to the children in their daily lives and in the cultural traditions of which they are a part. At the end of this chapter is a collection of sample activities that make use of materials identified through a survey of children's cultures done in one ALERTA classroom. Look closely at the examples, and then think about what materials you would use in place of those described to reflect the cultures of the children in *your* classroom.

The materials you identify can be made over a period of time through the combined efforts of the children, the parents, and your colleagues. It is important that you include materials construction in as many staff development workshops and parent meetings as possible. Many commerical resource books for teachers are available that cover techniques of materials construction. (See list of resources in the appendix of this source book.) Those techniques most frequently used in ALERTA classrooms are described in Chapter Five.

Designing Activities that Incorporate Elements of the Children's Culture

Having culturally specific materials alone will not be sufficient to integrate into your classroom use of the cultures represented by the children. You will also need to design ongoing cluster activities that make use of the children's knowledge. *Remember,* these are not "special" activities planned for such an occasion as Black History Month but are the activities that are used every day to teach concepts and skills to the children. The major difference is that the activities are connected to the children's direct experience at home and in the community and that they use materials derived from or reflecting that experience to teach the concepts or skills involved. Here is one example of a series of learning activities derived from the children's experience.

An observant teacher in one school saw that when the children left the school they would run up to the elderly gentleman selling piraguas *(snowcones) near the school. This was not surprising except that upon closer look, she saw how gentle he was with the children and how much he enjoyed talking and laughing with them. Some time after this she introduced herself to Don Paco and after talking to him awhile invited him to her classroom. She had the idea that Don Paco could explain to the children about making piraguas. On the day agreed upon, Don Paco came into the classroom with his cart full of brightly colored syrups and a great piece of ice. The children were allowed to shave the ice, pour the syrup, and smell and taste the delicious snow cones. Don Paco then told them how he had come from Puerto Rico, worked in New York, and later when he retired became a* piragüero. *The class talked about the different tastes and how the syrups were made from fruits. It was an interesting, enjoyable time for all.*

Out of this experience grew many activities introducing new concepts, skills, and vocabulary. Children made their own syrups out of fruits in season. They measured, weighed, predicted, and wrote. Thinking of Don Paco's stories prompted some children to ask their parents and grandparents why and how they had come to New York. Interviews were conducted, notes taken, maps made, and life histories written about. This activity truly used the experiences of the children as the basis for learning.

The full procedure for planning ALERTA cluster activities is described in Chapter Eight. You should, however, begin to use such learning activities that make direct use of the children's experience as soon as possible after you begin to use ALERTA's approach. Having such daily activities for small groups of children will help you refine your practice as you move through later chapters of this source book. Teaching through the cultures of the children in your class and exposing them to each others' cultures makes a strong statement of worth. It is a celebration of who we are. It is a celebration of our humanity.

For ALERTA's Level 2:
Examples of Ways the Types of Information Collected Through Workshops, Conversations, and Other Resources Can Be Incorporated into Teacher-directed Cluster Activities

The activities that follow illustrate how information gathered from parents, caregivers, and other resources can be incorporated into daily activities for small clusters of children. The examples are grouped according to the level of culture they represent (see Exercise 2).

1: Objects/Artifacts/Implements

Making Maracas

Maracas are a form of musical instrument popular in many Hispanic countries and in parts of the United States. Individual cultural groups have different ways of making and decorating maracas. The activity that follows presents two forms of maraca that you can help young children construct. Your choice of form will depend upon your observation of the children's developmental levels.

After an activity in which children have heard or used maracas, explain to them that they will make their own maracas. All materials should be prepared *before* the activity begins. When the alternative way to make maracas is chosen, the activity should be extended over a period of a week to allow for layering and drying of the papier-mâché.

Materials for Simple Maracas

small rocks or pebbles
small juice containers
thick cardboard cut to the diameter of
    the open ends of the juice containers
masking tape

Put a teaspoon of pebbles into a small juice can. Place previously cut cardboard at the open end of the can and secure with masking tape.

Materials for an Alternative Way to Make Maracas

small balloons (one for each child)   newspaper strips (1″ × 1½″ wide)
petroleum jelly   small pebbles
juice bar sticks   tape
papier-mâché mixture   paints and brushes

(It is suggested that the teaching team make a sample pair of this type of maracas for the children to see *before* the activity is initiated.)

Distribute a balloon to each child. Have the children blow up their balloons to the desired size of the maracas. Tie the ends. Each child should spread a thin layer of petroleum jelly over the entire balloon.

Have children place newspaper strips in the papier-mâché mixture. Next, the children layer these strips onto the greased balloon. No more than two layers should be wrapped around the balloon before allowing it to dry. The maracas should be smoothed as each layer is ad-

ded. Be sure the opening where the balloon is tied is large enough for pebbles to be inserted. Continue the layering process until a thickness of approximately one-quarter of an inch is reached. Be sure each layer has dried before adding new ones.

When the layering process is finished and the papier-mâché is completely dry, have the child puncture the balloon and gently remove it. He or she can drop five or six pebbles into this opening and insert the juice bar stick there as a handle. Tape the stick securely to the opening and layer papier-mâché around it. When this is dry, the child is ready to paint and decorate his or her maracas.

Making Cymbals and Jingles[2]

Instruments of this sort are common in both the English-speaking and Spanish-speaking Caribbean, Panama, and other parts of Central America. They are used to accompany songs of many types.

[2] Used with permission of D. R. B. Grant, *op. cit.*

Chapter Four

Materials for Making Cymbals

lids of cans (large cookie
   can or canister-type)

electrical tape
hammer

Before doing this activity, use a hammer to flatten the edges of the lids of the cans. Measure and cut a six-inch and a four-inch piece of electrical tape for each cymbal. Working with the children, put the sticky sides together, centering the short tape on the long tape and leaving an inch of tape on either side of the long piece. Have the children affix the two ends of the tape to the back of each cymbal, leaving a loop of tape large enough for a child's hand. Reinforce the ends of the tape with additional tape. Sounds can be made by crashing two lids together, tapping them together, or hitting one with a drumstick.

Materials for Making Jingles

24 bottle caps (those that one has to
   pry off)
nail for punching holes in bottle caps

hammer
about 18 inches of wire
tape

Use a hammer to flatten about twenty-four bottle caps, and then punch each one through the middle. A nail can be used for punching, with the bottle caps resting on a workbench or a bit of wood. (The teacher or a parent should punch the holes beforehand.) Children can string the bottle caps onto a length of wire measuring eighteen inches. Overlap the ends of the wire about five inches in either direction, and wrap securely with tape. Allow enough space for movement between bottle caps. To get the jingling sound, the child holds the wire and shakes it. The finished product looks like this:

Talk to the children about what they have made, and ask them how the instruments can be used. Encourage the children to use the instruments to accompany their singing. At a later date form a percussion band, using these instruments as well as maracas or other instruments the children have made.

Using Images from the Environment in Songs, Rhymes, Artwork, and Development of Other Skills

People of many cultural groups have noted sights or sounds that are distinctive of their region of origin and incorporated them into their folklore, songs, or artwork. In Puerto Rico, for example, there is a tiny tree frog that lives only on that island. The *coquí* is greenish-brown in color and sings it name over and over again as soon as the sun sets. Only the male sings to call his companion. The little frog rests in shallow water during the day when it sleeps. Coquíes are gentle little creatures; if you are very quick, you can handle them and put them back in their trees without frightening them. Puerto Rican children raised on the island know the coquí and listen to him at night. A curious fact regarding the coquí is that if it is taken from Puerto Rico, it no longer sings and soon dies.

The coquí appears in some songs and rhymes for children. Verses such as the following are easily taught to children who have had direct experience with coquíes.

El coquí, el coquí a mi me encanta
Es tan lindo el canter del coquí,
Por las noches al ir a acostarme,
Me adormece cantando asi:
¡Coquí! ¡Coquí! ¡Coquí! quí quí quí!
¡Coquí! ¡Coquí! ¡Coquí! quí quí quí!

Besides appearing in songs and rhymes, coquíes may also be seen sometimes in various forms of folk art. You might use your knowledge of this fact in a craft project done with children who are familiar with coquíes. If you or your partners have an artistic bent, you could carve a linoleum block with the image of a coquí. Working for a short period of time over several days, the children could print lengths of cloth for use as curtains in their classroom's housekeeping area or placemats for use at lunchtime.

Printing of this sort could be done with *any* design that has meaning for the children and parents participating in your program.[3]

---

[3] Suggestion to use local designs such as these West African Adinkra symbols was made by Vida Dzobo, an ALERTA trainer on sabbatical leave from work in her native country, Ghana.

Another possibility for use of culturally-related designs is in learning activities that focus on strengthening children's visual discrimination skills. In Japan, for instance, ancient heraldry designs or crests are sometimes used with young children to foster such skills; and some Japanese-Americans have retained that tradition.[4] You and your colleagues could create a card game where children match the designs that are *the same*, as in the example that follows.

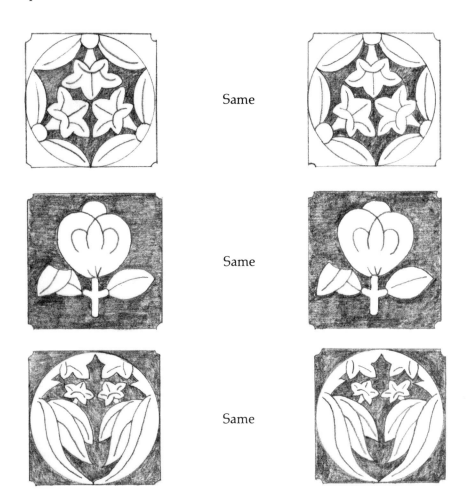

Same

Same

Same

2: Customs, Traditions, Ways of Doing Things

Head Wraps

Head wraps are a common form of clothing in many cultures. In some cultural groups, men wrap their heads. This is true of the Sikhs of India, for example. In other groups it is the women who wrap their heads. Women in different parts of Africa do it, as well as many women in the Dominican Republic, Cuba, Puerto Rico, Jamaica, and the United States. Your choice of wrapping style for use in your classroom will depend on what you have observed to be the preferred styles among the parents participating in the program.

[4] An excellent source of patterns for Japanese crests is Matsuya's *Japanese Design Motifs* (Fumie Adachi, Trans., New York: Dover Publications, Inc., 1972.)

Show the children how to tie a simple wrap.

Demonstrate a more complicated wrap, such as this one:

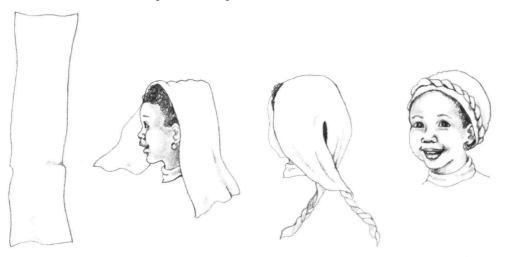

As you are wrapping a child's head, encourage the children to talk about where they have seen such a wrap before, how wrapping is done in their home, and so on. Invite the children to try wrapping each other's heads. When the activity is over, leave the scarves or lengths of cloth you used in the dress-up or dramatic play area of the classroom so that the children can work with them again during child-initiated portions of the day.

Family Reunions

When families have lived in a particular city or town for generations, they often retain close ties with relatives in the area of the country from which their family originally came. Many African-American families in New York, for example, go to family re-unions somewhere in the South during the summer or for holidays. The children go with their parents and have the chance to experience the richness of the family gathering. They may hear several different accents, enjoy foods that are prepared on special occasions, learn the ways of addressing different relatives, and hear family stories that have been passed down for generations. As children come quickly to anticipate this great adventure, they are likely to mention it in the classroom. The staff can pick up on the excitement of a child or several children by developing activities and learning materials around family reunions.

Photographs taken of landmarks along the way to such a reunion and at the family gathering should be requested ahead of time from the parents of the children who will be participating in the activity. It is important that you explain to the parents what the photos will be used for. Use the set of photographs to make one or more of the following things.

1. Sequence cards (for example: 1. leaving home, 2. driving to Alabama, 3. arriving at grandmother's house).

2. Individual books recording each child's journey and significant happenings at the reunion.

3. Lotto games.

(Techniques for making lotto games and other such materials from photographs are presented in Chapter Five.)

Materials such as these can be used in teacher-directed cluster activites to teach such skills as sequencing and matching, or they can be placed in the table toys/manipulatives area of the classroom for use during periods when the children select their own activities.

3. Underlying Systems and Values

Family Composition

The persons considered by children to be part of their families may differ from cultural group to cultural group. When asked who is in their family, some children may talk about their mothers, fathers, and brothers or sisters. Children from other groups, however, may include in their spontaneous descriptions grandparents, aunts and uncles, cousins, or persons who are not blood relations. Moreover, within all groups there is the possibility of single-parent families. Sensitivity to the possibility of such diversity both among and within given cultural groups requires that you prepare learning materials in such a way that the variation can be expressed.

In a flannelboard activity on the composition of families, for example, you could make cardboard figures (backed with flannel) to represent fathers, mothers, brothers, sisters, grandparents, aunts and uncles, cousins, and boarders. The figures should have the ethnic characteristics of the children in the center, offer an obvious range of ages, and display different body types (thin, heavy, tall, and short people).

Give each child the opportunity to put her or his family on the flannelboard. As the children work, encourage them to identify each family member.

Kwanzaa: "Gifts of Love"

Sometimes people deliberately choose to express certain of their values through a holiday. Kwanzaa is an example of such a celebration that has a relatively recent origin. It was started by Dr. M. Ron Karenja in 1966 and is now observed by some members of African-American communities in the United States, who see it as an opportunity to stress the unity of the Black family. Kwanzaa occurs between December 26 and January 1 of each year. The festival was derived from the harvest celebrations of agricultural African people. Each day of the holiday embodies a different principle and is characterized by its corresponding symbol. The seven principles and symbols of Kwanzaa are listed here.

Principles	Symbols
1. Umoja (unity)	Mazao (crops)
2. Kujichagulia (self-determination)	Mkeka (mat)
3. Ujima (collective work and responsibility)	Kimara (the candle holder)
4. Ujamaa (cooperative economics)	Vibunzi (ears of corn)
5. Nia (purpose)	Zawadi (gifts)
6. Kuumba (creativity)	Kimbombe cha umoja (the unity cup)
7. Imani (faith)	Mishumaa saba (the seven candles)

Prior to beginning Kwanzaa activities, it is recommended that parents in your program who celebrate the holiday be invited to talk with the children about the festival. They should explain that one of the things people do during Kwanzaa (on the last day) is to make "gifts of love" to give to someone special. (It is not necessary that this particular phrase be used, as long as the children understand that the idea is to make something for someone.)

After the parents' explanation, give the children a variety of "found objects" and basic art materials to work with. Encourage the children to use these materials to make a gift for their families. Tell the children they can make anything they want. Give as little direction as possible concerning the final product of their work, but assist if the children show they need a little help in manipulating the materials (e.g., use of the scissors, paintbrushes, etc.). By allowing the children to use the materials in whatever manner they prefer, you as the teacher are also allowing the children to exercise one of the principles of Kwanzaa; that is, creativity.

Because this is an open-ended activity requiring a great deal of different types of materials, it is recommended that it be carried out during a time of the day when the children will not run out of time before finishing their work. You may consider having the work continue for several consecutive days until the children feel they have given final shape to their work.

This activity should be conducted with small groups of children in order to allow you to pay individual attention to each child and therefore promote further understanding of its purpose. Other possibilities for Kwanzaa activities include the following.

1. Making necklaces, wrist and ankle bracelets, and costumes to wear at family gatherings during Kwanzaa.

2. Planting in September or October so you can harvest in December. You can plant beans, herbs such as parsley and dill, scallions, etc.

3. Harvesting the crops and having the feast celebration—e.g., making (with the children) a salad, soup, or stew, and eating it.

Wishing Luck and Prosperity: the Chinese New Year

Many Chinese-American families and some families from Southeast Asia (for example, Vietnamese and Cambodian families) continue to celebrate the new year as one of their major holidays. The Chinese New Year does not fall on January 1 but on a date later in the winter marking the start of the new year by the ancient lunar calendar.

Originally the celebration was held over a period of more than a month, but today it is more common to see festivities concentrated in the time between New Year's Eve and Lantern Festival (about fifteen days). Various customs are associated with this holiday, because it has been celebrated for thousands of years by people from many different regions of China and Southeast Asia. Therefore, there is no one "right way" to celebrate. As with any holiday, the traditions used in your program should reflect the actual practices of families of children in your classroom.

Whatever the specific customs followed, there is an underlying theme that unites them in the intent to wish luck and prosperity on others. Many of the ways of preparing food, decorating the home, and giving special greetings to friends and relatives are done specifically because they are considered lucky and thus will bring luck in the new year to all who observe them. Red is the color that brings prosperity and luck over this period. Household decorations and greeting cards are usually red with gold writing to convey good wishes.

An effective way of incorporating this celebration into your on-going program is to invite parents (and, if possible, grandparents) of children in the program into the classroom to speak with the class for a few minutes about the ways that their families enjoy the holiday. Each of these short talks should be focused on *one* of the many customs observed and should include an explanation of what the custom means (*why* people do it that way). The parents should be asked to bring with them photographs, pictures, and/or objects related to the custom they will be describing.

After each talk, the children should make or prepare (and add to the Housekeeping Area) one more element of the holiday that has been described. Over a week's period of time, for example, the children could work with you and the parents to:

1. cut and paste red paper strips with gold lettered greetings wishing luck, to hang on the walls of the classroom;

2. decorate a table for special foods with red candles and incense burners;

3. carefully clean the Housekeeping Area so that everything is perfect for the holiday;

4. set out ten or twelve dishes (always an *even* number) with pictures of the special foods, or even better, with the foods themselves, on the decorated table;

5. make red paper envelopes with gold lucky greetings for use in role plays where the children give each other "lucky money" (you would use play money) as they visit the Housekeeping Area of the classroom during this period; and

6. prepare a puppet show entertainment followed by a small bazaar of special foods for snacks. (For this activity, you should adapt a Chinese, Vietnamese, or Cambodian story to make it developmentally appropriate as a basis for the show.)

In preparing for such a celebration, you may wish to read the following source: Mann, Shiah. *Chinese New Year*. New York: A.R.T.S., Inc., 98 Madison Street, N.Y., 1976. Equally important are your continuing conversations with persons who know the holiday very well, so that you can add to and expand upon the activities described.

CHAPTER FIVE

Level 3: Identifying and Using Community Resources

*"My lion's **big**," Tyrone explained to the teacher. "I take him home with me on a leash."*

"My lion purrs," said Ana. "Except when she gets mad; then watch out!"

"I don't see any lions," said Sara. She stood with hands on her hips and radiated authority from every one of her 39 inches. "Where are they?"

"Outside," replied Tyrone. He smiled.

Tyrone's teachers were puzzled. This was the fourth morning that a group of four or five children had come into the classroom talking about lions. The lions seemed very real to the children. Not only did they talk about these marvelous lions but they also painted lions in the art area, and Ana made one out of clay. The rubber lion suddenly became a favored accessory in the block area.

"Maybe some parents took a group of children to the zoo," speculated Margaret, one of the teachers. But a conversation with Tyrone's mother, who came to pick him up at the end of each school day, revealed no visit. Nor could she recollect Tyrone's seeing a program about lions on T.V.—at least not recently.

The following Friday, the staff of the early childhood center met for their monthly in-service day. Their plan that morning was to go as a group on their third community walk to collect information, take photos, and make tapes of community sights and sounds important to the children in their center. A couple of members of the staff were not enthusiastic at the prospect.

"I've walked up that street on the way to work every day for seven years," said Margaret. "There's nothing I can learn from this walk that I don't already know."

The educational director thought about Margaret's comment for a moment.

"That's probably true from your point of view as an adult," she said. "Try to see that street as a three- or four-year-old may see it. You might be surprised."

Margaret's group walked slowly down the street, taking photos and talking together. Margaret stepped on a large pebble and turned her ankle. Grimacing, she sat down abruptly on a nearby bench to rub her ankle. She looked up at her companions to say something, and as she did her eyes focused on the building across the street. Over the door, on the cornices, above the windows, and under the eaves were beautiful old stone carvings of . . . lions.

The third level of use of ALERTA is identifying and using community resources. At first glance, this level of work may seem to be identical to the usual practice in early childhood education of taking the children to visit the firehouse or the post office. A deeper look, however, reveals an important difference in approach. ALERTA expects teachers and parents to look at the communities in which their children live from a child's point of view. The art of community observation involves picking out those aspects of a neighborhood that catch the children's rather than the adult's attention and then using what has been identified to create learning materials that have special meaning for children.

Reflection of the community in the curriculum is an important part of ALERTA's process. For adults and children alike, culture is not only the past and the traditions of a people but also the present, everyday environment in which they live. It is common knowledge that young children learn most easily when objects or situations familiar to them are used in the teaching process. The sights and sounds of day-to-day living are directly related to the ways children use their five senses, solve problems, and develop language. By paying careful attention to the elements that make up the community, teachers can find easy and intriguing ways to build upon the knowledge the children bring with them to the classroom or early childhood center. In this chapter you will be introduced to ways of observing the community, recording your observations, and transforming your observations into materials for your classroom and learning activities for young children.

EXERCISE 1

Observing the Community

The first requirement for incorporating the community into the curriculum is to be able to *see it* in ways different from your usual view of it.

A young teacher in a remote Alaskan village was walking along a tundra path with a small group of Head Start children one summer afternoon. She was in a hurry to reach their destination, because it was time for lunch and the food had yet to be prepared. Suddenly she realized that one child was not with the group. Looking back she saw Wassile crouching over a small clump of plants. She retraced her steps and crouched down with him to see what was so fascinating. Under the leaves of the cranberry bushes, tiny alpine flowers had emerged in stars of pink, white, and pale blue.

As adults, you may have lived in one community for many years. You are so familiar with the sights and sounds of your neighborhood, town, or village that in a sense you no longer see or hear them. Young children, on the other hand, experience their world as something new and fresh. Things that adults take for granted, children can use to add to their knowledge and refine their skills.

To start developing a child's-eye view of your community, ask yourself the questions on the next page.

Next, to confirm the accuracy of your memory, take a walk around the neighborhood where the children who come to your early childhood center or school live. It is helpful in taking such a walk to carry an observation guide like the one on pages 86–87. A guide provides a convenient way to take notes as you walk along. Not all the items suggested here may apply to your community. Before you take the walk, you may want to add to or change some of the items in the guide so that it will be more focused on your environment.

Although you can do the walk on your own, you will get the best effect from it if you go with a partner or a group of people using ALERTA. That way you will be able to collect not only your own perceptions but also those of other people. A shared walk will produce a larger pool of observations to draw from in the materials development that you will be doing later.

It may be that such a walk will give you a renewed appreciation of your neighborhood's diversity. Such a realization on your part can be a safeguard against stereotypes. A community that at first appears to have only one or two groups suddenly shows itself to be a rich multicultural mix. That diversity must appear in the learning activities you design to reflect your community.

Building on the work you did in Level 2, you may also come to the conclusion that some of the ideas you had about particular groups are either too general or are inaccurate for the context in which you work. Members of the same national or ethnic/cultural group may have very different experiences from one another. Children in your classroom, although they now live in a common community, may have come from different regions or countries. Within those regions or countries, they may have come from different rural or urban areas. Many children regularly travel back and forth between their home community (where the school or early-learning center is located) and the region or country from which their families came. Young children need to relate to all the environments they know. You need to know what those realities are for each family. For example, has the family lived here for more than a generation? Does the family travel to the country or to the region in the United States from which it originally came? What does the region where they go look like? What experiences have the children had there? Keeping your eyes and ears open to the clues presented in the community—in the children's play and in conversations with parents—will help you to answer these questions.

Guide for Community Observations

1. What sorts of buildings make up the neighborhood? (Tall, narrow buildings? Low, wide buildings? Apartments? Single-family dwellings?) Of what types of material are the buildings made?

_____

_____

2. What types of industry or agriculture are found in your community? What do they produce?

_____

_____

3. What types of goods are sold in the stores? Do some of the stores show an orientation toward particular cultural groups? If so, how?

_____

_____

4. What special service agencies are found nearby? (Hospital? Community center? Post office? Farmers' exchange?)

_____

_____

5. What easily recognizable occupations are in evidence in the neighborhood? (Doctors or nurses? firefighters? construction workers? farmers?)

_____

_____

6. What types of vehicles are seen in the neighborhood? (Buses? subways? cabs of different kinds? trucks?)

_____

_____

7. What special machinery is in evidence? (Streetcleaners? cranes or other construction units? tractors? road graders?)

_____

_____

8. What is the topography of the neighborhood? (Hilly? flat? straight streets? crooked streets?)

_____

9. What sorts of recreational facilities are available? (Movies? penny arcades? parks? swimming pools? basketball courts?)

_____

10. If there are parks, what kinds of plants and trees grow there? Are there any animals around? (Squirrels? dogs? cats?)

_____

_____

11. What kinds of games do children play in the streets?

_____

_____

12. What styles of clothing are popular?

_____

_____

13. What sorts of special events go on in the neighborhood? (Feast days? art carnivals? street fairs? block parties?)

_____

_____

14. What sounds can be heard in the neighborhood?

_____

_____

15. What colors are frequently used in building decoration?

_____

_____

16. What are common signs or symbols seen in the neighborhood?

_____

_____

EXERCISE 2

Observing a Home Visit

The home visits required in Head Start and other early childhood programs can also provide content important in creating continuity between home and school. Although many early childhood programs do expect teachers to make home visits, few prepare teachers to examine their own values and how those values might affect their perceptions during such visits. The ALERTA Program requires that staff become used to looking closely at variations in value systems, including their own, and seeing the relationship of those values to teaching and learning behaviors.

One of the reasons for making home visits is to acquire insights from parents that might be useful in teaching their children. The most obvious continuity sought in bilingual programs is in the area of language. You need to know what proportion of the children are from Spanish-dominant[1] and what proportion from English-dominant homes as well as what dialects or regional variations of the two languages are spoken. Observations of home language use provide the background to help you understand the child's linguistic functioning in the classroom.

You may recognize that there can be many forms of a single language and that the way people speak—the accent, the vocabulary, and the grammatical structures they use—are indications of the region in which they were raised. In this view, one form of the language is not "correct" whereas another is "wrong." Instead, you see that language patterns are learned in the context of specific situations. It is important from this perspective that you as a teacher learn what form of a given language is spoken at home. In the classroom you will want to accept the language the children bring with them at the same time you introduce a more universal form of language. Your aim is to have the children be able to choose later in their lives which language or which form of a single language they will use according to the situation in which they find themselves.

On the other hand, you may believe that there is only one correct, or pure, form of a language and that persons who use "dialects" are speaking badly. If you visit a home where people are not speaking the "standard," you may unconsciously dismiss much of the detail of language use that you observe, seeing it as unimportant or as not giving you any valuable information. In this case, you will lose an opportunity to build on an aspect of children's experience and run the risk of making them feel that what is done at home is somehow wrong.

Observations of children in their home settings can also provide you with information on child-rearing patterns used by parents of young children. Style of discipline used, the nature of the rewards, the way family is defined (extended or nuclear), and the behaviors parents expect of children (even if you consider them inappropriate to the child's age), can all provide information useful in the informal structuring of class behavior.

Once again, it is possible that your own views about how children should be raised or what sort of discipline should be used may interfere with your making accurate observations of home expectations. The ability to suspend judgment will allow you to recognize at a deep level that parents, relatives, and others in close contact with a child at home serve as role models. If there is a contradiction or a difference between the model presented at the school and that presented at home, the child may be confused about social relationships and expectations. Therefore, the child should be able to continue his or her identification with patterns learned at home while he or she observes and incorporates other forms of interaction patterns at the center, free of criticisms or pressures from the staff.

Teachers preparing to make home visits need to consider such issues and look at their own views as honestly as possible. One way to become sensitive to your own beliefs is to sit with a group of teachers or other staff members using ALERTA and try to answer the questions outlined in the "Home Visit" form as they relate to the children your school or center serves. Then try as an individual to answer the questions in relation to your own family. When you have finished, talk about any differences that may have appeared between the expectations of staff in regard to their own families and what you as a group expect to be true of the families you serve. You may discover in your discussion certain points of potential conflict between the points of view of

[1]Substitute the second language used in your program as appropriate.

Things to Note *Before* and *After* a Home Visit

1. What language(s) is (are) spoken at home?

_____

2. Is a regional variation of the language used in the home? What are some of its characteristics?

_____

3. What is the general composition of the family? (How many children are in the family? Do grandparents or other relatives live in the same home?)

_____

_____

4. Does the family travel a lot with the children? Where do they go? How often? What experiences have the children had as a result of traveling?

_____

_____

5. What types of toys and games are used in the home?

_____

_____

6. Do any of the activities at the center go against the parents' values or beliefs?

_____

_____

7. What approval or disapproval of certain types of behavior in children is given? What behaviors are particularly singled out for comment? What style of discipline is used at home?

_____

_____

8. What expectations are held for the children? Do the expectations differ according to sex, position in order of birth, etc.?

_____

_____

you and your colleagues or between you and the families you are going to visit. This experience may help you to be cautious and to reserve judgment in the actual visits.

Of course, it is also very possible that the characteristics you attributed to the families you will be visiting were not accurate representations of the individuals involved. You may have stereotyped expectations, especially if the families are from an ethnic or religious group unfamiliar to you. Having thought about what your expectations are ahead of time may in contrast allow you to see the actual patterns of an individual home more clearly.

During an actual visit, of course, you will not want to be writing down the details of people's conversations. Making notes while you talk together may discourage people from speaking freely to you. As soon as you return to your center or school or to your home, however, you should write down any information acquired that you think might relate to program planning for the children.

The preceding questions asked may assist you in recording your thoughts after a home visit. They are meant as suggestions only. You may want to add thoughts of your own and ideas arising from discussions with other members of your staff. It is unlikely that on a single home visit you will be able to gather all the information that is helpful in planning. It is more usual to accumulate the information over several visits and through informal day-to-day contact with the parents at the school or center. Your notes become cumulative and thus an increasingly richer source for designing new learning activities.

EXERCISE 3

Organizing Information on Community Observations

Now that you have collected some specific information on your community through initial walks and home visits or other conversations with parents, you should sit down (with a partner, if possible) and sort your observations into groups useful to you. One way to do this is to put the separate pieces of information into lists that relate to the various areas in your classroom, such as those listed here.

Housekeeping Area or Family Corner

Common clothing: jeans, T-shirts, wraparound skirts, blouses with short sleeves

Types of goods sold in stores: tropical fruits

Special service agencies: visiting nurses, infant center

Recreation: basketball court, "loadies" court

Art Area

Special events in the neighborhood: annual street fair, feast day celebration

Decorations: mural of city life on boys' club wall

Style of architecture: stone ornamentation on buildings

Colors used commonly in community decorations: red, black, and yellow.

Block-building Area

Building types: brownstones, highrises, warehouses

Common vehicles: delivery trucks, buses, subways, double-deckers

Special machinery: construction cranes, lifts

Topography: hilly, streets parallel

Table-toy Area

Animals found in area: cats, dogs, birds of many types

Plants: dogwood, mimosa

Common occupations: storekeepers, clerks, doctors

Sounds heard: fire sirens, buzz saws, crane bells

Signs/symbols: STOP, GO, FOOD

Another way to sort your observations is according to the types of skills that you hope to help children develop. An example follows of how that way of organizing the information might look.

Communication Skills	Social Skills
Common occupations	Traffic rules
Clothing common in neighborhood	Ways people purchase goods in stores
Signs/symbols commonly found	Public awareness in using parks
Special events in the neighborhood	Ways people visit each other

Science/Problem Solving	Premath Skills
Animals/plants found in area	Numbers of vehicles
Sounds heard in community	Heights of buildings
Route to the market	Classification of types of stores
Cooking/foods common to area	Construction projects

EXERCISE 4

Recording Community Information in Photographs and on Tape

In addition to taking notes on what they see, ALERTA developers recommend that staff and/or parents take photographs of the sights and tape the sounds of the neighborhood, which they can use later to make classroom materials. There is an important reason for doing this.

A group of graduate students opened the door to the room where they expected to attend a course lecture. To their surprise, they found that their usual meeting room had been rearranged. Their instructor had organized the movable tables and chairs into "interest areas," each containing a variety of materials for both children and adults.

The students stood for a moment and then followed their instructor's direction to pick an area that appealed to them and to begin exploring the materials in that area. Suddenly one of the students interrupted her task with a sound of surprise.

"Hey, look here! This book has a photograph of my neighborhood. That's my house, right there!"

Other students moved closer to see the photo, and a lively conversation followed.

At a Head Start Center in a large city in the Northeast a small boy followed his usual pattern of moving rapidly around the classroom, stopping briefly in the various areas but never long enough to become involved in the activity going on in each. Billy was a special child, one of several children with minimal brain dysfunction who had been mainstreamed with the normally developing children at the center. His teachers had noted that he was bright, that he had a very high energy level, and that his productive speech was still somewhat limited.

Billy moved toward a table where teacher-made puzzles had been set out for the children's use. In a somewhat noncommital fashion he began to put one of the puzzles together. Suddenly he stiffened and peered more closely at the puzzle he had assembled. Then he dashed for his teacher and pulled him over to the table.

"Raúl, do you see this? That's the place where my mommy . . . the place where we get the bus to come here! See? Right there. The bus!"

That was the first time Billy's teachers had heard him speak two complete sentences.

Adults and children alike are drawn to materials that make use of objects, scenes, or sounds familiar to them. Their recognition often brings enjoyment and frequently encourages language and other forms of social interaction. Such materials are a powerful medium for learning.

Recording community information photographically and on tape requires preparation. First, it should be noted that although color photographs are very appealing, they cost more to produce. Black and white photographs may serve your purpose equally well.

To take the photos, you should have a good 35-mm camera. Tape sounds on a thirty- or sixty-minute audiotape, using a recorder with new batteries. (Inexpensive brands of tape frequently do not record well.)

Always ask permission of shopkeepers, store managers, and homeowners before photographing their buildings. Naturally you should also ask individuals for permission to take their pictures or to record them. Not only will your openness express courtesy but also the very act of asking is likely to arouse community members' interest regarding the work of your center or school. As your work with ALERTA continues, these contacts may lead to local receptivity toward use of community resources.

Have the photographs developed with a *matte finish* in various sizes (4″ × 5″, 5″ × 7″, 8″ × 10″), depending on the use that will be made of them. Lotto games generally use 4″ × 5″ photos; language experience books use 5″ × 7″; puzzles use 8″ × 10″. If you have someone print the photos for you, specify that (a) double-weight paper be used for puzzle photos and (b) single-weight paper be used for lotto games and language experience photos.

Once your photographs have been developed, look them over carefully to select those that are clear, uncluttered, and well defined. Do not use fuzzy photos or photos that have captured only part of the scene you intended to appear. Also, try to select close-ups over long-distance shots whenever possible. In the same manner, select those tapes that have the clearest examples of the sounds you wished to record.

In the next exercise you will learn how the photos can be mounted on styrofoam boards for puzzles, on drawing board for lotto games, and on heavy drawing paper for language experience books. In the meantime, however, you should gather the materials needed for the construction process. Tips follow on where to find the supplies.

Supplies to use in Constructing Learning Materials

Materials   Best Place(s) to Purchase

Puzzles

Large sheets of styrofoam board 30″ × 40″	Art supply store
Sharp mat knife	Art supply store
Pencil and felt-tip marker	Stationery store
Rubber cement	Five-and-dime or department store
Rubber cement pickup	Five-and-dime or department store
Clear contact paper	Art supply store

Lotto Games

Mount boards (11″ × 14″ or larger size if you desire to mount more than four photos)	Art supply store, photographic supply store, or some bookstores. (Certain places sell large sheets that must be cut down to size with an art knife or paper cutter. Others sell boards cut to size.)
Mounting tissue	Photographic supply store
Art knife or single-edge razor blades	Art supply store or some bookstores
Spray fixative	Art supply store or some bookstores
Ruler	Stationery or art supply store
Pencil	Stationery store
Gum eraser	Stationery or five-and-dime store
Scissors	Art supply store or some bookstores
Iron, and sheet of white paper	Home or school supply

Language Experience Books

Spiral art tablet (bond paper— size depends on photos being used)	Art supply store
Mounting tissue	Photographic supply store
Art knife or single-edge razor blades	Art supply store or college bookstore
Spray fixative	Art supply store or some bookstores

Making Learning Materials from Photographs and Tapes

A great variety of learning materials can be made from photographs and tapes. Directions are given here for constructing puzzles and lotto games, two materials that are appealing and quickly assembled. Suggestions for a variety of other materials follow. You may have ideas of your own to add to the collection of possibilities, which you should note on the form provided.

How to Make Puzzles

Materials Needed

Puzzlemaking requires photograph, styrofoam board, a mat knife, rubber cement and rubber cement pickup, and clear contact paper.

Styrofoam board is best to use since it is a soft material that is easy to cut with a mat knife. Make certain that you buy enough styrofoam to make a tray-like frame for the mounted photograph.

Rubber cement is the means for adhering the photo to the styrofoam board. It can be purchased at any five-and-dime.

If you smear any rubber cement on the photo, the pickup is used to clean up the spill. *Rubber cement pickups* can be purchased in an art store or at a school supply company.

The *felt-tip marker* is for drawing the puzzle design on the back of the styrofoam, and the *mat knife* is used to cut the board into the puzzle pieces. A mat knife can be purchased in an art supply store or a five-and-dime.

The *contact paper* is used to protect the puzzle from wear and tear.

Steps in Assembly

1. Start by cutting two styrofoam board pieces 1 inch square larger than the photograph you will be using.

2. Place the photo on one of the cut styrofoam sheets and mark off the size of the photo with a pencil. Be sure that a border of 1 inch is left on all four sides. Trace the photo sides with a pencil.

3. Remove the photo and carefully cut the marked area with a mat knife. Now you will have a piece of styrofoam larger (by 1-inch) than the photo, a styrofoam piece the size of the photo, and a frame of styrofoam (1-inch in width).

4. Place rubber cement all over the styrofoam piece that has been cut to the size of the photo. Place the photo on the styrofoam and press down and out with your hands. Be sure that the photo edges adhere well to the styrofoam. (If you accidentally smear glue on the photo you can clean it up later with rubber cement pickup.)

5. Place clear contact over the photo, making sure that there are no trapped air bubbles.

6. Now place rubber cement evenly on the 1-inch frame and place this frame on the styrofoam piece that is larger than your photo. Press, making sure all the edges are glued down. You will now have a frame-tray for the puzzle.

7. Next, turn the mounted, contact-covered photo over and use the felt-tip marker to draw the puzzle pieces on the foam side in as many pieces as you think the children can handle. Be careful to make a design that suits the develop-

mental level of the children for whom the puzzle is intended. Younger children will need puzzles with only three-to-five pieces of easily recognizable shapes. (Straight line cuts are not advised, nor are cuts ending in sharp points. Gentle curves are best.)

8. Cut the pieces with a mat knife. Be sure to cut slowly down through the photo. The puzzle pieces will fit snugly into the frame-tray.

9. While the children are working to put the pieces together, the puzzle can be used to encourage conversation about places the children have visited in the neighborhood.

How to Make Lotto Games

Materials Needed

Several materials in addition to matched photographs are needed for making lotto games: *Mount board* is a semi-hard board on which the photos are mounted. It can be purchased at a photo shop or an art store.

A *ruler* and *pencil* are used to measure and mark spots where you want to place your photos on the mount board.

Dry mount tissue or *seal* adheres your photo to the mount board. The tissue also can be purchased at a photo shop or an art store.

An *iron* is used to activate the adhesive in the dry mount tissue. A sheet of *white paper* between the iron and the photo keeps the iron from leaving marks on the lotto game and also prevents it from burning the photograph. (This should be a dry iron—do not use a steam setting.)

A *gum eraser* can be used to remove any stray pencil marks or smudges. The gum eraser can be purchased at a five-and-dime.

Spray fixative is used to help preserve the photographs over time.

Steps in Assembly

1. Spray all the photographs you plan to use with the fixative and put them aside to dry.

2. Measuring with the ruler, put small pencil marks on the board where you want to mount the photos.

3. Next, take the dry mount tissue and cut it with scissors to the size of each photo.

4. Put the iron on a low setting. Place a piece of mount tissue on the back of each photo, and gently tack the center of the tissue with the iron. If the tissue turns out to be a little larger than the photo, cut the excess tissue off with scissors.

5. Keep the iron on the low setting. Take a photo and place it on the mount board on the area you have marked.

6. Put the sheet of white paper over the photo that is going to be mounted and then gently iron the photo, starting at the top of the picture and ending at the bottom.

7. Continue in this manner to mount all the photos for the lotto game on the board.

8. Stray marks can be removed with the gum eraser.

9. In order to make the matching photos more durable, you can mount them on either cardboard or mount board using the same basic technique. First, cut a piece of board to the size of your photo.

10. Place a piece of mount tissue on the back of the photo and tack it in place.

11. As before, trim any excess tissue with scissors.

12. Put the photo and its piece of tacked-on tissue on the precut board, and cover it with the white paper. Gently iron the photo into the board. Repeat the process until all the matching photos have been mounted.

Other Suggestions

Language experience books can easily be made following the same basic technique described for constructing lotto games. Instead of mount board, use a spiral-bound art notebook. First, arrange your photographs in a sequence that illustrates an event in the children's lives. Then mount one photograph on the right-hand side of each two-page section, moving from section to section to complete your sequence. The space to the left of each photo is used to record the children's stories about each scene.

Sight/sound lotto is a variation of the traditional lotto game. Select a set of pictures that clearly corresponds to sounds you have recorded on audiotapes. Mount the pictures on separate pieces of mount board as you would do for the matching pictures described previously. To play the game you play back the audiotape, stopping it after each sound. The children pick out the picture that matches the sound they hear.

Game boards on which the children advance from scene to scene can also be constructed using photographs of places or objects familiar to the children. Arrange your photographs on a winding path that moves over the surface of a

**Your Suggestions for Learning Materials
Using Photographs or Audiotapes**

_____
_____
_____
_____
_____
_____
_____
_____
_____
_____
_____
_____
_____
_____
_____
_____
_____
_____
_____
_____
_____
_____
_____
_____
_____

heavy piece of oaktag. Mount the photos, and then carefully outline the steps along your path with a felt-tip marker. Children can use dice or a spinner with matching photographs to move from "Start" to "Finish." A variation on this game is for the children to advance to the photograph that corresponds to a sound they hear on an audiotape.

You will want to make your learning materials as durable as possible so they can be used by the children repeatedly and so you will not need to make them over and over again. Using heavy-duty material (styrofoam, heavy oaktag, or cardboard), spraying photos or drawings with a fixative, and covering game boards with clear contact paper are all important in adding to the durability of the materials.

EXERCISE 6

Using Community Walks as Learning Activities with Small Groups of Children

As important as it is for adults to look at their community through the eyes of children, it is even more important that the children be encouraged to continue to gain knowledge of their neighborhood. ALERTA developers recommend that community walks with small groups of children be frequent occurrences throughout the school year.

Such walks need not be very long. Often a ten- or fifteen-minute walk may be more impressive to children than a longer field trip. Each trip should be planned for a particular purpose, and that purpose should be communicated in simple terms to the children ahead of time. At the conclusion of each excursion, the children in the cluster (small group) can represent what they have seen through a follow-up activity.

Children symbolize objects and events with which they are familiar in different ways—through role plays; language; and the creation of paintings, drawings, or models. Making a model of their own neighborhood is an especially powerful way that children can express an understanding of their world. This exercise outlines a typical sequence teachers might follow to carry out the construction of such a model with the children.

A building project requires planning and a long-range perspective on the teacher's part. You should collect ahead of time a variety of materials that will be needed for construction. Some suggestions are the following.

–milk cartons	–newspaper
–egg cartons	–dried twigs
–empty thread spools	–crepe or tissue paper (green, blue)
–clay	–scraps of wood
–bottle caps	–juice bar sticks
–empty cans	–tongue depressors
–toilet paper cylinders	

It is crucial that your materials gathering be followed by a practice session in which you take a community walk without the children, return to your classroom, and actually do a little of the construction. The experience will give you a more realistic idea of what the children will be encountering with the task and will prepare you to meet any technical problems that might arise.

The following steps illustrate an appropriate sequence to follow in undertaking such a project with young children.

1. Take a series of walks in the neighborhood with the children. The area to be covered should be well defined (for example, the block on which the center is located or the street in front of the center).

2. Each trip should have a specific focus so that the children are concerned with only a few things at a time.

3. There should be much interaction with the children (in both languages, as appropriate) during the course of the trip so that the things being looked at are clearly pointed out and so that the things that capture the children's interest can be noted by the teachers. Inviting parents to accompany the group and talk with the children about what they see would be helpful in getting a variety of views on the neighborhood.

4. When the children return to the classroom after each trip, the teachers should present them with an activity to encourage them to record what they have seen. In this case, the children would work on another piece of the construction of the model.

5. Teachers/parents should identify particular goals and objectives for each of the construction sessions so that emphasis can be on the children's using and expanding their present concepts (for example, concepts of position, left-right, grouping/classification, etc.) and the languages that were part of their experience during the walk. (See Chapter Eight for a list of ALERTA's goals and objectives.)

Additional sample learning activities incorporating aspects of the community are described at the end of this chapter.

To Illustrate How Information Coming From Community Walks Can Be Used in the Classroom

The following activities arose from learning experiences that teachers designed as followups to community trips they had taken with small groups of children. In each instance the teachers had followed the procedure of taking community walks for such purposes as visiting a store, watching the way traffic lights regulate traffic, looking for particular signs, or (in rural settings) looking for wild onions, watching geese flying north, or visiting a cow and her newborn calf. Purposes for community walks were defined through observation of interests the children had expressed in their work and play. For that reason, the activities described here may not be ones appropriate for use in your own classroom. Instead, this collection is meant to show possibilities, in addition to those already mentioned in Chapter Five, that are inherent in the simplest of community sights and sounds and to illustrate how those common experiences can be transformed into learning activities for the children.

People and Things in My Neighborhood

After the children have been taken on a number of short walks around their neighborhood, parents and teachers can construct flannelboard figures illustrating some of the features that interested the children. To make an item meaningful, it should have the particularities to which children are accustomed in their own surroundings. For example, the color of police cars differs from city to city, and designs on such cars also vary. In drawing any item, the purpose is to make it real and familiar for the child. Teachers must also think about items to include that are unique to their city, town, or village. For example, pushcarts may be found both in New York City and San Francisco. Although in both cities the items are pushcarts, they may be depicted differently for each city. In New York City, the carts may sell frankfurters, soda, ice cream, and pretzels. These carts may be seen either at street corners or in motion. In San Francisco, carts may be stationary and selling flowers. Whatever the children have actually seen should be used in the set of materials you develop.

The items you have drawn create a setting or context for telling stories using the flannelboard figures. Such activities will support language development by giving children opportunities to tell stories, follow action sequentially, learn labels, etc. You may do this activity in several ways.

1. Set out materials and ask the children to set up a story on the board. They can then relate the story.

2. Create a setting by putting up a few items and then ask a child to make up a story using the figures.

3. Set up figures and items and then have the children think and talk about what may be happening.

4. Tell a story in one language; during another activity time, retell the story in the second language.

Visiting a Grocery Store

Take the children in small groups to visit a neighborhood grocery store twice. Prior to the visits you should speak to the owner of the grocery store to ask if the children can tour the store, ask questions, and have a brief discussion with him or her. You may buy items for the children to handle and/or match their weight, size, texture, content, amount, length, thickness, height, form, shape, color, etc. The children may have an opportunity to guess, measure, estimate, check, and verify. Once the group has returned to the classroom, hold a brief discussion on what everyone saw on the trips and how the children felt about the trip. They should describe the store and find similarities and differences with others they may have seen.

1. Invite the children to construct or build a grocery store out of large blocks or hard cardboard. Once the "store" is built, the children will select the products that would be found in it, based on their cultural background and experiences. They should choose an appropriate name for the "store." Pictures of the different foods, signs, etc., should be placed on its walls.

2. At other times, children may construct a clothing store, puppet theatre, post office, and (in the spring) a flower shop where plant sales can be held. These activities would grow out of trips, discussions, and the children's questions.

Street Games

As children walk through their neighborhood, they may see older children playing games they have created or learned from generations of children before them. Often these games can be easily adapted for use with younger children. The following descriptions give two examples of such adaptations.

"Skelly"

"Skelly" or "Loadies" is a game played by many children in the streets of New York. A large outline of a square is divided into smaller sections, and each of the smaller sections is numbered.

The playing pieces are made by dripping wax from a lighted candle into a soda-bottle cap until the cap is full and then letting the wax harden.

Start Here

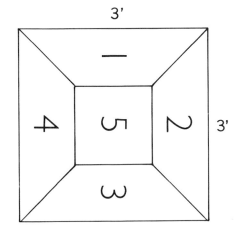

A child kneeling at point X calls out a number (in this case, 1 to 5) and then flicks his or her bottle cap into the square with that number on it. The bottle cap cannot be thrown. It must be flicked (as a marble would be flicked) with thumb and forefinger. The bottle cap must stop moving within the boundaries of the square named. The game rules get much more complicated for older children, but for preschoolers we can stop at this. At the teacher's discretion (according to the individual abilities of children playing), the child's "shooting" position can be changed. When the children are first learning to recognize numerals, there might be only two squares. Eventually, the children can shoot at the numbers in sequence.

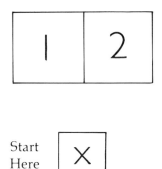

"Hopscotch"

This game may be used as a cluster activity. The child chosen to be first tosses his or her pebble into square 1, hops into square 2, and continues hopping to REST. At REST he or she turns and attempts to hop back to square 2, where he or she picks up the pebble that is in square 1. Next, the child tosses the pebble into square 2, hops into square 1, hops to square 3 and on to REST and again returns to square 3, picks up the pebble in square 2, hops to square 1, and hops out. She or he continues until she or he has reached square 5 and then begins backwards (from square 5 to square 1). The first child to finish is the winner. When a child misses a square he or she is aiming at, the next child follows.

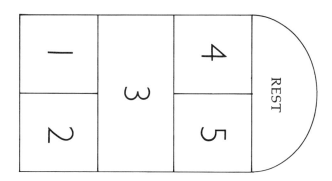

Local Animals

As the children are walking through their neighborhood they are likely to notice the animals and birds common to the area. The children's knowledge can be used to foster their ability to recognize categories or groups of animals that have characteristics different from one another.

Design a community walk specifically to look for animals, birds, and (if appropriate to your area) fish. When the children return to the classroom, ask them to recall all the animals, birds, and fish they have seen. Use a rhyme or chant such as the following one to help the children categorize the animals according to whether they are found on land, in the air, or in water. After each verse, have the children name the local animals that the rhyme fits.

"Los animalitos"	"Little Animals"
I	I
Los animalitos que van por el aire vuelan, vuelan, vuelan . . .	Little animals that go by air fly, fly, fly . . .
II	II
Los animalitos que ven por el agua nadan, nadan, nadan . . .	Little animals that go through the water swim, swim, swim . . .
III	III
Los animalitos que van por la tierra marchan, marchan, marchan . . .	Little animals that walk on the land march, march, march . . .

As the children name the various *animalitos* they can also imitate the movement of each.

Local Food Crops

In many areas of the country children commonly see food crops being grown and are aware of the seasonal farming activities. Once again, the children's knowledge can be used to foster what may be a new skill: placement of a series of events in a sequence.

The following example uses avocados to illustrate a sequence. Any other crop grown in your area (potatoes, corn, apples, peaches, etc.) could easily be substituted in the activity to achieve the same purpose. Follow these steps.

1. Take the children to visit an avocado orchard.

2. Take the children to a local store to buy avocados.

3. Make an avocado salad with a cluster group.

4. Have children place avocado seeds in water (flat end in water, point exposed).

5. Periodically work with your cluster to observe the avocado's progress.

6. Once the avocado has established roots and sprouted, have your cluster group plant it in soil. At each point in the process take photos (or draw pictures) of (1) an avocado tree with fruit; (2) buying an avocado in the store; (3) the avocado; (4) the avocado cut in

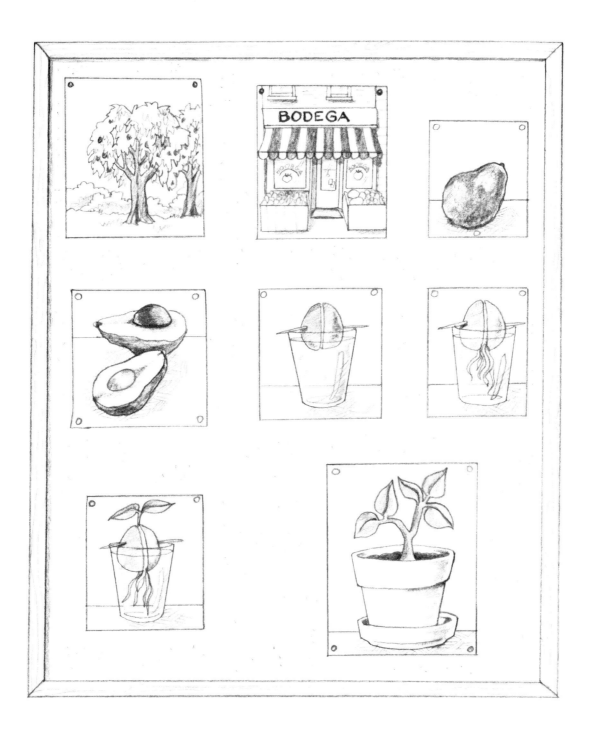

half, showing the seed; (5) the avocado in water; (6) the beginning root system; (7) the sprouted avocado; and (8) the avocado in soil. Later, in a cluster activity, have the children place the photos or drawings in the correct sequence and then tell the story of the avocado.

A photo series can be made later showing the increase in growth. The children can put these photos in sequence and tell their story as well.

Note: To make these materials more durable you should mount the photos on cardboard and laminate them.

CHAPTER SIX

Level 4: Preparing a Multicultural, Bilingual Learning Environment for Young Children

Your work with Levels 1, 2, and 3 of ALERTA has given you a great deal of information about yourself and your colleagues, about the cultures of the families participating in your program, and about the community of which you are a part. You are probably already drawing upon these resources in your choices of activities for the children in selection or construction of new learning materials and in your interaction with parents. Now it is time to pause in the process and consider the implications of your knowledge for the total design of a learning environment for the children.

Whether you are located in a child development center, a private nursery/kindergarten, or a public school, you have undoubtedly been assigned a space, a room that is your home base. This chapter offers you a way to pull together the information you have collected and use it in a classroom setting. The purpose of your work in Level 4 is to provide the children in your program with as many reflections of their personal worlds as possible so that a continuity between their former experience and their new learning is maintained. A fully prepared environment is also important so that you will have the resources at hand for designing learning activities that build upon the experiences the children bring with them into the classroom.

This chapter is organized to assist you in (1) surveying your classroom to determine the extent to which it already reflects your children, (2) identifying areas of the classroom and learning materials that need further preparation, (3) securing the needed learning materials, and (4) transforming your classroom.

Most early childhood classrooms in the United States are organized around various "interest centers," where the children work on self-selected activities for a portion of each day. ALERTA sees such an arrangement as very important in the achievement of its basic goals. The exercises that follow, therefore, assume that your classroom incorporates use of centers or classroom areas as a major part of your curriculum approach. The classroom areas discussed in this chapter are the following.

1. Housekeeping
2. Blockbuilding
3. Sand
4. Water
5. Art
6. Table materials/manipulatives
7. Music and movement
8. Library
9. Large-muscle area
10. Woodworking
11. Science

Areas 1 through 10 are physical locations in the room. Area 9 can exist both within the room and outdoors. Area 10 is an important area but not necessarily essential to the curriculum of three- and four-year olds; that is, we place it in a category of "preferred but optional." Area 7 is an activity that may be set up in a variety of ways within the total curriculum. Number 11, science, is conceived of not as an area but as an approach that may permeate all areas of the curriculum. This approach is discussed at the end of the chapter, with suggested activities that deal with science content on the three- to five-year-old level.

Other centers could be added to this list, and some of those listed could be combined to make the best use of available space. You will notice, however, that *nowhere* does ALERTA advocate use of separate "culture" or "community" classroom areas. Instead, perspectives drawn from study of cultures and communities are integrated into *all* the other learning centers so that the children come to understand these concepts as an ordinary part of daily life.

EXERCISE 1

Survey of the Classroom

The first step in the preparation of your classroom is to take a close look at each of your classroom areas to see if it has the internal arrangement and learning materials that support ALERTA's basic goals. (See Chapter One for a summary of ALERTA's program goals.) Is each of those areas designed to reflect the cultures, interests, surroundings, and needs of the children served by your program? You can use the following classroom survey to help yourself answer that question fairly. Fill out as much of the survey as you can while actually walking around your own classroom. Leave any items you do not understand until you have completed Exercise 2.

Survey of the Classroom Environment

1. Housekeeping Area or Family Corner

Is the space large enough for several children to move around in easily?
Yes ☐ No ☐

Is it located near the blockbuilding area, which may serve to stimulate the dramatic play in each of the areas? Yes ☐ No ☐

In addition to the usual furniture, dishes, pots, pans, and cutlery, does the area include many of the following? (Check the articles that do appear.)

☐ "Grownup" clothing commonly worn (every day and for festivals or holidays) by people of the cultures represented in the program.

☐ Boy and girl dolls that have the skin color, hairstyles, facial features, and varieties of clothing of the cultural groups represented in the program.

☐ Puppets that have the skin color, hairstyles, and facial features of the people, and varieties of clothing of the cultural groups represented in the program.

☐ Food packages (cans, boxes, etc.) that have labels in the children's native language as well as those that have labels in English (e.g., popular brands found in local supermarkets or grocery stores).

☐ Additional kitchen utensils commonly used in the kitchens of people from the cultures represented in your program.

☐ Furniture typical or distinctive of the cultures of the families in your program.

☐ Materials that show men and women in nurturing roles and in various types of family structures (e.g., photographs or illustrations of men feeding children; single-parent families; families including grandparents, etc.).

☐ Decoration reflecting colors, patterns, and family scenes common in the cultures represented in your center.

2. Blockbuilding Area

Is this area large enough for five or six children to use it at one time?
Yes ☐ No ☐

Is the area located as far as possible away from the quiet area or library corner?
Yes ☐ No ☐

In addition to the usual building blocks, are there sets of scaled-down objects reflecting the place where your program is located (trees, animals, etc.) to be used in fantasy play?
Yes ☐ No ☐

Are there scaled-down, multiracial figures of people? Yes ☐ No ☐

Do the figures avoid sex-role stereotyping? Yes ☐ No ☐

Is the area decorated with illustrations of typical building styles from your area, such as photographs of the children's homes or easily recognizable landmarks?
Yes ☐ No ☐

3. Sand Area

Is this area easily accessible to the children? Yes ☐ No ☐

Are a variety of materials for measuring, filling, and pouring provided (e.g., "squirty" bottles, tubing, pitchers, food coloring, bubble pipe, measuring cups, etc.)?
Yes ☐ No ☐

Is there any setup in the area that makes use of the role of sand or earth within the children's cultural traditions? Yes ☐ No ☐

4. Water Area

Is this area easily accessible to the children? Yes ☐ No ☐

Are a variety of materials for measuring, filling, and pouring provided (e.g., "squirty" bottles, tubing, pitchers, food coloring, bubble pipe, measuring cups, etc.)? Yes ☐ No ☐

Is there any setup in the area that makes use of the role of water within the children's cultural traditions? Yes ☐ No ☐

5. Art Area

Is this area set up near a source of water (faucets or tubs of water)? Yes ☐ No ☐

Is the area well lit by natural light? Yes ☐ No ☐

In addition to paints, crayons, collage material, and clay, are any designs or motifs displayed that are part of the cultures represented? Yes ☐ No ☐

In the area are children exposed to crafts (e.g., weaving, pottery, basketry, beadwork, metalwork, woodworking, etc.) common in the cultures of their families?
Yes ☐ No ☐

6. Table Materials/Manipulatives

Are there materials that allow the small muscles to be used in several different ways?
Yes ☐ No ☐

Are there at least three different types of materials for each of the learning opportunities listed below?

Classify objects Yes ☐ No ☐
Classify pictures Yes ☐ No ☐
Put objects in a series (e.g., by length) Yes ☐ No ☐
Put pictures of objects in a series Yes ☐ No ☐
Sequence or form patterns Yes ☐ No ☐
Experiment with spatial orientations Yes ☐ No ☐
Try out their memory Yes ☐ No ☐

Do many illustrations on the materials reflect the children's environment (urban, suburban, or rural)? Yes ☐ No ☐

Do many illustrations on the materials reflect the various racial/cultural groups represented in the center? Yes ☐ No ☐

Are any words appearing on the materials written in the two languages used in your program? Yes ☐ No ☐

Do the collected materials have several levels of complexity so that children will still find some of the materials challenging even after they have developed skill with others? Yes ☐ No ☐

Are the materials displayed in a way that makes the choice evident to the children (clearly visible and easily reached)? Yes ☐ No ☐

7. Music and Movement Area

Are there records of the various types of music common in the cultures represented? List the types that do appear:

_____

_____

Are there records that use culturally distinctive instruments? Yes ☐ No ☐

Is there a variety of culturally appropriate instruments for the children's use? Yes ☐ No ☐

Are dances distinctive of all the cultures represented taught at some time? Yes ☐ No ☐

Are games (including rhythmic and/or musical games) taught that are distinctive of the various cultures represented? Yes ☐ No ☐

8. Library Area

Is this area placed in a quiet spot, out of the mainstream of activity? Yes ☐ No ☐

Is the area soft, cozy, and inviting? Yes ☐ No ☐

Do the bookshelves allow the books to be broadly displayed at the children's eye level? Yes ☐ No ☐

Does each classroom have available at least two books for every child, although they may not all be displayed at once? Yes ☐ No ☐

How many of the books are bilingual (written in both languages used in the program)? _____

How many of the books are written in English? _____

How many of the books are written in the second language used? _____

Do the illustrations in at least half of the books reflect the children's environment (e.g., urban, suburban, or rural)? Yes ☐ No ☐

Do the illustrations in many of the books reflect the various cultures and races represented in the center? Yes ☐ No ☐

Does the content of many of the books represent the children's life experiences (cultural and environmental)? Yes ☐ No ☐

Do the books give positive messages about particular cultural groups and about the roles of women? Yes ☐ No ☐

If the answer to the above question is no, make notes about the books in question.

9. Large-muscle Area

Is space available for the children to play games that require use of their large muscles? Yes ☐ No ☐

If Yes, is the space indoors ☐? Outdoors ☐?

Are games taught that are distinctive of the various cultures represented by the children in your program? Yes ☐ No ☐

What games are played by the children?

_____

_____

_____

12. Rotating Point of Interest

Is the children's work displayed in a way that they can easily see it? Yes ☐   No ☐

Are the work displays changed frequently? Yes ☐   No ☐

Is there any picture of an event that has special significance to the children in your program? Yes ☐   No ☐

Are such displays or pictures used in story times or discussions? Yes ☐   No ☐

Is there a space somewhere in your school or center especially devoted to the interests and cultural backgrounds of the *parents* of the children in your program? Yes ☐   No ☐

Do menus available reflect foods common in each of the cultures represented? Yes ☐   No ☐

What equipment is available for those games?

_____

_____

_____

10. Woodworking Area

Is there room enough in the area for two or three children to use it at one time? Yes ☐   No ☐

Is there a woodworking table available? Yes ☐   No ☐

Which of the following tools are available for the children's use?

☐ vise attached to workbench   ☐ sandpaper (various grains)

☐ hammers   ☐ assortment of nails

☐ saws   ☐ supply of soft wood

☐ c-clamps

Have rules for use of the area been posted in picture form where the children can easily see them? Yes ☐   No ☐

Is the area decorated with wooden objects or pictures of wooden objects distinctive of the cultures represented in your program? Yes ☐   No ☐

11. Science

Are special opportunities and activities made available in most or all of the areas named above that allow the children to experiment, hypothesize, solve problems, try out various possibilities for action, etc.? Yes ☐   No ☐

Do the opportunities available make use of a variety of materials drawn from the children's natural environment (such as leaves, twigs, pebbles, seashells, etc.)? Yes ☐   No ☐

List the opportunities and activities especially set up for these purposes today.

_____

_____

_____

_____

_____

Identifying Classroom Areas and Materials Needing Further Preparation

In doing the survey you may identify areas in your room that need more preparation. This exercise contains detailed suggestions for each classroom area. Even if you feel that your classroom meets the requirements of the environmental survey, you should read each section carefully to see if there are ideas here that you have not previously considered.

The material presented in this exercise is divided into several parts. The first section offers some general comments on the purposes that underlie the preparation of a learning environment. Following those comments are descriptions of each classroom area. The descriptions use examples drawn from two distinct populations. Group 1 is located in a large urban center on the eastern seaboard of the United States. Its public school kindergarten program serves Spanish- and English-speaking families from the Caribbean and African-American families with roots in both the city and the rural South. There are also a few families in the program who recently immigrated from West Africa. Group 2 is located in the upper midwestern United States. Its Head Start program is conducted in eight child-development centers scattered over a wide geographical area. The families in the program share a rural environment but come from a variety of Native-American and European-American traditions.

Your own community may resemble those described in some ways but be significantly different in other ways. Your task in this exercise will be to look at the examples and then, as appropriate, to *make use of the information you have collected that reflects the children you serve* in the various classroom areas. Opportunity is provided at each point along the way for you to consider the suggestions made in the light of specific knowledge you now have about the children's cultures and community. The exercise ends with a review of some additional factors that will also influence your preparation of the environment.

General Comments

A learning environment makes a statement about the underlying assumptions, values, and priorities of the educator. By selecting some materials over others, favoring certain types of interactions over others, and focusing on chosen knowledge areas, you define (1) your role in the education process, (2) the nature of the learner, and (3) what is deemed worthy of knowing. Even without the presence of children and adults the environment makes these statements, which are then more fully realized when human interactions occur.

In a multicultural, bilingual early childhood classroom, the learning environment must be given especially careful attention so that it will serve two purposes: (1) provide opportunities for the socioemotional, cognitive/linguistic, and psychomotor growth of preschool children and (2) convey an acceptance of and respect for the various cultures represented in the early-learning center. The exact formula for achieving these purposes will vary from classroom to classroom. The following suggestions are given to orient you to possibilities that will fulfill the intent of this curriculum.

Intrinsic to our curriculum approach is the availability of choice for children and adults; therefore, in ALERTA all areas may be used both for child-initiated activities and for adult-directed ones. Further, it is possible that with sufficient understanding and experience you will be able to set up these areas so that each can be used by children with minimal adult direction after the initial introduction to school (which, of course, will vary for each child). Most of the areas should be available to children on a daily basis. This point speaks specifically to our view of early childhood learning: children need repeated opportunities over a period of time, without the pressure of a timetable, to achieve mastery and understanding.

At the same time one must keep in mind that it is possible to periodically vary some of the materials within areas. The change can prevent boredom when a number of children become overfamiliar with some equipment to the point that they lose interest in it. Careful observation of the children's interactions within areas will provide cues for you to introduce a new material or temporarily remove an old one. More is said about changing materials in Levels 5 through 8.

Housekeeping

Description of Area

The housekeeping area should be located in a bright corner of the classroom with enough space for several children to move around easily. Placing it near the block area might encourage interaction in the dramatic play that occurs in both areas.

Materials Needed (for Group 1)

1. Commercial materials:
-dolls that vary in shape, size, style, and material of construction
-dolls with skin color, hair types, and facial features that reflect the physical characteristics of the children in the classroom
-dolls that resemble male and female babies, children, and adults
-doll clothing that represents both the modern and traditional dress used by members of the children's cultures
-dolls' basket cradles, cribs, carriages
-mirrors
-dressers
-crockery and cutlery
-tables and chairs
-clothing for dress-up play (e.g., shoes, dresses, pants, shirts, cloth for head-wraps, etc.)
-pictures showing both men and women in a variety of nurturing roles

-pictures showing both men and women in a variety of occupations

2. Teacher-and/or parent-made materials:
-puppets (characters from folktales the children know)
-dolls (to be made by the teacher and children)
-doll clothes
-cots, beds, shelves, cupboards
-special clothing for dramatic play, such as carnival costumes typical in festivals the children have seen, and caps or hats representing various occupations

3. Food products or packages (vegetables and fruits may be made by the children out of papier-mâché):
-products with Spanish and English labels
-sugar box
-avocados
-papayas
-plantains
-bean bags (different types)
-cooking oil
-cornmeal
-rice
-butter

-milk containers
-oatmeal

4. Additional kitchen utensils (besides the usual pots and pans):
-mortar and pestle
-grater
-ladle
-cutting board
-rolling pin
-meat grinder
-coffee strainer
-frying pan
-barbecue grill

Materials Needed (for Group 2)

1. Commercial materials:
-dolls that vary in shape, size, style, and material of construction
-dolls with skin color, hair types, and facial features that reflect the physical characteristics of the children in the classroom
-dolls that resemble male and female babies, children, and adults
-doll clothing that represents both the modern and traditional dress used by members of the children's cultures
-dolls' basket cradles, cribs, strollers, infant seats, woven baby baskets, cradle boards
-mirrors
-dressers
-dishes and cutlery
-tables and chairs
-clothing for dress-up play (e.g., shoes and mocassins, dresses, pants, shirts, scarves, shawls)
-pictures showing both men and women in a variety of nurturing roles
-pictures showing both men and women in a variety of occupations

2. Teacher- and/or parent-made materials:
-puppets (characters from folktales the children know)
-dolls (to be made by the teacher and children)
-doll clothes, quilts for doll beds
-cots, beds, shelves, cupboards
-special clothing for dramatic play, such as those typical in the events or celebrations the children have seen, and caps or hats representing various occupations

3. Food products or packages (vegetables and fruits may be made by the children out of papier-mâché):
-products with labels
-cheese
-cereal
-vegetable cans
-bags of beans (different types)
-cooking oil
-rice
-macaroni
-butter
-milk containers
-oatmeal
-corn
-dried meat
-wasna
-recipe charts

4. Additional kitchen utensils (besides the usual pots and pans):
-grater
-ladle
-cutting board
-rolling pin
-meat grinder
-frying pan
-barbecue grill
-soup kettle
-coffeepot
-cake pans
-pie plates
-muffin pans

Planning for the Housekeeping Area

Review the materials suggested for the two sample groups. Now think of the children in *your* program and note materials other than those you already have in the housekeeping area that would reflect the children's cultural and community experiences.

1. Commercial materials: _____

_____

_____

_____

_____

2. Teacher- and/or parent-made materials: _____

_____

_____

_____

_____

3. Food products or packages: _____

_____

_____

_____

_____

4. Additional kitchen utensils (besides the usual pots and pans): _____

_____

_____

_____

_____

Blockbuilding

Description of Area

The size of this area depends largely upon the number of children that will be using the area at a given time. In a classroom group of twenty to twenty-five students you can anticipate five or six children in the blockbuilding area.

In determining the amount of space needed, it might be helpful to notice the nature of construction with respect to the age and developmental abilities of the children. Three-year-olds may often build wider, covering more territory than the older, more experienced four- and five-year-olds, who may build taller and more symmetrically. The younger (three-year-old) builders likewise may use fewer materials in their constructions. A single block may represent a car, a hospital, or a school. Four- to five-year-olds are more differentiated and might try to present more detailed aspects of their impressions. Allocation of space and selection of materials should reflect these two considerations.

Materials and Equipment Needed

For a classroom of twenty to twenty-five three-, four-, or five-year-old children there should be at least one whole set of standard wooden unit blocks. At times you may wish to supplement a set by adding preferred, frequently used shapes. These blocks should be displayed on open shelf storage units. Furniture should be arranged to allow convenient access to the blocks. Unless the shelves are anchored to the floor, the storage units might be safer if pushed against a wall.

The area should not have furniture other than that used for storage or transport of materials. A level floor (without splinters!) provides the most secure building foundation. A smooth foam-backed carpet that fits snugly to the floor (without raised corners or buckling seams) is commonly found in block-building areas. Carpeting tends to decrease the amount of noise often heard in an uncarpeted area, although it also tends to reduce the steadiness of the blocks. The area should be well lighted.

The basic material in the blockbuild-ing area is the hardwood unit block set. For early childhood classrooms, the intermediate set consisting of 350 pieces in 23 shapes is recommended, which allows for an adequate distribution of materials among the children. Wooden blocks should be sanded smooth and free of splinters. Other blocks or building units may also be placed in the blockbuilding area. Plastic units (2″ × 5″) such as those commercially produced by several companies add color and variety to the area.

Objects and wedge figures such as appropriately scaled people, animals local to the area where the center is located, transportation vehicles, trees, and furniture generally tend to make blockbuild-ing more functional, as these props suggest various themes. Figures should be multiracial and should avoid sex-role stereotyping. Display photographs of buildings or structures that are familiar to the children (such as skyscrapers, bridges, and brownstones for Group 1 or

tribal council buildings, schools, and stores for Group 2) and that show the same shapes as the blocks in their building materials as well as pictures of building projects done by members of the group. Such pictures should be hung at the children's eye level and changed frequently; they can be used as a basis for discussions about blockbuilding.

Below is a list of common block types and the recommended amount of each kind.

Square	50
Oblong	60
Doublong	20
Quadlong	14
Roof board	14
Pillar	34
Half-pillar	12
Quarter-pillar	12
Diagonal	20
Triangle	18
Ramp	20
Column	20
Large column	4
Gothic arch	4
Gothic arch door	4
Y-switch	–
Half-arch	4
Small buttress	4
Quarter-circle curve	4
Large buttress	–
Roman arch	6
Small half-circle	6
Half-circle curve	–
Double roof board	–
Double triangle	8
Elliptical curve	8
Number of blocks	350
Number of shapes	23

Included in the materials for Group 1 may be erector sets for building bridges, materials for making signboards, models of streetlights and traffic signs, and siding of various sorts to represent different types of building materials. Group 2 might have flexible reeds or sticks for construction of fences, sweat lodges, boweries, or arbors; small, notched "logs" for making log cabins or ceremonial buildings; and cloth for various types of tents. Parents and teachers for either group can supplement these materials with replicas of landmarks or buildings in the city, town, or village in which the center is located; the replicas can be drawn or painted on heavy cardboard and scaled to the size of the blocks. The cutout figures can be made to stand up by attaching a cardboard flap to the back of each one.

Planning for the Blockbuilding Area

Review the materials suggested for the two sample groups. Now think of the children in *your* program and note materials other than those you already have in the blockbuilding area that would reflect the children's cultural and community experiences.

1. Additional wooden unit blocks needed: _____

_____

_____

_____

_____

_____

_____

_____

2. Supplemental building materials to reflect the children's environment: _____

_____

_____

_____

_____

_____

_____

3. Photographs of landmarks or buildings well known to the children: _____

_____

_____

_____

_____

_____

_____

Sand

Description of Area

The sand area requires a rectangular container appropriate in size and shape for the number of children that will be using it at one time. The container should be lined at the sides only and be a suitable height for small children. For safety reasons, the container should be placed in a corner of the classroom or set apart from other areas by movable room dividers. The teacher must be careful that in partitioning he or she does not remove this activity from the life of the classroom.

Materials Needed
–anything hollow
–spades
–spoons
–shells
–rubber or plastic
  buckets
–funnels
–saucepans
–pie pans
–tin cans (painted)
–ice-cream containers

} for wet or dry sand

–sieves
–salt shakers
–pitchers
–tin cans with holes

} for dry sand

Periodicallly there can be special setups in the sand area that echo the children's past experiences with sand or earth. For Group 1, for example, a miniature beach area might be constructed, combining a sandscape with an "ocean," boats, fishing nets, seashells, beach umbrellas, and so on. Or a construction site could be modeled in the sand area with miniature earth movers, trucks, and other such equipment. Group 2 might be equally interested in a construction site or might respond to a model of a nearby riverbank supplied with natural structures (rocks and models of trees) and the types of boats they have seen there. Such special setups would be used to follow up particular community walks taken with the children and as much as possible should involve the children in their construction as previously described in Level 3.

Planning for the Sand Area

Review the materials suggested for the two sample groups. Now think of the children in *your* program and note materials other than those you already have in the sand area that would reflect the children's cultural and community experiences.

1. Basic sand materials needed: _____

_____

_____

_____

_____

_____

_____

_____

_____

_____

_____

2. Materials for possible special setups: _____

_____

_____

_____

_____

_____

_____

_____

_____

_____

_____

_____

Water

Description of Area

The water area should have a water trough (square or oblong) supported by a wooden frame, a baby bathtub, or a car tire sawed in half. Water play should be near the water supply and would be safest out of the main traffic lanes so that accidents are minimized.

Materials Needed

- mild liquid detergent
- food coloring
- teapots
- coffee percolator or drip coffee pot
- funnels
- tubes (for siphoning)
- strainers
- pitchers
- "squirty" bottles
- spoons
- a piece of hosepipe
- plastic fruit shapes
- plastic glasses
- plastic dishes
- tin cans of different heights
- improvised boats from walnut shells, newspaper, leaves, matchboxes
- bubble pipe or straws
- base of bathmats for safety and protection
- sponges

As in the sand area, the water area may be used periodically for special kinds of experiences to follow up a trip or walk taken by the children. The children might reenact a boat race they have seen or construct a waterfall like the one they have visited. The success of such projects will, of course, be dependent on the care you have taken to provide the props or building materials needed for the expe-rience. These special setups are also ex-amples of instances in which more teach-er interaction may be needed than is usually recommended during child-initiated use of the centers. Once such a project has been cooperatively devel-oped, however, it can be used by chil-dren in a variety of ways that they initiate themselves.

Planning for the Water Area

Review the suggested materials. Now think of the children in *your* program and note materials other than those you already have in the water area that would reflect the children's cultural and community experiences.

1. Basic water materials needed: _____

_____

_____

_____

_____

_____

_____

_____

_____

_____

_____

_____

_____

2. Materials for possible special setups: _____

_____

_____

_____

_____

_____

_____

_____

_____

_____

_____

_____

Art

This section describes an area for art where the children are encouraged to try out several means of artistic expression or produce various art forms. It is important, however, that art moves beyond a certain area of the room. Art should be interwoven through the curriculum in instances ranging from room decoration to the types of illustrations in books that you request be bought for the program.

The description of the art area includes discussion of several art forms: painting, clay molding, drawing, and collage making. While each form is treated separately, some initial remarks may be generally applicable.

Description of Area

Whenever possible, an art area should be located near windows so that children can work with colors under natural light. The area should also have easy access to water for washing up. Either place the area near a sink, or provide tubs or pails of water in rooms that do not have indoor sinks. Make sure that materials are accessible to the children so they may independently initiate activities, and provide materials to assist children in cleaning up once they have completed activities. Also provide space in which finished materials may be placed.

A further consideration is that the art materials should not be near the library area. This is a precaution, as accidental spills and splattering of paints do occur within the course of a day.

Painting

Painting may be set up as an activity at an easel, at a table, or on the floor. Some classrooms use all these possibilities, and others remain with one preferred mode.

Easels may be commercially purchased or constructed by nailing into the wall a slanted board with a base that extends to hold point jars and brushes. Table and floor painting require a tray to hold paint in containers, brushes, a jar or clean water, and a sponge to absorb water from brushes that are rinsed. Table and floor painting helps children change the direction of their paper (e.g., they can use it vertically rather than horizontally). Paper should be available at child height so that children may help themselves. Basic materials to include in the area are the following.

-18″ × 24″ newsprint
-tempera paint in primary colors (red, yellow, blue, and later black and white)
-brushes (choice of two sizes of bristle brushes, 1/2-inch and 3/4-inch)

We do *not* recommend using ready-made colors such as orange, green, purple, brown, etc. Rather, it is suggested that you provide primary colors along with empty jars in which children may mix their own colors. This is an example of how you can help children become actively involved in a process and have the opportunity to make discoveries.

If the budget permits, children may on occasion use 12″ × 24″ manila paper for painting. As an economy measure, sheets from a printed newspaper may be used for painting. Pages should be selected that are from the financial or classified sections, as the fine, continuous print on these pages does not create distraction.

The area may be decorated with the children's work and designs and/or artwork drawn from the cultures represented at the center. Particularly important in some communities might be designs that have a symbolic meaning well understood in the community. Making the designs and their meanings available to children can be an important first step in the process of learning to read. The purpose of displaying artwork of the children's cultures is *not* to encourage the children to copy such works but to continue exposing the children to the aesthetics of the groups of which they are a part and to introduce them to the colors and forms enjoyed by groups other than their own. As with other aspects of their learning, it is important for children to see that there are many ways to express beauty.

Clay

This section refers to natural clay—not plasticene. Clay should be placed in an intact plastic bag with moistened towels over it. The plastic bag should be placed in an airtight container or pail with a tight-fitting cover. Some staff members prefer to have the clay formed into grapefruit-sized balls, and others have the children scoop out their own supply.

At these young ages, children do not need any special tools or equipment for playing with clay. They use it directly on a table, molding it with their hands. The adults at the center or school should maintain the clay's proper consistency. Clay should be soft but not slippery; the children should be able to easily mold, pull, and stretch the material.

If pottery making has a strong place in the community your program serves, the area could be decorated now and then with fine examples of local work. In some Native-American communities of the southwestern United States and Mexico, for example, clay occupies a central position in the working lives of many people, and the children may be very interested in it.

Drawing

Materials for drawing should include manila paper in assorted sizes (18″ × 24″ and also that size halved and quartered) and crayons (standard set of eight colors, large size). Depending on the values of the adults and the school's budget, a set of crayons may be provided for each child, or several sets may be made available for the group. Another possibility

for drawing is using chalk on black paper, which offers children a new way to look at line, form, and color.

Collage

The children can create collages using cardboard, construction paper, or manila paper for a base; paste and small brushes; and assorted materials such as the following.

- assorted scraps of cloth (focus on color/texture/thickness)
- natural materials found in the area in which the center is located: grass, leaves, straw, cork, seeds
- assorted papers with varied textures (focus on color/texture/shape)
- string, wool, thread
- cutouts from magazines (selected by the children)

No matter what materials are made available to children, they should be presented in some organized manner. Materials should be placed in clear plastic containers that will help children see what is available and make it easy for them to choose and carry the materials of their choice. Attention should be given to achieving a balance in what is offered—variety in color and textures, yet not so much that the child may feel overwhelmed by choice.

It is worthwhile to point out again that the children's use of all the media described will be enriched by their exposure to examples of the art characteristic of their cultures both in decoration of the area and in some of the materials provided. It is *not* intended that the children try to copy such work (their own creations are to be encouraged) but rather that they continue to develop a feel for the artistic expressions of their cultures as they do in their own homes.

Planning for the Art Area

Review the suggested materials and techniques. Now think of the children in *your* program and note materials other than those you already have in the art area that would reflect the children's cultural and community experiences.

1. Basic art materials needed: _____

_____

_____

_____

_____

_____

_____

2. Materials from the children's environment for use in art: _____

_____

_____

_____

_____

_____

_____

_____

3. Decorations for the area drawn from the community: _____

_____

_____

_____

_____

_____

_____

Table Materials/Manipulatives

The phrase *table materials* is a general label given to a variety of manipulative equipment found in early childhood classrooms: puzzles, pegs and pegboards, string and wooden beads, one-inch blocks, parquetry blocks, Tinkertoys, simple lotto games, activities involving geometric shapes, various Montessori-inspired activities and matching games, Cuisenaire rods, and other materials known by commercial names. The label *table materials* both points out the place where the materials are generally used and implies that their size is small enough to be accommodated on a tabletop.

Generally, most table materials set a task for the child; that is, the activities are prestructured or defined. The degree of definition varies. For example, a puzzle, pegs and board, and stringing beads are all activities that are rather structured. A puzzle is to be taken apart and put together; pegs are to be inserted into the holes in the board; beads are to be strung. A puzzle allows no leeway other than putting it together again. Pegs require the dexterity to place pegs in holes. Children may give themselves the additional task of creating a design in color while inserting the pegs (e.g., outside border all green, inside all orange, or alternating a pattern of colors).

Less-defined or less-structured materials are Tinkertoys, parquetry blocks, and Cuisenaire rods, with which the child's task is to build, create a design or pattern, etc. Games such as lotto, sorting of geometric shapes, and sequence cards focus on finding relationships between objects. The latter task may be approached in a variety of ways. Even from this brief description, it is obvious that many and varied materials fall into the category of manipulatives. How do you select materials that are appropriate, challenging, and satisfying to the children?

Teachers must consider the developmental level of the children in the group.

Generally, what may one expect in psychomotor skills of three-, four-, and five-year-olds? What are they capable of in terms of understanding similarities and differences, attributes of objects, and relationships between objects? Having assessed expected levels of ability, one should ask which materials offer children (1) opportunities to practice and strengthen such skills and (2) a challenge to move them forward in the sequence of development. Further considerations in the selection of materials are the following.

1. Do the chosen materials approach a given task from varied vantage points?

2. Do they cover a range of development, offering possibilities for increasing complexity?

3. Are the materials durable and well constructed?

4. Is the content relevant to the life experiences of the children?

5. Do illustrations reflect the populations represented in the center?

6. When labeling appears, is it in both English and the second language used in the program?

When commercial materials meeting requirements 4, 5, and 6 are not available, teacher- or parent-made materials can be constructed that have as much (if not more) appeal as commercial sets. Suggestions for several types of these materials have been given in previous chapters of this source book (see Levels 2 and 3). Puzzles, lotto games, board games, sorting and sequencing materials and many other manipulatives can easily be made from local materials (such as leaves, pebbles, seeds, and bottle caps) and photographs of local scenes. Completing the ALERTA Classroom Survey can help you identify exactly which sorts of manipulatives your center is lacking, and parents and teachers can work together to create the variety of materials needed for different developmental levels.

Once materials are selected or created, the next questions to arise are (1) Where shall this area be placed and (2) How shall the materials be made available?

It is advisable to have these materials away from the art activities and areas of high activity and movement. You may want to place them within or next to space designated as a quiet corner or a library area. Additionally, there must be adequate space for several children to work independently or in small groups. Though labeled *table materials*, most, if not all, may also be used on smooth flooring. In fact, the area may be set up so as to offer children the option of using the materials on either the table or floor.

The various materials chosen must be displayed so that choices are evident to the children. This may mean storing puzzles in a rack so that children may easily choose one, or stacking pegboards near plastic containers holding pegs. Materials stored in clear plastic containers let children easily see the contents of a game or activity. Various materials, activities, and games may be attractively displayed on shelves near the area in which they are to be used.

Children may need initial guidance and reminders to return materials to their designated places on shelves. You should periodically check games, activities, and materials to see if there are missing pieces or damaged parts. The self-checking nature of many of these materials and the purpose of the activity may be defeated when there are missing or inadequate parts. It is difficult for a child to develop skills with puzzles when not all the puzzle pieces are available. In displaying materials, attention should be given to the following.

1. *Respond to the range and level of skills within the group.* (E.g., available at any one time should be simple puzzles consisting of a few pieces and also puzzles of increasing complexity both in pictures and number of pieces. Puzzles should be rotated and changed periodically to match the developing skills of the children. Although the range from simple to complex is maintained throughout the year in principle, the content must change to sustain the interest of the children.)

2. *Offer choice in variety of skills being developed* (discrimination, fine motor, matching, etc.).

3. *Offer several choices in activities for the same skill.* (E.g., eye-hand coordination may be practiced and strengthened by using beads and string, pegs and boards, simple sewing of wool on canvas, etc.).

4. *Provide materials that also offer children the possibility to set their own challenge or task.*

Music and Movement

Description of Area

The music area can be set up in a variety of ways, depending upon its intended purpose. If you wish to provide the opportunity for child-initiated activities, you may define a space containing equipment accessible to the children. Music may also be an adult-initiated activity in a larger, less-defined area, with instruments or other equipment used only by the teacher. A blending of the two in which you temporarily designate a portion of the room as the music area is also possible.

If musical instruments are to be accessible to the children, they should be displayed on a low rack. You might wish to have the instruments in an easily opened box or chest and records on the rack, near the record player.

Materials Needed (for Group 1)

Categories you might consider when stocking the shelves are listed here.

1. Music for listening, drawn from the various cultures represented at the center:

–recurring themes
–rich melodies
–distinct rhythms (*el merengue, la plena, la bomba, la salsa,* blues, soul, jazz, etc.)
–full-bodied sound (use of many instruments)
–pop music (music to which the children are exposed through the media)
–vocal music (songs)
–game music (for finger plays, clapping games, etc.)
–exercise music (for marching, stamping, skipping, etc.)

2. Instruments for creation of music:
–drums
–maracas
–calabash
–guitar
–cuatro
–triangles
–cymbals

–tambourines
–bells
–xylophones
–claves
–conch
–horn (trumpet)
–bass
–flute
–kalimba

Materials Needed (for Group 2)
Categories you might consider when stocking the shelves are listed here.

1. Music for listening, drawn from the various cultures represented at the center:
–recurring themes
–rich melodies
–distinct rhythms (square dance, jigs, round dance, "fancy" dancing, etc.)

–full-bodied sound (use of many instruments)
–popular music (music to which the children are exposed through the media, such as country-western)
–vocal music (songs)
–game music (for finger plays, clapping games, etc.)
–exercise music (for marching, stamping, skipping, etc.)

2. Instruments for creation of music:
–small drums and large drums for co-operative drumming
–bone whistles
–wooden flutes
–guitar
–triangles
–cymbals
–tambourines
–bells
–xylophones
–horn (trumpet)
–fiddles

Planning for the Music and Movement Area

Review the materials suggested for the two sample groups. Now think of the children in *your* program and note materials other than those you already have in the music and movement area that would reflect the children's cultural and community experiences.

1. Music for listening: _____

_____

_____

_____

_____

_____

_____

_____

_____

_____

_____

_____

_____

2. Instruments for creation of music: _____

_____

_____

_____

_____

_____

_____

_____

_____

_____

_____

_____

_____

Library

Description of Area

The size of the library area depends largely upon how it will be used. A quiet, intimate library tends to be snug and comfortable with enough space for three to five children. Some teachers prefer this area to be used for active learning and therefore make it larger and more open. It is not unusual for the larger area to accommodate from twelve to fifteen children.

The quiet and intimate library or reading area is generally in a small area away from the noisier activities. This type of library should have at least one shelf of books arranged so that the children can easily identify and reach the selections. A table with two to four chairs might be placed in the area. The setup should reflect comfort and relaxation. A couch, throw pillows, and shag rugs could be included for this purpose. The setting encourages a reflective type of learning.

An active library area generally suggests movement and exploration. Chairs should be available for the group sharing of stories or other related activities, such as use of records or cassette recordings. In this area two or three open-shelf units may be available for storage. Bookshelves that allow the books to be broadly displayed are preferred. Although tables and chairs may be present, the floor can also be used for individual investigation. (The children could spread small mats on the floor to define a working area.)

All libraries should be adequately stocked with enough books to cover a range of topics. A minimally stocked library should have about two books per child, although they may not all be displayed at once. The book selection should include fiction and nonfiction, special-interest books, and books about and/or made by the children themselves. Magazines, catalogs, and newspapers may also be included.

In a multicultural, bilingual program, special care should be taken to provide many books that are written in the two languages used in the program. When a variation of a language is used in the community and the community supports its use in the center, one should attempt to find that variation in print. (For example, teachers in early childhood centers in the United States should regard with caution books printed in continental Spanish dialects or British English, unless, of course, the children come from regions in which those variations are spoken.)

Attention must be given as well to illustrations and the "hidden curriculum" in the content of books. Illustrations should reflect as much as possible the ethnicity of the children. The content should enhance the children's self-esteem and not subtly demean it or contradict cultural values that parents wish to preserve. Content that mirrors the children's immediate environment (e.g., life in urban neighborhoods as well as life in the Caribbean islands or on the rural high plains) is important.

Unfortunately, there are not at present a great number of commercially available books that meet the expectations of this curriculum. For that reason, classroom staff may wish to have workshops in which they create books that will more adequately address the children's interests and surroundings than those that can be purchased. Such books can be made from photographs taken at the center or in the neighborhood, from magazine pictures that reflect the children's environment, or from pictures that the children have drawn. Simple texts can be written by the staff in the children's own words. Making such books is an activity that parents may enjoy at their workshops.

Tape recordings of local traditions and stories, simplified when necessary for the understanding and enjoyment of young children, can also be made available. The children will learn to insert the cassette into a recorder and push the button to start the tape. Headsets can be used so that the area will remain quiet for the other children using it, and hand puppets made by parents or teachers can also be made available so that children can act out the story as they listen to it.

Planning for the Library Area

Review the suggestions for the library area. Now think of the children in *your* program and note types of books or other materials you need to acquire in order to reflect the children's cultural and community experiences.

1. Books positively representing the children's cultural and racial groups: _____

_____

_____

_____

2. Books positively representing the setting where your program is located (urban, suburban, rural): _____

_____

_____

_____

3. Books written in the second language used in your program: _____

_____

_____

_____

4. Books made by children, parents, or teachers of events in the children's lives: _____

_____

_____

_____

5. Tapes of stories from the oral traditions of families in the program: _____

_____

_____

_____

Large-muscle Area

Description of Area

The indoor large-muscle area should be large enough so that four to six children can move freely without fear of upsetting equipment or endangering the safety of others in the group. The setup of the area should permit the children to run, jump, hop, skip, and use various forms of equipment.

In determining area size, it is important to consider the nature of the equipment that will go into it and the type of activity that will go on there. If the area is to be primarily a building space for giant blocks or interlockers, a smaller space might be used. If the space includes the use of riding toys such as tricycles and wagons, it will need to be considerably larger. Activities such as running, rope jumping, hopscotch, and dance require more space than does construction work.

In addition, the age and developmental stage of the children who will be participating in the area will influence you as you prepare area size and materials. Older children will require more space, as their skills and mobility are greater. Older children are also more likely to test themselves against the equipment and their fellow players.

It is unusual for the average preschool classroom to have enough space for a permanent large-muscle area in the classroom. Because the area requires so much space, it is usually a temporary area that can be set up quickly during certain portions of the day. Setup is often accomplished by removing tables, chairs, and other pieces of furniture from some part of the classroom for the length of time prescribed for this activity. Thus, any classroom area can become a large muscle-area, providing it is large enough and free of obstruction.

It is not unusual for one to find portions of the large-muscle area taped off to divide the building area from the area in which the large muscle toys (tricycles, etc.) are being used. Large circles, hopscotch or skelly (loadies) outlines, and forms for other such games can be taped or painted onto the floor.

Materials/Equipment Needed
The range of possible materials for this area is quite large. Because the classroom covers a span of ages, it is likely that the materials can be used according to the needs of individual children. Riding toys, movable stairs, balance beams, balls, jump ropes, and other such toys add richness and variety to the area. Giant blocks and interlocking pieces and giant Tinkertoys provide opportunities for the children to participate actively in the spatial concepts that are a part of the total preschool curriculum.

In centers with an outdoor space that can be used for a portion of the year, a playground can be created using materials that can easily be scrounged from the area. Old tires, for example, can be bolted together and hung vertically or horizontally from trees or large posts. Cable spools can be bolted together and secured in the ground to make an attractive jungle gym. Many other locally available materials can be collected by parents and teachers to make a variety of forms for climbing, crawling, and jumping.

Some cultural groups use specific equipment in the pursuit of favorite forms of exercise; whenever possible and appropriate, such materials should be available in programs serving children of those groups. For example, many South American families favor soccer as a sport. Soccer balls would be valued outdoor equipment in programs serving their children. Some Filipino groups, on the other hand, use long bamboo poles in children's jumping games, and their children should have the poles available as a choice in outdoor play. As with all other classroom materials, your selection of outdoor equipment should be based on observations you have made of the cultures and community your program serves.

Planning for the Large-Muscle Area

Review the materials and techniques suggested for the children's large-muscle development. Now think of the children in *your* program and note materials other than those you already have available for large-muscle development that would reflect the children's cultural and community experiences.

1. Special equipment needed: _____

_____

_____

_____

_____

_____

_____

_____

_____

_____

_____

_____

2. Boundaries or game outlines needed: _____

_____

_____

_____

_____

_____

_____

_____

_____

_____

_____

_____

Woodworking

Description of Area

The woodworking area or carpentry corner needs to be large enough to accommodate as many children as can safely be supervised. Children should be able to move from one material to another without interfering with the work of others. Adequate space will reduce the possibility of accidents.

The area should include at least one woodworking table with dimensions of about 27″ H × 21½″ W × 43″ L. A vise attached to this bench or table is recommended. Containers should be provided to allow for storage of various sizes and types of nails. Cans, boxes, and plastic containers are excellent for this purpose. Storage facilities must be provided for tools. For preschoolers, outlines of the various tools could be posted on pegboard or some similar material so that children will know exactly where to return each tool.

Wooden articles characteristic of the cultures represented at the center may be used to decorate the area along with the children's own work.

Though wood is not generally considered a manipulative material, children learn that a piece of wood can be reduced in size, sawed, shaped, joined, etc., by using appropriate tools. These actions can give children a real sense of mastery over the material.

Fundamental to working in the woodworking area is gaining respect for the tools that the children employ. Staff should discuss with the children the proper way to handle equipment in the area. As children see staff members using these materials correctly they will learn appropriate use.

The woodworking area should encourage construction in which the child selects the project. Many children will learn that their hands cannot exactly replicate ideas they have in mind. Some children may become discouraged upon realizing this and may elect not to use the area at all. Your role could be to demonstrate some of the possibilities within the children's range so that they can experience success in their work.

Materials Needed

- workbench
- 2 hammers (claw), medium weight
- 2 saws (rip or crosscut)
- 2 c-clamps
- sandpaper of various grains
- assortment of nails
- ample supply of soft wood in manageable sizes
- storage facility where tools can be put away when not in use
- ample supply of storage containers for nails

Tools and materials should be real and of good quality. Rules in picture form for use of the area should be posted in the area for all to see.

Planning for the Woodworking Area

Review the suggested materials. Now think of the children in *your* program and note materials other than those you already have in the woodworking area that would reflect the children's cultural and community experiences.

1. Basic woodworking materials needed: _____
   _____
   _____
   _____
   _____
   _____
   _____
   _____
   _____
   _____
   _____
   _____

2. Materials reflecting the children's cultural or environmental experiences with wood:
   _____
   _____
   _____
   _____
   _____
   _____
   _____
   _____
   _____
   _____
   _____
   _____

Science

As mentioned earlier in the chapter, *science* is not understood to be a particular area in the room or a specific corner but rather an approach that permeates the entire curriculum. In this approach, emphasis is given to the scientific method with its steps of observing, questioning, exploring, hypothesizing, experimenting, and validating. In whatever area the children are working they should be encouraged to observe, question, think about what they perceive through their senses, play with ideas, take imaginative leaps, and try out their hunches. Likewise, they should be encouraged to seek relationships, make discoveries, experiment with possibilities, try out ideas in a variety of settings, and attend to process. Participation in such an approach necessitates the development of skills for categorization, discrimination, and generalization as well as the ability to think inductively and make inferences.

This curriculum is specifically developed for children who (by Piaget's definition) are in the preoperational stage of development and who, therefore, do not yet have full command of many of the skills just cited. The curriculum thus focuses on facilitating such development and providing opportunities for the use of these skills. (In no way is this to be understood as accelerating such development.)

For example, when children are outdoors they will be helped not only to make observations of seasonal changes but also to talk and think about them and (when they return to their classroom) dictate stories about their observations. To give another example, in the block-building area a child who is bridging two blocks with a third and experiences difficulty may be helped in a variety of ways to see cause and effect relationships (connections to be found among the three blocks) that will help the children to complete the bridging successfully.

When one turns specifically to the content of science (concepts of buoyancy, evaporation, condensation, change, growth) and/or to related mathematical concepts (such as volume and capacity), the provision of certain materials—concentrating on those natural materials available from the local environment—just as much as teacher-directed activities will help the children to make discoveries and find connections. For example, in helping children to understand concepts of growth and change, staff members may offer a variety of activities centered around planting; water play offers opportunities to understand the meaning of buoyancy. In the creation of the environment itself questions are posed, challenges created, discrepancies noted, and thought stimulated.

Planning for Science

Review the techniques suggested for incorporating science into the various areas of the classroom. Now think of the children in *your* program and note materials drawn from the local environment that would foster the children's problem-solving abilities in each area below.

1. Housekeeping: _____

_____

_____

_____

2. Blockbuilding: _____

_____

_____

_____

3. Sand: _____

_____

_____

_____

4. Water: _____

_____

_____

_____

5. Art: _____

_____

_____

_____

6. Table materials: _____

_____

_____

_____

7. Music and movement: _____

_____

_____

_____

8. Library: _____

_____

_____

_____

9. Large-muscle area: _____

_____

_____

_____

10. Woodworking: _____

_____

_____

_____

A Few Additional Comments on the Environment

Most of the material in this exercise has been description of ways you might set up a learning environment in order to encourage the children to achieve the goals set for their development. Some other aspects of a classroom setup or environment, less obvious than the areas of the room or the type of activity within areas, are also important to think about as you prepare your program. Among these are nutrition, safety, cleanliness and order in the environment, the treatment of plants and animals in the classroom, and the decoration of hallways and offices. As you look at your classroom you should consider carefully and plan each part of this hidden environment.

Nutrition

Nutrition is a subject frequently talked about in program training sessions. Members of the program staff who have attended such sessions are likely to know the importance of the children's receiving a balanced diet in the snacks and meals they receive at school. It is common for the teaching staff to integrate the preparation of foods into learning activities for the children.

One aspect of nutrition that is overlooked in many programs is the appeal of certain dishes or types of food to children from different cultures. A meal that is beautifully balanced nutritionally may not be eaten by many children in the program, because the food is unfamiliar. Sometimes programs attempt to produce food distinctive of the children's cultures but adjust the seasoning so much the children no longer recognize the dish.

In a multicultural preschool program, menus must be planned with nutritionally balanced foods typical of the various cultures represented at the center. Both snacks and the main meals of the day should be balanced and varied. When the cooks are preparing foods foreign to them, they should use cookbooks with authentic recipes from the original regions of the families served by the center. Parents may be willing to help the cooks by sharing some of their families' favorite recipes. (See Level 1 for suggestions.)

Safety

Safety in the preschool classroom is vital to the curriculum described in this source book. Safety can be looked at in two ways.

1. The environment: an arrangement and selection of materials that will allow interaction between the total classroom elements but will not endanger the child or others with whom he or she is interacting.

2. Procedural considerations: care given to the use of materials, routines, and equipment as an integral part of the curriculum in order to reduce (and hopefully eliminate) the possibility of physical or psychological harm to the child.

First of all, you must consider safety as you arrange the classroom. Such questions as the following should all be asked as you set out the areas described in this chapter. Are corners padded? Is there adequate space for a particular activity? What is the size of the group? What is the condition of the equipment? What is the energy level of the children in the classroom? What is the focus of the curriculum activity? How many persons are available to supervise?

To help establish safe procedures you should develop a chart to acquaint each child with features of toys that might cause harm or injury if the toys are not used or cared for in an appropriate manner (e.g., if the blocks are not sanded smoothly, they can give splinters). The children should be taught to respond to an unsafe condition either by correcting the situation themselves or by bringing it to the attention of someone who can correct it.

More than the establishment of procedures is required for a safe environment. You should provide opportunities for the group to talk about, suggest, and dramatize safe and unsafe conditions and uses of materials, which will make the children understand the need for safety. Further, discussions will make the need personal and important to them because of the responsibility you give them to help you provide a safe classroom. Opportunities to practice such procedures as fire drills also should be provided frequently. The children should know how to respond to your cues in such circumstances.

Cleanliness and Order

Some responsibilities in a preschool setting are givens for the teacher and the children. Arranging and cleaning up after an activity are examples of such responsibilities. Keeping the classroom clean and orderly through the efforts of both the teaching team and children will enable the program to run smoothly and efficiently.

The health component of the overall early childhood program should also be strongly considered in this aspect of the environment. Along with standards for cleanliness and order in the classroom, standards for care of one's own body should be modeled by the staff and incorporated into both the environment and directed-learning activities. For example, the children should have the opportunity to brush their teeth after lunch, and handwashing should be supervised until the children show that they have mastered the technique. Doctor/nurse and dentist materials (in toy form) can be made available in the dress-up or role-playing areas. These materials may become the focus for small or large group discussions.

Care of Plants and Animals

Many classrooms for young children have small animals (gerbils, guinea pigs, mice, garter snakes, or rabbits) and a variety of plants for the children to observe and care for. Often the plants are those that the children themselves have started from seeds. Proper care of both the plants and the animals is something that can be a subject of large group discussions. Their care must be constantly reinforced through the arrangement of the areas in which the plants and animals are kept, the classroom staff's demonstration of appropriate behavior toward living things, and the adults' being watchful whenever children are working with either animals or plants.

Hallways and Offices

Messages of respect for cultural diversity in an educational setting come to parents and children in many ways. The setup of the classroom is, of course, very important, and most of this exercise has been devoted to a close look at classroom environments. It is important to remember, however, that a school's hallways and offices also can be important indicators of your program's appreciation of individuals and groups. Displays of the children's work, evidence of parent workshops such as those discussed in Chapter Three, posters reflecting the region of origin of parents and staff, decorations characteristic of participating cultural groups, and reflections of community scenes are all ways to acknowledge the importance of the collective experience of individuals in the creation of a program of heightened awareness.

EXERCISE 3

Securing Needed Learning Materials

Some of the materials you need for your classroom are commercially available. To assist you in your search for materials to reflect the children in your program, commercial resources and publishers are listed in an appendix to this source book. You should also gather catalogs from as many publishers of educational materials as possible and review them carefully with your partners to select books, games, and other equipment. In making such selections, you must keep in mind the developmental characteristics of your children and the multicultural (and perhaps bilingual) requirements of your program. In all cases you should ask yourself the questions on the material assessment form provided before ordering any material. Many times this will mean that you must see the material and have a chance to review it before you order it. If your review is positive, you can then place the order using a form like the sample one or the form that is preferred by your program's administrators.

Materials that cannot be purchased commercially can often be made by teachers and parents in the sorts of workshops described in ALERTA's Levels 1, 2, and 3. The success of such workshops, of course, depends on the care you take prior to the meeting to secure all the materials needed for the work in large enough quantity for all the participants to be actively involved in the task. A sample form is provided for you to list the items to be made and note the materials you will need to collect ahead of time.

Assessing the Appropriateness of a
Material's Use in Your ALERTA Program

1. Will this material help the children meet one of ALERTA's goals? _____

   _____

   _____

   _____

   _____

2. Does this material reflect some aspect of my children's direct (cultural/com-
   munity/environmental) experience? _____

   _____

   _____

   _____

   _____

3. Is this material accurate and nonstereotypic in its portrayal of cultural groups or
   geographic settings? _____

   _____

   _____

   _____

   _____

4. Is this material developmentally appropriate for the children in my program? ____

   _____

   _____

   _____

   _____

   _____

Placing an Order

Check your material budget with your director or principal. Determine your budget allowance, and prepare a list of materials to be ordered.

Item Name	Company Producing Material	Number of Items	Price per Item	Total Price

Preparation for Materials-Making Workshops

Type of Item	Materials to Be Collected Ahead of Time

Transforming Your Classroom

It is important to take a close look at your learning environment and identify materials that you need to carry out the program. Equally important is the task of making specific plans for bringing about the changes you want in your classroom. Change will not occur at the pace you expect unless you take steps to determine *when, how,* and *with whom* you will work to create your new environment. On the final pages of this chapter are questions that may help you organize each aspect of the transformation of your classroom. These questions are your blueprint for carrying out the day-to-day work of using ALERTA's Level 4.

Planning for Change

1. What are your priorities in materials making? (What type of materials do you want to make first, next, and so on?)

   _____

2. How do you plan to make the materials that you need for the various areas of the classroom? (Parent/teacher workshops? use of resource people? individual work after class?)

   _____

3. Who has special expertise that might be able to help you with each type of materials construction?

   _____

4. What dates have you identified for materials-making sessions?

   _____

5. What printed resources might you draw upon for materials making? (Idea books, commercial materials that might be adapted to meet ALERTA's goals, stories and traditions collected from parents, etc?)

   _____

   _____

6. What procedures do you need to follow to insure that needed materials are ordered according to school or center policy?

   _____

   _____

7. When will specific changes in your classroom be made?

   _____

8. Who will help you do any needed rearranging of your classroom?

   _____

CHAPTER SEVEN

Level 5: Observing Children's Interests, Developmental Levels, and Language Use

Once the learning environment has been prepared to reflect the community and cultures of the children in the program, teachers and parents have a unique opportunity to observe their children's emerging interests and capabilities. Observation in ALERTA does not begin with Level 5, of course. As soon as you initiated the program in your center or classroom you began drawing upon a growing awareness of self and others, which was a form of observation. Moving through Levels 2 and 3, you sharpened your observational skills in identifying elements of the cultures represented by your participating families and in recognizing community resources that could be integrated into daily learning activities for the children. In Level 4 you transformed your perceptions into a learning environment specifically designed to promote new concepts, skills, and attitudes in the children through use of familiar objects and events.

The difference in Level 5 is that, in addition to looking at the characteristics of cultures and communities that are reflected in the children, you now also focus on the children's personal and developmental characteristics. Children reveal these personal and developmental characteristics most readily in a learning environment that recognizes the distinctiveness of both groups and individuals. It is the task of adults in the program to be able to see and utilize what the children reveal of themselves.

As a child-centered program, ALERTA expects daily child observations to be the basis for program planning. This expectation grows out of child development and early education literature that has consistently indicated that young children learn most rapidly and easily when learning activities are designed around their immediate interests and are neither too complex nor too simple for their level of development. This chapter presents an introduction to the child-centered observation used in ALERTA, with descriptions of child characteristics to look for and techniques for making observational notes on a regular basis. The exercises for teachers and parents are organized in four groups: (1) making child observations in anecdotal form, (2) observation of child interests, (3) observation of skills and developmental levels, and (4) observation of present language use and proficiency. How these observations are subsequently used in program planning will be discussed in Chapter Eight.

As you begin Level 5 it is recommended that you videotape in your own classrooms instances of children working during child-initiated portions of the day. For the purpose of the activities to come, five to ten minutes of footage focusing on one or two children is needed. If videotaping is not possible, try to locate a film that shows children at work in an early childhood setting; identify for viewing a five-minute segment showing clear instances of child behaviors.

Although the following exercises can be done by a person alone, they will have their greatest effect if done with at least one partner.

Making Child Observations in Anecdotal Form

There are at least two ways of making reliable child observations. The first is to make notes periodically on what individual children have said or done in a particular situation. Often these notes focus on an anecdote, an incident that tells a story about a child's abilities or interests or records something that happened in-

volving the child. For that reason, such notes are known as *anecdotal records*.

A second way of making observations is to use an *observation guide* or checklist that focuses on particular aspects of the child's interests or capabilities. The items on the guide may indicate specific settings for observation of children's activ-

---

Observer: R.D.   Bill *(monolingual English)*

October 27

At lunch, asked R.D. when everybody was going to go on the trip to buy fish for the new aquarium.

In afternoon, sat "reading" the book Miguel's Mountain *for most of work period.*

November 2

When came into classroom in the morning, asked R.D. if he could help set up the aquarium. R. responded "yes." Helped spread gravel and set plants in tank. Carried several pitchers of water from dechlorination tub to aquarium without spilling a drop.

Later, watched fish and smiled.

---

ities or may relate to the goals of the program. This exercise provides practice in the first type of child observation—anecdotal records. Examples of the second type of observation are illustrated in later exercises.

To begin this exercise, look at these sample anecdotal records and characterize the style in which the observations were written. (*Note:* These samples, and those that follow, are meant to simulate the front and back of index cards. In actuality, you will want to identify only one side of the card, and post your observations consecutively to that side of the card, continuing onto the other side when necessary.)

You may have noted the following.

1. The observations collected here were of incidents that occurred over brief spans of time.

2. Only what the child *did* or *said* was recorded and not the observer's interpretations of the action.

Observer: R.D. *Elliott (English-dominant bilingual)*

October 28

In morning work period, helped R.D. assemble the fruit for a tropical salad. Touched the pineapple and asked, "How do you get the prickles off?" R. gave him a plastic knife and a slice of pineapple to peel. E. worked with knife for a while without removing any of the peel. Left the table saying, "I'm not hungry now. Good-bye."

After lunch asked if he could put on the counting games record. Started record and sat working with a lotto game that included a photo of his house. Sang along with record as he worked.

Later listened to Halloween story and said (in Spanish) that his "abuelita" (grannie) had given him a candy skull for "El dia de los muertos" (The Day of the Dead).

November 5

Watched Teresa and Marta begin to put away materials in the housekeeping area at cleanup time. Walked into area and folded doll blankets neatly. Placed blankets on doll bed. Said to Marta, "¿Qué tu haces? You want me to help?"

At various points during the day, the observer tried to focus on one incident at a time. This is not always possible, as in the natural course of children's activity many activities are likely to be going on simultaneously. If an observer tries to record too many situations at one time, he or she runs the risk of not seeing any one happening very clearly.

Several items should be included on all anecdotal records of this sort: the child's name and note of his or her language proficiency,[1] the observer's name, and the date. This information is important when the notes are being used for program planning, discussed in the next chapter.

Now view your videotape or film segment and record on an index card exactly what was done or said by a particular child. (If you are working with a partner, you both should observe the same child. You may wish to view the videotape twice.) Assess the adequacy of your observations against the following criteria.

1. Accuracy in reporting what was actually observed.

2. Use of strictly descriptive rather than interpretive or inferential language. (E.g., "Johnny smiled" instead of "Johnny seemed happier.")

3. Attempted focus on a particular incident that revealed evidence of the child's development in the socioemotional, cognitive, linguistic, or psychomotor domains.

When a lack of accuracy, clarity, or focus in an observation is revealed, rewrite the observation to remove the difficulty. (In the case of several partners working together, a representative of each small group can present an example of a reworked observation, explaining to the group as a whole what changes were made and why they were necessary.)

If you experienced feelings of uncertainty as you undertook this exercise, we recommend that you review the elements of child observation in these three popular texts.

Almy, Millie and Genishi, Celia. *Ways of Studying Children.* New York: Teachers College Press, 1979.

Boehm, Ann E. and Weinberg, Richard A. *The Classroom Observer: A Guide for Developing Observation Skills.* New York: Teachers College Press, 1977.

Cohen, Dorothy H. and Stern, Virginia. *Observing and Recording the Behavior of Young Children.* New York: Teachers College Press, 1973.

These resources provide abundant examples of observations, distinguishing between descriptions of what children have actually said or done and inferences that you as a teacher may eventually draw from those descriptions.

In Level 5, ALERTA's staff members are expected to write clear descriptions of child characteristics and behaviors. Each staff person writes anecdotal notes on at least two children each day. Interpretation and use of those observations in ongoing program planning is discussed in the next chapter of this source book.

As soon as you feel comfortable with the elements of descriptive anecdotal records, it is time for you to put your perceptions to the test by actually recording the interests and characteristics of the children in your classroom. The next three exercises provide opportunities for you to recognize and capture in writing significant moments in children's activity within their multicultural environment.

---

[1]How you determine a child's language proficiency is explained in Exercise 4.

Observing Children's Interests

It was pointed out in Chapter Two that children's interests are often keys to unlocking their inner worlds and that learning appears to proceed with greatest effect when it grows out of strong interests. Young children may have quite different sets of interests according to the events they have witnessed or directly experienced in their day-to-day lives. Clearly, the impact of culture on children's interests is likely to be strong. Young children in South Dakota's ranching country, for example, may be fascinated by rodeos, and children in Newark, New Jersey, may be attracted to the activity at construction sites. Children in San Diego, California may find boats especially interesting.

The easiest way to discover children's interests is to have a learning environment rich in materials and opportunities for the children's direct extension of their previous experiences. Examples of such environments were discussed in Chapter Six. Effective use of ALERTA's Level 5 relies on the existence of such an environment in your classroom or early-learning center.

Two techniques for recording the interests that children spontaneously express are described here. The first method is to carry index cards and a pen in your pocket as you work each day. At different times during the day conduct a five-minute observation on each of the children you are observing that day. Inevitably you will record expressed interests of the children. A typical anecdotal record might look like the following example. Note how many interests are evident in this observation.

Sometimes observers include information relating to a child's developmental level on the same card as they note an interest. Turn now to the sample child observations at the end of this chapter. See if you can pick out the children's interests in each set of notes. Circle the *interests* only.

Another way to record child interests

Observer: L.W.   *Raúl (Spanish-dominant bilingual)*

September 22

Went to the art area in the morning and began working with clay there. Made an airplane and remarked to Juanito, "Mi Papa va a Santo Domingo mañana." ("My Daddy's going to Santo Domingo tomorrow.")

At lunchtime, volunteered, "¡Mi gatita tuvo cuatro gatitos chiquititititos ayer y son míos!" ("My kitty had four little tiny kittens yesterday and they're mine!")

---

over the period of a week is to use an observation guide like the one that follows. When you use a guide like this, you are not able to associate particular interests with individual children, but you can see patterns of interest over a short period of time. You also can see which areas of a room are attracting the most children. Some classroom areas may need to be made more interesting to the children so they will want to work in all of them.

An example of how information is recorded on this chart is provided. In the first column, the observer has kept a tally of the number of times that week children used each area for an extended period of time (at least ten minutes) during *child-initiated* portions of the day. The second column provides notes on which materials in each area were especially appealing to the children. The third column records topics raised by the children that reveal current interests.

Now that you have been introduced to two ways of recording child interests, you should practice them in your own classroom at various times throughout the day. Over the next week or two, use the anecdotal recording approach with two children each day. When you feel comfortable doing the brief anecdotes, add five minutes or so of observation with the guide every day during child-initiated work periods. When you review the cards and chart at the end of each week, circle the children's interests you recorded. Keep your notes from these practice sessions for use in the program planning exercises that are presented in Chapter Eight.

The ALERTA Program

Observations of Child Interests Over a Week

Observer(s) _____   Dates _____

Center/School _____   Classroom _____

	Tally of Times Children Used Area for Extended Work	Materials Selected by Children for Frequent Use	Topics Raised in Children's Spontaneous Conversations
Housekeeping/ Family			
Blockbuilding			
Art/Music			
Library			
Water/Sand			
Manipulatives/ Table Toys			
Other:			
Community Walks/ Field Trips	Not applicable	Not applicable	

Observations of Child Interests Over a Week

Observer(s) ___M. C.___   Dates ___June 28 – July 2___

Center/School ___Webster___   Classroom ___B___

	Tally of Times Children Used Area for Extended Work	Materials Selected by Children for Frequent Use	Topics Raised in Children's Spontaneous Conversations
Housekeeping/ Family	ⅬⱧ ⅬⱧ ⅬⱧ ⅬⱧ III ㉓	coffee maker/colador family puppets "food" for "picnic"	what people take on a picnic going to the beach with family
Blockbuilding	ⅬⱧ III ⑧	stand-up figures of men/women toy train toy boats	bridge (for trains) going fishing with father/mother/brothers
Art/Music	ⅬⱧ ⅬⱧ IIII ⑭	clay sand painting materials marimba	barbecues (making hamburgers) going to Georgia for family reunion
Library	ⅬⱧ ⅬⱧ ⅬⱧ II ⑰	"I Am Adopted" "Is That Your Sister?" "Good-night Moon!"	new baby sister born last week birthdays
Water/Sand	ⅬⱧ ⑤	sea shells as scoops bubble pipes/colored water/soap solution	fireworks
Manipulatives/ Table Toys	ⅬⱧ ⅬⱧ ⅬⱧ ⅬⱧ ⅬⱧ IIII ㉙	board games using dice puzzles of children's homes	ways to travel different kinds of travel
Other: Woodworking	ⅬⱧ IIII ⑨	heavy cardboard hammers saws	building boats
Community Walks/ Field Trips	Not applicable	Not applicable	going with mother to buy new bathing suit piragua stand on street corner

EXERCISE 3

Observing Children's Skills and Developmental Levels

As children grow they go through levels or stages in their development that have been well described by many observers. These stages affect the ways children handle their emotions and relate to other people (their socioemotional development), how children see the world and approach problems to be solved (their cognitive development), the skill with which children control their bodies (their psychomotor development), and the extent and complexity of their language use (their linguistic development). Some of the characteristics that are typical of young children in each of these domains of development have been described in Chapter Two and should be reviewed before you undertake the following exercise.

The activities in this exercise provide situations in which you can refine your own ability to see the patterns that individual children present in each domain of their development. As you will see in Chapter Eight, your collected notes on these patterns will be very useful in the planning of learning activities to extend the children's skills.

Socioemotional Development

For healthy social and emotional development it is very important that young children feel pride in who they are and what they are able to do. In some early childhood literature this trait is referred to as the children's "feeling good about themselves." Signs to watch for that might reveal how children feel about themselves could include whether they do the following:

–try activities that are new to them
–initiate activities when they have a

choice of things to do
–show others the work they are doing
–ask to take their work home
–express pleasure in the display of their work
–recognize or point out in illustrations people that resemble themselves
–feature themselves accurately in drawings or role plays they do

Another set of characteristics revolves around children's relationships with other people. Here you might be interested in whether the children do the following:

–show trust of other people
–invite other children to play or work with them
–treat other people with respect
–share materials with other people most of the time
–play or work with children from cultural or racial groups different from their own
–speak well of members of their own and other groups
–usually control emotions that could be harmful to others
–accept direction from others when appropriate
–mention family members and friends

As you think about these characteristics of healthy socioemotional development, you should remember that although all children are likely to experience common human emotions, the way they express or reveal those feelings might vary from culture to culture. One child might show respect by speaking up, for example, and another child might show respect by remaining silent. One child might show pride by asking that her picture be hung on the wall, and a proud child from another culture might consider it rude to ask for work to be displayed. Any interpretation of the children's behavior that you do later for the purposes of planning must be done with the behavioral expectations of particular cultures in mind. At the same time, you must avoid stereotypes. Remember that all people of one group or culture do *not* act in the same way.

Turn again now to the sample observations found at the end of this chapter. Underline in red pencil all the observations of children's *socioemotional* characteristics. Do not be surprised if you find that you have already identified some of these as child interests in the previous exercise. The interests that children express are closely tied to their socioemotional development, and there may be a good deal of overlap between the two.

If you have been able to videotape children at work in your classroom, it will be very useful for you and a partner to look at the tape again and record on index cards all the instances that relate to the children's socioemotional development. Compare your notes with those of your partner to see if you recorded similar descriptions, and discuss any differences in perception.

Over the next week continue to write your anecdotal observations. At the end of the week underline in red all examples that you see of the children's socioemotional development. As before, you should make records on at least two children a day for about five minutes at various points during the day. Keep your notes for use when you move on to Level 6.

Cognitive Development

There are many indicators of the developmental level of children's thinking skills. Among the most commonly considered are the ways children:

- identify and describe objects and events (including development of vocabulary and sensory discrimination skills)
- associate objects and events with one another (such as "things to wear when it's raining")
- group objects by traits they have in common (such as "all the objects made of wood")
- describe the position of objects in space (as in "I'm moving my combine *across* the cornfield" or "My boat just went *under* the bridge.")
- express notions of time (as in active recognition of the fact that *first* you peel the plantain, *then* you slice it, and *finally* you fry it)
- reproduce visual patterns (as in doing a puzzle or making a border print of local design on curtains for the housekeeping area)
- reproduce sound patterns (such as songs, rhymes, or the sounds of a "new" language)
- reproduce motion patterns (as in dances or games)
- predict the likely outcomes of an observed activity (for example, saying what will happen if an egg rolls off the table)
- pose alternative ways to solve a given problem (as when there are not enough tortillas for every child at snack time)
- use objects symbolically (for example, using a wooden block to represent a telephone receiver)

Examples of all these characteristics are in the sample child observations found at the end of this chapter. Turn to those observtions and put a box around all the notations that record an instance of children's *cognitive* development.

Once again, you may discover yourself marking an observation that you previously identified as socioemotional development or a child interest, but don't worry. Observation of the same event may reveal several different kinds of information at once, which is why it is important to record descriptions of (rather than interpretations of or inferences from) child activity. Having descriptive observations allows a teacher to use a set of observations in several different ways and encourages economical use of time available for observation.

To refine your ability to record instances in which children reveal aspects of their cognitive development, view your videotape again with a partner, and note specific cognitive occurrences. Compare records to see if you picked out the same incidents, and explain to one another how you see those behaviors as yielding information about the children's present cognitive development.

Although children naturally tend to display their emerging cognitive abilities, they will not necessarily do so in the absence of stimulating materials to work with. Moreover, young children may show their thinking skills most fully when dealing with objects or events they recognize from their experience at home or in their community. Anthropological field workers have recounted instances in which young children seemed at a loss when given small plastic bears for forming groups of "more than" or "less than" a certain number. The same children were observed to recognize who had the winning hand in a card game with no difficulty whatsoever. Card games of many sorts were a popular form of family recreation in their community. In another community, a child who on the basis of use of some typical school materials was thought to have poor auditory skills was later discovered to be a featured singer in a Native-American singing society, a membership that required extraordinarily acute auditory skills. Occurrences such as these should remind us as teachers that although our ultimate goal is to develop children's flexibility in working with a great variety of materials, we should insure that materials familiar to the children are well represented in a learning center, especially during the children's early years. With this con-

sideration in mind, you may want to review once again the materials you have available for the children's use in your classroom to see that culturally and environmentally specific materials are plentiful.

The next step in refinement of your observational skills is for you to continue to observe at least two children a day for about five minutes at intervals throughout the day. When you review your index cards at the end of the week, put a box around all examples you have found of the children's cognitive skills. Once again, keep your notes for use in the next level of program implementation.

Psychomotor Development

Young children's natural disposition toward active work and play provides many opportunities for observation of psychomotor development. The distinction between gross-motor (large-muscle) and fine-motor (small-muscle) development in children is a common one to most people who have worked in early childhood settings. Less common but perhaps more useful in program planning is recognition of different types of motor skills in relation to the setting or situation in which the activity is occurring. In Chapter Two a number of examples were given of children's gradual mastery or control of their bodies in space, moving from defining their working space (and that of others) to controlling their bodies as a whole while moving and while stationary, to independently using their limbs while moving and while stationary, and finally to controlling their bodies while the environment around them was moving.

After reviewing the examples of each category of activity given in Chapter Two, consider the following list of possibilities.

–putting on/taking off clothing
–doing role plays or pantomimes
–setting a table for lunch

-going down an escalator
-using manipulative learning materials at a table
-sitting to listen to a story
-marching
-working with a small group in a corner of the room
-rocking in a rocking chair
-handing out name tags to other children
-swinging on a swing
-dancing
-stirring cookie dough
-putting away blocks at cleanup time
-toileting, brushing teeth, etc.
-playing obstacle course games
-doing finger plays and hand games
-playing circle games

See if you can sort these activities into the five categories in the following sample chart.

As might be expected, examples of several of the previous categories are found in the set of observations at the end of this chapter. Turn to those observations one more time and underline in blue all the notes you see relating to *psychomotor* development. You will again experience the overlap between domains of development that we discussed previously, as observations relating to a child's psychomotor development may also reveal something about his or her cognitive or socioemotional development.

Psychomotor Development

Control of the Body within a Defined Space

Control of the Body While Moving through Space

Independent Use of the Limbs within a Defined Space

Independent Use of the Limbs While Moving the Body through Space

Control of the Body as a Whole While Surroundings Are Moving

Now view your videotape once more with your partner and note the specific instances you see of psychomotor development in the children. As you did earlier, compare your records and discuss your perceptions of the capabilities the children were revealing. You may notice in this portion of your work that you see only one or two categories of activity discussed above, which may be because you have been presenting the children with limited opportunities for the other kinds of activity or because the children were involved in more quiet kinds of work when you videotaped. You may also notice in reviewing your tape instances of children using culturally specific motions or gestures to convey meaning. If distinctive gestures appear, they might form one of the bases for an exploration with other teachers or parents of nonverbal communication in various cultural groups.

Your ability to distinguish the several types of psychomotor development will be strengthened when you turn your attention to the psychomotor skills of the children in your own classroom. Follow the same procedure as you did previously, making ongoing anecdotal observations to review at the end of the week. Try to observe at least two children a day for about five minutes each at different times of the day. Remember that although you will be noting child interests and socioemotional, cognitive, and psychomotor development, this time at the end of the week you will underline in blue only the instances you saw in the psychomotor domain. As before, keep your notes for use in Level 6.

To conclude this exercise you should note that, as with observation of child interests, it is also possible to observe children's socioemotional, cognitive, and psychomotor development by using a checklist or guide. Such a guide should be constructed on the basis of goals and objectives identified for the children's development. An example of such a checklist is presented in the following chapter after procedures for deriving goals and objectives for children's learning have been discussed.

EXERCISE 4

Observing Children's Language Proficiency

In order to use ALERTA's bilingual component it is necessary for you to know the degree of proficiency the children in your classroom have with English and with the other language to be used in the program. The purpose of this exercise is to introduce you to a way of gathering initial information on the extent and contexts of the children's present use of language.

Refer to the Guide for Clustering Children for Combination (Adult-Directed) Sessions on the next page. You will notice that this observation guide has four categories: Language Child Uses at Home, Child's Use of Language with Others in Classroom, Child's Use of Language According to Classroom Setting, and Complexity of Child's Use of Language in Classroom. The first three categories come from ALERTA's use of insights from sociolinguistic theory as described in Chapter Two. It was noted there that children (and adults) may switch languages or language variations according to the context (persons with whom they are speaking or settings in which they are working) of their language use. Observing language use in such contexts is likely to provide a fuller

The ALERTA Program

Guide for Clustering Children for Combination (Adult-Directed) Sessions

Child's Name _____ Observer _____

Classroom/Center _____ Date _____

Directions: Place either number 1 or 2 in each category below that applies to your observations of this child. 1 = understands the language 2 = speaks and understands the language Total each column as you finish it; then combine your totals. Use the totals to select an appropriate language cluster for adult-directed work with the child.

Languages Child Uses at Home:

	English	Spanish	Other
with mother			
with father			
with brothers/sisters			
with grandparents			
with aunts/uncles			
with others			
Totals			

Child's Use of Language with Others in Classroom:

with _____ (Teacher's name)

while he/she is speaking _____ (Language)

with _____ (Teacher's name)

while he/she is speaking _____ (Language)

with _____ (Peer's name)

while he/she is speaking _____ (Language)

with _____ (Peer's name)

while he/she is speaking _____ (Language)

Totals

Child's Use of Language According to Classroom Setting:

	English	Spanish	Other
Blockbuilding			
Art			
Science			
Library			
Housekeeping/Dramatic Arts			
Sand/Water			
Music			
Manipulatives			
Outdoors			
Snacks/Meals/Routines			
Totals			

Complexity of Child's Use of Language in Classroom:
(NOTE: Here circle the number that *best* represents how the child uses each language. Count only circled numbers in totals.)

	English	Spanish	Other
Single words	1	1	1
Phrases/sentences	3	3	3
Full conversations	5	5	5
Totals			

The Combined totals are: _____

The **Combined totals** indicate that this child should *initially* be placed in an:

☐ English monolingual cluster ☐ English-dominant bilingual cluster

☐ Spanish monolingual cluster ☐ Spanish-dominant bilingual cluster

☐ _____ monolingual cluster ☐ _____-dominant bilingual cluster

☐ _____ monolingual cluster ☐ _____-dominant bilingual cluster

example of language proficiency than would otherwise be the case. The fourth category focuses on the developmental characteristics of language acquisition in young children.

Use of this guide with individual children over several weeks' time will give you a sufficient amount of information for initial identification of a language cluster for each child.[2] These cluster identifications will change as the children move through the program. Spanish monolingual children, for instance, will most likely become Spanish-dominant bilingual speakers. The initial first cut identification, however, permits children with similar patterns of language proficiency to work together with a teacher for a short time each day in adult-directed activities.

Look at the example of a completed observation guide (on pp. 158–159). The guide was filled out on the basis of the observations summarized in the next sections.

Background Information

Alicia is a four-year-old girl who was born in the Dominican Republic. Her family came to New York when Alicia was two years old. She and her family live near the Head Start Center in a predominantly Hispanic neighborhood.

Alicia began coming to the Head Start Center in September. The observations recorded were made during the last two weeks of October. Alicia's classroom has approximately 50 percent native English speakers and 50 percent native Spanish speakers.

The head teacher in Alicia's class is monolingual English speaking. The assistant teacher is bilingual in Spanish and English. Although the assistant teacher was born in the Dominican Republic, most of her formal schooling took place in New York. She never studied Spanish in the course of her educational experience.

October 20 (8:45 A.M.)

Alicia enters the classroom with her grandmother, who speaks no English.

Grandmother: *"Quédate quieta y déjame desabotonarte el abrigo. Pórtate bien y no te ensucies el traje."* (Be still and let me unbutton your coat. Be good and don't get your clothes dirty.)

Alicia enters the classroom, skips up to the head teacher, and touches his knee lightly.

The teacher smiles and responds.

Teacher: *"Hi, Alicia! How're you doing? What would you like to do this morning?"*

Alicia smiles at teacher, looks around the room, and points to the housekeeping corner.

Teacher: *"What do you want to do?"*

Alicia: *(while still pointing):* *"Play!"*

October 29 (10:30A.M.)

Alicia is seated at the table having a snack with two English-speaking children and a Spanish-speaking child. The two English-speaking children are talking.

First English-speaking child: *"Did you see the monster last night? That was scary!"*

Second English-speaking child: *"Yeah, I saw it! That big old monster smashed that house, and it went crash, bang!*

Alicia has been listening intently, although she has not entered the conversation. She turns to the Spanish-speaking child.

Alicia: *"Yo tampoco le tengo miedo. Yo lo cojo y lo mato."* (I'm not scared of it either. I'll catch him and kill him.)

[2]Examples of language cluster designations are English monolingual speakers, English-dominant bilingual speakers, Spanish-dominant bilingual speakers, and Spanish monolingual speakers.

Guide for Clustering Children for Combination (Adult-Directed) Sessions

Child's Name _____ *Alicia* _____   Observer _____ *L. W.* _____

Classroom/Center _____ *Escuelita* _____   Date _____ *September 30* _____

Directions: Place either number 1 or 2 in each category below that applies to your observations of this child. 1 = understands the language 2 = speaks and understands the language. Total each column as you finish it; then combine your totals. Use the totals to select an appropriate language cluster for adult-directed work with the child.

Languages Child Uses at Home:	English	Spanish	Other
with mother		2	
with father		2	
with brothers/sisters		2	
with grandparents		2	
with aunts/uncles			
with others			
Totals		8	

Child's Use of Language with Others in Classroom:

with _____ *Ron* _____
  (Teacher's name)
while ⟨he⟩/she is speaking _____ *English* _____   1
  (Language)

with _____
  (Teacher's name)
while he/she is speaking _____
  (Language)

with _____ *Peter and Sally* _____
  (Peer's name)
while ~~he/she is~~ *they are* speaking _____ *English* _____   1
  (Language)

with _____ *Marta* _____
  (Peer's name)
while he/⟨she⟩ is speaking _____ *Spanish* _____   2
  (Language)

Totals	2	2	

Child's Use of Language According to Classroom Setting:

	English	Spanish	Other
Blockbuilding			
Art			
Science			
Library			
Housekeeping/Dramatic Arts	1		
Sand/Water			
Music			
Manipulatives			
Outdoors			
Snacks/Meals/Routines		2	
Totals	1	2	

Complexity of Child's Use of Language in Classroom:
(NOTE: Here circle the number that *best* represents how the child uses each language. Count only circled numbers in totals.)

	English	Spanish	Other
Single words	①	1	1
Phrases/sentences	3	3	3
Full conversations	5	⑤	5
Totals	1	5	

The Combined totals are: 4   17   _____

The **Combined totals** indicate that this child should *initially* be placed in an:

☐ English monolingual cluster   ☐ English-dominant bilingual cluster

☒ Spanish monolingual cluster   ☐ Spanish-dominant bilingual cluster

☐ _____ monolingual cluster   ☐ _____-dominant bilingual cluster

☐ _____ monolingual cluster   ☐ _____-dominant bilingual cluster

Note: Alicia is beginning to understand English and may be moved to the Spanish-dominant bilingual cluster soon.

Additional Information

Alicia's father picked her up after school on October 23. He speaks and understands English. He says that is wife uses only Spanish in the home, as she has not yet learned English. He also said that Alicia's older brother can already understand English well but does not speak it at home.

In the example of the completed observation guide, the totals under each column have been added up and entered on the form. The totals indicate that this child may be considered either a Spanish monolingual speaker or a Spanish-dominant bilingual speaker. Observations of Alicia's socioemotional development indicate that she would be more comfortable, for the time being, in the Spanish monolingual cluster. Soon she may be switched to the Spanish-dominant bilingual cluster.

For approximately two weeks, use this guide to summarize observations on ten to twenty children in your class. At the end of that time sit down (with your partners, if you have them) and examine your completed observation guides. Make a chart like the one below on newsprint, and place the names of the children you have observed in the appropriate cluster.

As you consider your results, it will undoubtedly become evident that it is not easy to determine the dominant language of some bilingual children and that you need to make your best educated guess to place the child in a compatible cluster. It is fairly common for staffs completing this exercise to find that their children divide fairly evenly into the four groups. It is not necessary that all four clusters be represented, however. To be most effective, each cluster should have no more than six children in it. In reviewing this procedure you should consider the following points.

English Monolingual	Spanish Monolingual*
English-dominant Bilingual	Spanish-dominant* Bilingual

*Substitute language appropriate to your group.

1. The purpose of this procedure is to form small clusters of children in each classroom to work together for a short time each day in adult-directed learning activities.

2. Staff members in each classroom should complete their intial observations on the children's use of language and record those observations on the guide(s) for clustering children within the first eight weeks of the school year.

3. As soon as the language observations are complete, clusters should be formed in each classroom and daily adult-directed activities should be planned that take into account language characteristics of the children in each cluster.

4. A child's membership within a language cluster should not be considered fixed. As children become increasingly proficient in the second language, the two monolingual clusters may be phased out and all four clusters may be bilingual.

5. Children in all four clusters should participate in adult-directed activities that continue the expansion of the first language as well as in adult-directed activities for the acquisition of the second language.

Management of Ongoing Child Observations over Time

Although ALERTA developers expect that child observations will be ongoing throughout the program year, they are realistic in their recognition that teachers do not have time available to record observations on each child every day. A plan can be adopted that makes the task easily manageable at the same time as it gives—over a week's time—the information needed for program planning.

In typical early childhood classrooms of approximately twenty children, there is often a teacher and an assistant. If the teacher and the assistant were to sit down at the beginning of the week and divide the group in two, each of them would have ten children as her or his special observational responsibility. If both the teacher and the assistant made a point of keeping a special eye on two of the ten children each day (different children would be observed each day), all the children would have a special observation made on them each week.

The teacher and assistant could each observe her or his children during the regular course of the day's activities. The observers could keep index cards or a clipboard with an observation guide readily available to jot down a quick note when something happens with one of the children during the day. Using this plan, staff members would each spend only about ten minutes daily in concentrated observation.

If a teacher is working alone in a self-contained classroom, the same plan could be followed with the understanding that only half the children would be observed at the end of a week. In that case, each round of observations would be completed every two weeks instead of every week.

You should begin your daily child observations as close as possible to the beginning of the program year. During the first four to six weeks of your program you can begin to collect observations of the children's interests, skills, and developmental levels. From approximately the sixth to the eighth week of the program you can observe the children's language proficiency for the purpose of forming language clusters. For the remaining weeks you can continue to conduct daily observations to observe child interests and developmental levels. The children's rapidly growing proficiency in using a second language can be assessed periodically as part of the ongoing observational process, and adjustment of the language clusters can be made as appropriate. The following chart summarizes this observational plan.

In the next chapter we will look at how child observations are sorted and used in weekly and daily program planning to continue to shape both learning activities and the classroom environment to children's interests and needs. Recommended procedures for observation and planning over the course of the program year are also presented.

A Plan for Ongoing Child Observations:
Continuous Use of ALERTA's Level 5

Weeks	Observers	Circle Only Observations of Child Interests	Underline Only Observations of Skills/ Developmental Levels	Circle Observations of Interests and Underline Skills/Develop- mental Levels	Observations of Language Proficiency
1 and 2	Teacher 1 (T1) Teacher 2 (T2)	T1: anecdotal records of 10 children each week T2: anecdotal records of 10 children each week			
3 and 4			T1: anecdotal records of 10 children each week T2: anecdotal records of 10 children each week		
5 and 6				T1: anecdotal records of 10 children each week T2: anecdotal records of 10 children each week	
7 and 8		T1: Week 7 Child Interests Guide T2: Week 8 Child Interests Guide			T1: Clustering Guide, 10 children each week T2: Clustering Guide, 10 children each week
9 and 10					
11 and 12[3]					Formation of language clusters

[3]After week 12, teachers continue observing the children's interests, skills, and developmental levels throughout the year. Language proficiency observations can be incorporated into the ongoing anecdotal observations.

Sample Child Observations

Observations of Monolingual
English Speakers

Observer: J.M. *Frank (monolingual English)*

February 5

Worked in the housekeeping area with "doctor" materials, taking Jerry's temperature and giving him a "shot." Called an "ambulance" to take Jerry to the "hospital."

Speaks almost nonstop as he works.

At library corner fought with Jerry over the book Goodnight Moon. *Cried when I let neither have it.*

February 9

Came in the morning with three toy trucks. Would not share them.

At snack time, talked about watching Emergency One *on T.V. and hummed the theme song.*

Ran all the time outdoors.

Watched the fish in the aquarium for 10 minutes before leaving room. Made his mother wait.

Observer J.M.   Beatrice (monolingual English)

February 2

Doesn't stop talking. Talked about her brother and how he goes to the "big kids' school." Said she was going to the park on Sunday.

Wrapped herself in blankets in the housekeeping area and played with Jackie ("hospital"). Played mommy to David. Wanted him to get into carriage.

February 10

Loves dressing up. Puts on different hats.

Imitates what she thinks is Spanish. Makes "Spanish" sounds.

Painted and wanted to tell teacher about painting: "Lady in a house."

Observer: J.M.   Harriet (monolingual English)

February 12

(New child in class. This is only her fifth day.)

Seems shy. Answers teacher by shaking head. Smiles. (Began talking to caregiver who came to pick her up at 2:30.)

Played with small colored cubes. Played at water table for 10 minutes.

Did not talk much to other children.

February 17

Loves to hear music. Asked to play triangle during marching time.

When asked about the picture she painted, whispered the picture was of herself and her baby brother. Said her baby brother speaks Spanish (!)

Likes to play with simple puzzles. When she has difficulty, she does not finish but quickly puts puzzle away.

Observer J.M.   *Jerry (monolingual English)*

February 1

On walk to market with small group of children and teacher said, "That's like B.J. and the Bear's. It's got lots of wheels." (He was pointing to a large trailer truck across the street.)

Showed Ms. Davis how he puts on jacket. Put it on twice.

February 8

Went to the woodworking area and nailed a tin circle to a wooden block. Sawed at a piece of wood (halfway through). Stopped work, sighed, and put tools back on workbench.

Made a road with blocks. Walked on it and put toy cars on it.

Observations of English-Dominant Bilingual Speakers

Observer: C.J.   *Maria (English-dominant bilingual)*

February 4

Spilled her juice at snack time. Puckered her face as if about to cry. Spilled milk at lunch. (No fuss made by adults.)

Had difficulty sitting during meeting time.

February 16

Loves to sing in both Spanish and English.

Played at water table most of the day.

While in the housekeeping area, had a monologue about washing her hair and using the hair dryer. Comment overheard: "Listen, I'm going out, so I have to dry my hair. Look, Michael, don't bother me. I'm going out."

Observer: C.J.   *William (English-dominant bilingual)*

February 13

Played in blockbuilding area during child-initiated play. Laid blocks out flat to cover a portion of floor. Later, lay on them. Said (in English) there was water all around and he was floating on blocks.

Did not want to eat lunch. Said he liked what his mother made. When asked what that was, shrugged shoulders.

February 16

Built boat again with blocks. Said (in English) that he and his brother were going fishing.

Used the large wooden blocks as small blocks on table. Made a car and shooting sounds as he worked.

Observer: C.J.   *Jackie (English-dominant bilingual)*

February 3

Tends to hit when other children don't do what she wants. Put herself in a corner when reprimanded for hitting.

Talked to group about her big sister Jeanie. Jeanie sometimes picks her up after school. Talked about going to a burger stand with Jeanie.

February 17

Loves rhythm games, especially "Head to Shoulders" and "Little Sally Walker." Is beginning to sing repetitive Spanish game songs.

Tends to be bossy, particularly with Beatrice.

Said (in English) she was going to Texas to her grandmother's house for Easter vacation.

Observer: C.J.   *Teresa (English-dominant bilingual)*

February 1

Answers in English when teacher addresses her in Spanish. Speaks Spanish with her grandmother.

Plays in blockbuilding area by herself. Builds in flat, horizontal manner. Uses large, rectangular blocks only.

February 11

Convinced José to be the baby. Put him in a carriage and baby-talked to him. "Spanked" him.

Has begun to build vertically in the blockbuilding area. Knocked down Frank's and Jerry's towers repeatedly. Became upset when Jerry cried, and tried to hit Jerry.

Observations of Spanish-Dominant
Bilingual Speakers

Observer: G.M.　　　　　　*José (Spanish-dominant bilingual)*

February 2

Smiled and hummed frequently as he worked.

Inspected the blockbuilding area and table games but did not stay with either long.

Tried to speak English to everyone. Did not want to come for story in Spanish. Sat close to group and listened.

February 9

Made structure with Tinkertoys. Said (in Spanish) it was a crane for lifting up bricks to make a building.

Generally avoids using Spanish. Twice this week joined an English first language cluster during combination session.

Loves to say "Shut up!"

Observer: G.M.   *Juanito (Spanish-dominant bilingual)*

February 3

Worked in blockbuilding area making a large boat. Boat fell apart several times, but kept rebuilding it.

Worked quietly, hardly speaking to anyone.

Watched L.A. clean the aquarium. Smiled when talked to.

February 13

Chose Crystal Climbers for work during child-initiated time. Spoke to Elliott about what he was making. "Esta es mi casa." ("This is my house.")

Chose teacher-made sequence game ("Paving Our Street"), looked at it, and put it back.

Observer: G.M.   *Antonio (Spanish-dominant bilingual)*

February 9

Puts on firefighter's hat each day. Plays at driving a bus. Sits on chair backwards to make bus.

Outside wore blanket tied around shoulders. Said (in Spanish) he was Batman.

February 18

Played with clay. Pounded a great deal. Said (in Spanish) that he was cooking.

Wears cowboy hat now.

Invited Bill to join him in afternoon when working on floor with Lego blocks. Made a spaceship and said he was going to fly to Puerto Rico. Bill asked if he could come. A. replied "Yep . . just you 'n me!"

Observer: G.M.   *Marta (Spanish-dominant bilingual)*

February 12

Talked about what kind of candy her mother was going to give her on Valentine's Day. Said she had gone with her mother to the store to pick out the candy. Spoke in Spanish.

February 16

Worked in the grocery store setup in one corner of the room. Arranged and rearranged the cans and packages until Bill came over to buy some food. Gave Bill a can of peaches and said (in English), "You've got to give me money. It costs money. Give me five dollars!"

Smiled and clapped her hands when told that her cluster would be making kites today. Throughout work period, talked (in Spanish) about going with her papa and brothers to fly kites in the park.

Observations of Spanish
Monolingual Speakers

Observer: L.A.   *Georgina (monolingual Spanish)*

February 10

Spent full child-initiated period working with manipulatives. Built a variety of structures, dismantled them, and rebuilt them.

Started crying again, right before lunch.

February 19

Has made friends with Alicia. Spends a lot of time with her in the housekeeping area.

Continues to be concerned about staying clean. Avoids paint, clay, and paste.

Does not eat well in school.

Speaks very softly and timidly.

Observer: L.A. *Carmen (monolingual Spanish)*

February 11

Wants to play with Alicia. Followed her around in the house-keeping area. Talked with teacher about the new dress her mother had bought her.

February 23

Completed a 12-piece puzzle quickly. Did not put it away afterwards.

Tends to be bossy with Georgina. Takes her hand, leads her to where she wants to play.

Observer: L.A.   Alicia (monolingual Spanish)

February 17

Speaks almost completely in Spanish, beginning to understand many English phruses.

Worked in housekeeping area, dressed up in heels and hat, and admired self in mirror. Noticed the fashionable shoes of a classroom visitor. Approached the visitor, smiled, and whispered to her, "¡Esos zapatos son lindos!" (Those shoes are pretty!)

February 24

Talked (in Spanish) to teacher about her grandmother. Said she went shopping with her.

Later became angry with Georgina because G. would not play the way A. wanted.

In the afternoon avoided teacher's invitation to play in the block-building area.

Sings "If You're Happy" in English at large group time. Continues to interact directly only with Spanish speakers.

Observer: L.A.   Roberto (monolingual Spanish)

February 19

Worked in sand area using tin cans for dipping and pouring sand. Asked Alicia if he could use her funnel. Took Jerry's spoon when J. put it down, and gave it back to him immediately when J. said (in English), "That's mine!"

Right before lunch, took out hand puppets that had been used in his cluster. Practiced moving them and supplying different voices for each puppet.

February 25

Played with Tinkertoys at table with José and Maria. Built a car and told the others that he was going to Mexico in his car. Asked the other children if they had built a car.

On walk to community garden, said his uncle had a big garden where all kinds of vegetables grew.

CHAPTER EIGHT

Level 6: Planning for Learning Across All Domains

A distinctive feature of child-centered programs is that ongoing observational records are used for planning activities and learning environments for the children. As you worked with ALERTA's Level 5, you practiced preparing observational records and identifying examples of young children's interests, skills, and developmental levels. At the conclusion of the chapter the following was noted.

1. Doing short, simple anecdotal observations need take only about ten minutes of your time each day.

2. A team of two persons in the classroom could decide which two children each staff member would observe on a given day. A single person working in a classroom could also observe two children each day without spending an inordinate amount of time at the task.

3. At the end of five days it would thus be possible to have anecdotal observations on twenty children. A person working alone would have observations on all the children in about ten days.

ALERTA's Level 6 illustrates how collected child observations are converted into learning activities through a child-centered planning process.

To develop appropriate materials and learning environments, adult-directed activities, and the interactions needed in child-initiated work, you need a planning procedure that will allow you to organize your notes on the children's interests and developmental levels. The procedure must offer you a simple and usable way to make use of the specific interests and capabilities of individual children at any point in time.

Many teachers feel they do not need such a procedure—that they always "know" what the children in their classroom can do. It has been observed, however, that when teachers saying this sit down to plan their programs, they frequently focus solely on activities rather than on the interests and progressing development of the children and the relationship of each of those to the choice of activities. It is for this reason that the Head Start program nationally now requires each center staff to have a system of record keeping in order to be in compliance with the Head Start Program Performance Standards. Many private early childhood programs have a similar requirement.

This chapter presents ALERTA's basic planning procedure in five parts: (1) deriving themes for learning activities from child interests, (2) defining a range of goals and objectives for children's learning, (3) identifying goals and objectives from observations of skills and developmental levels, (4) using themes and goals/objectives to design learning activities, and (5) establishing weekly and daily planning procedures. Each step along the way has been designed to remain sensitive to the realities of teachers' working lives. When you are first learning the procedure, you may find that it takes longer to complete than you expected. With a little practice you will discover that the procedure described here is both efficient and economical of time. As with other levels of program implementation, working with a partner in the following exercises is recommended. The exercises can also be done by a teacher or parent working alone.

EXERCISE 1

Deriving Activity Themes
from Observations of Child Interests

ALERTA teachers use observed child interests to identify themes (topics or content) for adult-directed cluster work conducted with small groups of children, for adult-directed large group activities, and for selecting new materials to include in the various areas of the classroom. Every week or two the teachers assemble the anecdotal records they have made of child interests or review their completed Observations of Child Interests guide. On newsprint or a simple note pad, they then list the prominent interests each child has spontaneously displayed over the time period.

To illustrate the process, the sample child observations found at the end of the previous chapter can be regarded as two weeks' worth of anecdotal records from a single class. Review of these notes readily reveals at least six areas of interest:

- doctors, hospitals, and medical practices
- older or younger brothers and sisters and their activities
- the children's homes/houses
- vehicles including cars, trucks, ambulances, buses, boats, and cranes
- travel to other places to see relatives
- buying and selling goods

General themes can be quickly derived from those areas:

- health care
- family members

- homes
- transportation
- family origins
- stores

The teacher(s) in this hypothetical case would select one of these general themes for use with the whole class for several days, or longer if the children's interest is sustained. (Which theme is selected from the list would be determined largely by the degree of interest that it had been seen to evoke in the children.) The other themes would be held in reserve for future planning sessions. Let us suppose in this instance that the general theme selected for the class was family members.

The next step would be for the teacher(s) to individualize the theme according to the specific interests of children in the four language clusters. One possibility for such an individualization can be seen in the following diagram.

Variations of the theme chosen would be seen in the adult-directed learning activities subsequently planned for the children in each cluster. It would also be seen, however, in the selection of music, games, fingerplays, or role plays used in large group activities and in the materials made available for the children's use in various areas of the room.

At another point of time in the program, the same procedure would have been followed by teachers reviewing the Observation of Child Interests guide

```
                    ┌─────────────────┐
                    │ General Theme:  │
                    │ Family Members  │
                    └─────────────────┘
```

Monolingual English	**English-dominant Bilingual**	**Spanish-dominant Bilingual**	**Monolingual Spanish**
• family composition	• family composition	• family composition	• family composition
• babies/children/ adults	• big brothers/ sisters	• house family lives in	• family activities
• people in family who take care of someone who is sick	• where other relatives live (travel)	• shopping with family members	• where other relatives live (travel)

presented in the previous chapter. General themes that appear there might be identified as family excursions and summer activities. Once again, the theme may be individualized for each cluster, though in this case you would not have much information on individual interests. You would, however, have some indication of whether areas of the room need to be made more attractive to the children, possibly by adding materials to reflect current interests.

ALERTA teachers often review both their anecdotal records and their guides for recording interests at the same time, which gives a fuller picture of recurring themes in the children's thought. In the next exercise you might wish to do the same.

Assemble the observations you made of the children in your classroom during the use of Level 5. Separate out the child interests you recorded. List on the following sample chart the interests of the children in your four language clusters. Review the lists for general themes and select one for use. Individualize the theme you select as appropriate to your clusters.

Collected Child Interests

English Monolingual Cluster	English-dominant Bilingual Cluster
Spanish-dominant Bilingual Cluster*	Spanish Monolingual Cluster*

*Substitute as appropriate the second language used in your program.

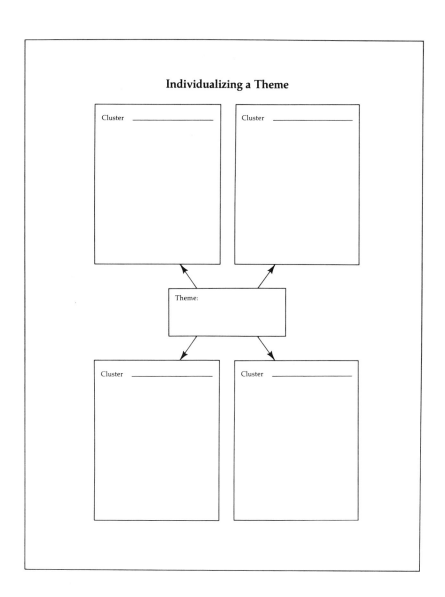

EXERCISE 2

Defining a Range of Goals and Objectives for the Children's Learning

Themes alone do not provide enough guidance for good planning of learning activities. Teachers need goals and objectives for the children's learning as well. Over the past few years, a great deal of attention has been given to the importance of goals and objectives in education, but teachers have often been presented with detailed checklists without explanation of what the stated goals and objectives represent. This exercise is devoted to a close look at how goals and objectives are defined in the ALERTA program and what those goals and objectives say about ALERTA's values.

Goals are things that you work toward. They represent some change that you want to occur in your life or in the lives of others for whom you are responsible. *Objectives* are the various steps you take to reach that overall goal. When teachers have goals for children's learning, those goals are the knowledge, attitudes, and skills they want the children in their classroom to have by the end of the school year. Many times, individual teachers do not decide on the goals for the children in their classroom. Instead, a school as a whole or a city-wide (or state-wide) educational system sets the goals for learning.

When teachers, parents, or administrators set goals and objectives for the children's learning, they make a statement about what characteristics they want the children coming out of their educational system to have. Some decision makers focus on one area of children's development, such as the acquisition of formal academic skills (for example, being able to recognize the alphabet or count to ten). Other decision

makers believe that in order for young children to be competent learners as they proceed through the school system they must help children develop attitudes and skills across the socioemotional, cognitive, linguistic, and psychomotor domains of learning. Teachers, parents, and administrators taking this view concentrate on creating learning situations in which young children are required to put into practice what they learn about their world. Children in these programs learn ways of relating positively to a variety of other people and develop their thinking skills so that they can work well in a variety of situations. They learn to recognize and use their own capabilities in many areas instead of in one or two areas of study, and they develop their linguistic and creative abilities as well.

It is probably clear at this point that ALERTA takes the second of these two views. ALERTA values positive social interaction, flexible and well-developed thinking skills, fluent use of language, and creative expression as avenues for enabling young children to continue developing as truly competent learners. Given that orientation, it was natural that ALERTA should develop a set of goals and objectives that reflect its deep-seated view of the kind of person it wishes to produce.

In Chapter One, the following four goal areas were presented as ALERTA's expected outcomes for children.

1. Appreciation of self as a person capable of a wide variety of intellectual and physical activities.

2. Positive recognition of the ways people from various groups are the same as well as the ways they are different from one another.

3. Active engagement with the events that make up their lives as a context for developing their capabilities in problem solving and communication.

4. Acquisition of specific knowledge and skills to help them deal successfully with school in today's culturally plural society.

(Two additional goals dealing specifically with bilingual capabilities are discussed as part of Level 7.) These goal areas illustrate once again the way that development in the socioemotional, cognitive, linguistic, and psychomotor domains are closely tied to one another. Goal Area 1, for example, draws heavily on the socioemotional domain, but it also draws on the cognitive, linguistic, and psychomotor domains. Goal Area 2 combines socioemotional, cognitive, and linguistic capabilities about equally. Goal Area 3 combines cognitive, linguistic, and psy-

chomotor outcomes, and Goal Area 4 draws on all four domains to promote skills and attitudes specifically related to success in diverse learning situations.

In the following section each of the four goal areas has been refined into a set of possible objectives, or elements that contribute to the achievement of the overall goal. These objectives are not meant to be the *only* objectives possible for each goal area. Rather, they should be viewed as one range of possibilities for the development of three- to five-year-old children. They offer a framework for viewing the children's capabilities on the assumption that the children who enter the program already possess learning and a set of experiences upon which we should build. The listing is *not* to be regarded as a statement of deficits that must be remedied in the course of the school year. Following this understanding, it is not expected that each child in the program will attain every one of the objectives by the time he or she leaves the program. Rather, it is expected that each child will show a balanced profile of achievement in each of the goal areas.

The ALERTA Program Goals and Objectives

Goal Area 1:   Appreciation of Self as a Person Capable of a Wide Variety of Intellectual and Physical Activities

Objectives: The children will:

1.   Show willingness to try new activities

2.   Communicate to others the belief that they can do the new activity

3.   Show pride in work completed

4.   Describe things they like to do

5.   Define a space in which they can work without interfering with the work of others

6.   Initiate and call a halt to activities

7.   Participate in both quiet and active experiences

8.   Work in all areas of the classroom

Goal Area 2:   Positive Recognition of the Ways People from Various Groups Are the Same or Different

Objectives: The children will:

1.   Describe some of their favorite family customs

2.   Associate themselves and their family with a particular cultural group (or groups)

3.   Describe characteristics of themselves and members of their family

4.   Describe ways in which people are alike (e.g., all have names, all can feel happy or sad, all live somewhere, etc.)

5.   Identify something unique about themselves

6.   Describe ways in which people may be different from one another (e.g., differences in height or coloring; differences associated with infancy, childhood, or maturity; differences in ways of doing things at home, etc.)

7.   Associate friends with particular cultural groups, events, or customs

8.   Associate objects, events, or customs new to them with particular cultural groups

Goal Area 3:   Communication and Problem Solving

Objectives: The children will:

1. Describe the uses of most of the common objects found in their classroom and homes
   (*Note:* Regional variations in vocabulary are to be expected, and alternative words for the same object will be introduced.)

2. Describe the common attributes of objects (e.g., color, shape, size, weight, texture, taste, smell, etc.)

3. Describe situations or events that are a part of their environment (e.g., workers repairing their street, their apartment's being painted, etc.)

4. Describe processes in which they participate (e.g., what happens when they siphon water from one container to another, how they help feed the baby, etc.)

5. Create and/or carry out a role play in which they use language and nonverbal communication to represent various characters

6. Develop ways to answer their questions about objects by "experimenting" with them (e.g., finding out which objects are heavier than others by weighing them on a balance scale)

7. Group objects in various ways (by attribute, function, or association)

8. Arrange objects in an identifiable sequence (from tallest to shortest, thickest to thinnest, etc.)

9. Use comparative and superlative terms (e.g., "John, please give me the *biggest* ball you can find!")

10. Use terms that show spatial relationships (e.g., "Please put the mop *in* the pail." "The spoons are *in front of* the glass.")

(*Note:* Hill and others have pointed out that there may be cultural differences in the perception of "in front of" and "behind." People of some cultures see the front of an object as the portion of the object that faces them, and people of other cultures see the front of an object as the portion of the object that faces away from them.[†]

11. Use terms that show a relationship to time (e.g., "We will eat *after* we set the tables.")

12. Demonstrate a one-to-one correspondence between common objects (e.g., providing a full set of clothing for each doll)

13. Demonstrate their understanding of the concepts "more than," "less than"/ "fewer than," and "the same as"/"as many as" in relation to weight, volume, and number of objects when the arrangement of the objects or the containers holding the objects are identical

14. Follow as many as three simple directions in sequence (e.g., "Henry, please pick up the books, take them to the library corner, and place them on the top shelf.")

15. Use language as part of the problem-solving process (to predict, hypothesize, etc.) when they are faced with objects or events that they do not understand (e.g., "I think that . . .", "What will happen is . . .", "Maybe next week . . .")

16. Give directions to each other in order to assist in solving a problem (e.g., "You need a ramp to make the road smooth.")

17. Move from use of simple materials to use of materials of increasing complexity

18. Use materials symbolically as well as literally (e.g., using a block as a truck as well as using it to build a structure)

[†]Clifford Hill, *Up/Down, Front/Back, Left/Right: A Contrastive Study of Hausa and English.* Paper of the Institute of African Studies, Teachers College, Columbia University, n.d.

Goal Area 4: Acquisition of Specific Attitudes and Skills for Success in School within a Culturally Plural Society

Objectives: The children will:

1. Show trust for one another and for adults by inviting interaction with them

2. Work cooperatively with others when appropriate

3. Work independently when appropriate

4. Show and talk about their feelings

5. Describe how another child may be feeling in a given situation

6. Accept that they may not have objects or experiences that are unsafe or otherwise inappropriate in a given situation

7. Use language to work out difficulties that arise with other children

8. Invite children of different racial, cultural or linguistic backgrounds to play or work with them

9. Attend to their own hygiene (such as toileting, toothbrushing, handwashing, and so on)

10. Put on or take off outside clothing with a minimum of adult assistance

11. Serve themselves at snacks or lunch without spilling food or drink

12. Get out materials to work with and put them away when finished

13. Show respect for their environment by keeping it clean and taking care of the animals and plants within it

14. Use materials that require coordination of the fingers

15. Use materials that require use of the whole body

16. Reproduce and create body movements that go together in a sequence (as in a dance or game)

17. Reproduce and create sound patterns (as in repeating songs or rhymes and in making up sounds to accompany a story)

18. Reproduce and create visual patterns (as in putting together a puzzle, weaving a mat, or stringing beads in a particular order)

These lists of learning goals and objectives are meant to be viewed as a flexible first definition of possibilities for young children's development within a multicultural context. Use of ALERTA with older children or children with handicapping conditions may require revision of the goals and objectives to suit developmental needs. Revision may also be required to meet needs or preferences of some communities using ALERTA. In order to have this listing fit the developmental levels and any special needs of the group of children your program serves, it is important that the goals and objectives presented here be reviewed by your center staff, an associated parent group, and the school's administrators and/or advisory board for appropriate additions or other revisions reflecting your community.

The following is a step-by-step procedure for reviewing ALERTA's goals and objectives in relation to the children you teach. Read the procedure carefully and then make arrangements to carry out all parts of it that apply to your situation. Your end product will be a revised list of goals and objectives especially tailored to the developmental levels of your children and the expressed preferences of your community.

Procedure for Adapting and/or
Revising the Learning Goals and Objectives

Talk with other people working in the classroom(s) at your school or center.

1. Do the children in your classroom appear to be at the same developmental level as the children for whom these goals and objectives were designed? Yes ☐   No ☐

2. Write the names of all of the children in your class on slips of paper and put the paper slips into a bag. Without looking at the names, draw out ten of the slips. Using the list of goals and objectives from the source book, discuss which objectives have already been achieved by each of the ten children you picked out.

_____

_____

3. On the basis of what you have found about the achievements of a sample of children in your program, how should you change the objectives listed in the chapter to better fit the developmental levels of your children?

_____

_____

Talk with the parents of the children in your classroom.

1. Give the parents copies of the goals and objectives. (You might want to spread this activity out over several meetings so that people will not have too much to react to at once.)

2. Discuss the goals and objectives with the parents, asking which ones they would change and what their reasoning is for the change.

Goals and objectives to be changed: _____

_____

Reasons for suggested changes: _____

_____

3. Ask the parents for suggestions of other goals and objectives to be added.

Goals and objectives to be added: _____

_____

_____

_____

Talk with your administrators and/or advisory board.

1. Give your administrators and/or advisory board copies of the goals and objectives. (Again, the board might prefer to read them section by section.)

2. Do the administrators or board members see any special needs of the children or circumstances in their community that are not reflected in the goals and objectives?

Suggestions: _____

_____

_____

_____

3. Do the administrators and/or board members have in mind specific changes for goals and objectives?

Changes suggested: _____

_____

Reasons for suggested changes: _____

_____

Put it all together.

1. One person from your school or center should take notes from all three types of meetings and put the suggestions together on a master copy of the goals and objectives.

2. The revised version of the listing should be typed up and given to each member of the staff. The revised listing should also be made available to the parents and members of the advisory board.

3. Space is provided below for the staff member who is putting all the suggestions together to make notes.

_____

_____

_____

_____

_____

_____

_____

_____

Use an additional piece of paper to complete any of these items.

Once you have a revised list of goals and objectives for the childrens' development you will have a resource that can be used in a variety of ways. For instance, it was noted in the discussion of child observations in Level 5 that child observation guides can be prepared for periodic use in assessing the achievement of individual children over time. Two sample pages from such guides are provided. In these examples a separate copy of the complete observation guide would be kept for each individual child. As teachers observe the children's achievements over time they would enter dates and brief notes as illustrated. Such a guide can be constructed using a simple "dates observed" format like that shown in the first example or with a wider range of possibilities such as those shown in the second example.

Sample Page from Guide for Observing Children's Skills and Attitudes

Goal Area 2: Positive Recognition of the Ways People from Various Groups Are the Same or Different

1. The child describes a favorite family custom.

Dates Observed: Specific instances:

_____10/25_____   _Said, " My mama makes scrambled eggs with green chilies!"_

_____   _____

_____   _____

_____   _____

2. The child associates self/family with a particular cultural group (or groups).

Dates Observed: Specific instances:

_____   _____

_____   _____

_____   _____

_____   _____

3. The child describes characteristics of self/members of family.

Dates Observed: Specific instances:

_____9/16_____   _Said, "My brother's tall! I'm gonna be tall like him."_

_____   _____

_____   _____

_____   _____

Sample Page from Guide for Observing Children's Skills and Attitudes

Goal Area 3: Communication and Problem Solving

Key: Beg = Beginning to   Freq = Frequently   Al = Always

6. The child develops ways to answer his or her questions about objects by "experimenting" with them.

Dates Observed:

Beg	Freq	Al
11/13		

Examples:

a. *Found out how much class turtle weighed by putting it on the scales.*

b. _____

_____

c. _____

_____

d. _____

_____

7. The child is able to group objects in various ways.

Beg	Freq	Al
	9/9	
	9/27	
10/14		
11/5		

a. Color

b. Size

c. Shape

d. Texture

e. Weight

f. Function

g. Association

You may decide that you wish to incorporate periodic use of a goal-based observation guide into your total observational and planning procedure. If you do, you should construct the guide following your revised listing of goals and objectives. (A complete guide using the goals and objectives presented in this chapter is found in the appendix of this source book.) You might conduct observations using the guide at several points over the year, perhaps in October (during weeks 5 and 6 of the program), in January, and again in May. Comparison of the results for each child at three points in time would give a clear indication of the child's progress over the year. It is also possible to use the guide more frequently, in the same manner as you use the child interests guide, to provide additional information that can be used in weekly planning sessions.

The advantages of incorporating the use of such a guide into your record keeping system are many.

1.   A goal-based child observation guide such as this can be used to synthesize anecdotal observations and thus show the patterns of a child's progress.

2.   If the guides were placed in individual children's folders at the beginning of the year, staff could make one or two entries for two children each day. Using the guides in this manner (in conjunction with the activity plans followed that day,

in which the staff had the opportunity to observe the children achieving certain objectives) would take only five to ten minutes of the team's time each day.

3.   Review of the guides every two weeks or so should show a *balance* in the various objectives being achieved by individual children across the four goal areas and three domains of development (socioemotional, cognitive/linguistic, and psychomotor).

4.   Any displayed lack of balance would allow teachers to change the planning of activities for individual children to encourage a broader range of development.

5.   An alternative way to use the guides would be to make entries for each child on the basis of collected anecdotal observations three times a year.

6.   Frequent use of the guides allows for direct weekly input into activity planning.

7.   Periodic use of the guides (e.g., three times yearly) allows for assessment of the progress of individual children within the program over time.

8.   In neither case are children expected to achieve all the objectives. Instead, it is expected that children will show a *balanced profile* of achievement across the three domains of development, which can be easily communicated to parents.

EXERCISE 3

Identifying Learning Goals and Objectives from Observations of Children's Skills and Developmental Levels

As with choice of themes, your selection of particular learning goals and objectives for the children in your classroom should be based on the child observations you have made. ALERTA teachers not only sort their anecdotal records into child interests but also separate out the notes they have made on the *capabilities* (skills and developmental levels) of individual children in the program. They survey the children's strengths and apparent needs as revealed in the observations and then pick out objectives from the various ALERTA goal areas that will extend the children's learning into new areas or give them additional practice in skills they are beginning to master.

It should be noted that when ALERTA teachers sort observations of the children's skills and developmental levels, they separate their notes according to the language clusters in which they have placed their children. This sorting by cluster allows them to individualize their selection to goals and objectives and (as is shown in the next exercise) makes it possible for them to select or create learning activities specially tailored to the emerging capabilities of the children within the various small clusters.

Once again, the sample child observations found at the end of the previous chapter can be used to illustrate this process. By looking carefully at each set of observations for clues about the children's socioemotional, cognitive, linguistic, and psychomotor development and skills, the following information can be noted for the children in the four language clusters.

Monolingual English Speakers

- difficulty in sharing materials (Frank)
- ability to represent scenes from environment symbolically (Beatrice, Frank, and Jerry)
- difficulty in completing tasks (Harriet and Jerry)
- not yet comfortable about interacting with other children (Harriet)
- competent in putting on clothing (Jerry)

English-dominant Bilingual Speakers

- difficulty in controlling body as a whole in a defined space (Maria)
- ability to reproduce songs in Spanish and English (Maria and Jackie)
- ability to use materials symbolically (William)
- difficulty in working cooperatively with others (Jackie and Teresa)
- ability to communicate verbally the intent of their actions (Maria and William)

Spanish-dominant Bilingual Speakers

- ability to represent scenes from environment symbolically (José, Antonio, and Marta)
- reluctant to use Spanish in the classroom (José)
- ability to work persistently at a task even when experiencing difficulty (Juanito)
- practicing use of small manipulative materials (Antonio, José, and Juanito)

Monolingual Spanish Speakers

- difficulty in working cooperatively with others (Alicia and Carmen)
- avoidance of certain classroom areas or activities (Georgina and Alicia)
- relates observations to family events (Roberto)
- role plays situations (Roberto and Alicia)
- "experiments" with manipulative materials (Georgina and Roberto)
- beginning to know and understand English phrases (Alicia and Roberto)

As you read through these lists you will notice that capabilities and needs have been listed that refer to the children's work in all three developmental domains (socioemotional, cognitive/linguistic, and psychomotor). One domain has not been emphasized at the expense of the others.

Once you have listed the skills and needs of the children in each of your language clusters you are ready to review your list of goals and objectives and pick out two or three *for each language cluster*, which you will work on for the next week or two.

Ordinarily, of course, you do not have so little information on the children as you have in this example. While you are reviewing the observations made over the past two weeks, you also have access to your collected knowledge from previous records on each child; therefore, you are able to put the most recent information into a broader context than is seen here.

Even the limited information we have here combined with what we know of the children's interests can suggest some goal areas and objectives to use as a basis for planning activities for each cluster.

For the Monolingual English Speakers

Goal **Area 2:** Objective 6 (Describe ways in which people may be different from one another.)
Goal **Area 4:** Objective 1 (Show trust for one another and for adults by inviting interaction with them.)
Goal **Area 4:** Objective 3 (Work cooperatively with others when appropriate.)

The first goal and objective was picked because the children in this cluster had already shown an interest in the ways people may be different from one another (babies/children/adults), which could be built upon to encourage them to make such a comparison. The other two objectives were chosen because of difficulties experienced by individual children that could hamper the functioning of the cluster in future activities.

For the English-dominant Bilingual Speakers

Goal **Area 2:** Objective 1 (Describe some of their favorite family customs.)
Goal **Area 4:** Objective 2 (Work cooperatively with others when appropriate.)

The first goal and objective was selected because the children had indicated an awareness of different parts of their families (perhaps even living in different locales), which could be connected easily to favorite customs. The other goal and objective was picked for the same reason that it was appropriate for the English monolingual cluster.

For the Spanish-dominant Bilingual Speakers

Goal **Area 3:** Objective 3 (Describe situations or events that are part of their environment.)
Goal **Area 3:** Objective 6 (Develop ways to answer questions about objects by "experimenting" with them.)

These goals and objectives are good points of focus, because the children in that cluster already appear to be showing a lively interest in events and situations surrounding them (their houses, for example), which can be used to further their learning. Several of the children also are showing some facility in the use of materials, which can be drawn upon for development of new concepts.

For the Monolingual Spanish Speakers

Goal **Area 2:** Objective 3 (Describe characteristics of themselves and members of their family.)
Goal **Area 3:** Objective 4 (Describe processes in which they participate.)
Goal **Area 4:** Objective 2 (Work cooperatively with others when appropriate.)

Once more, the goals and objectives were selected because they combine current interests of the children with skills and attitudes yet to be achieved that had been noted in the observations.

You may have wondered why no objectives were selected from Goal Area 1. It should be pointed out that Goal Area 1 is not used so much in the specific planning of adult-directed activities as it is in preparing the classroom environment for child-initiated work. More will be said in Chapter Ten (Level 8) about how the objectives in Goal Area 1 are embodied in the learning environment.

Following the procedure described for identifying goal areas and objectives, you should now assemble the anecdotal observations that you made of the capabilities of your children in Level 5. As you review your collected observations, refer also to the summary sheet entitled "Individualizing a Theme," which you prepared when you sorted out your notes on child interests. Select one to three goals and objectives that you now feel would be appropriate for work with each of your clusters of children over the next week or two. List those goals and objectives on a chart.

**Summary of Goals and Objectives to Use
in Activity Planning over the Next Week**

English Monolingual Cluster

Goal Area: _____   Objective _____

Goal Area: _____   Objective _____

Goal Area: _____   Objective _____

English-dominant Bilingual Cluster

Goal Area: _____   Objective _____

Goal Area: _____   Objective _____

Goal Area: _____   Objective _____

Spanish-dominant Bilingual Cluster

Goal Area: _____   Objective _____

Goal Area: _____   Objective _____

Goal Area: _____   Objective _____

Spanish Monolingual Cluster

Goal Area: _____   Objective _____

Goal Area: _____   Objective _____

Goal Area: _____   Objective _____

Using Themes and Goals and Objectives to Design Learning Activities

So far in this chapter we have illustrated how collected child observations are used to derive activity themes and the goals and objectives that embody the purpose of learning activities. Now it is time to combine a theme with the goals and objectives for a particular cluster of children in order to design a series of learning activities specifically suited to those children. The connections between themes, goals and objectives, and learning activities can be seen in this chart.

You will notice that the learning activity is *not* the same as the goal and objective. Sometimes people confuse activities with objectives. In ALERTA an activity is designed or selected on the basis of themes and goals and objectives,

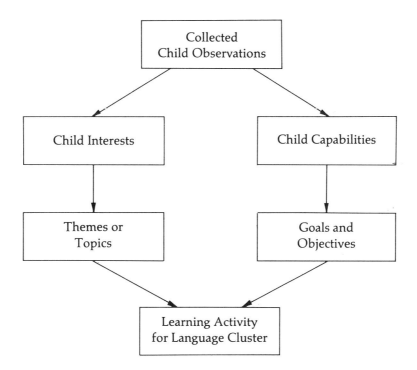

but it is not the *same* as those elements. Following are examples of activities that were planned for use over one week with the English monolingual speakers and the Spanish-dominant bilingual speakers. The same sort of planning, of course, would be done for the other two clusters as well.

In the examples you will notice that the theme, identification of the language cluster, and names of the children are all noted. For each day, the goals and objectives being used are recorded in shorthand notation (by goal area and objective number), and a learning activity is briefly described that as often as possible uses materials from the children's cultures and environment as a setting for carrying out the activity's purpose.

Look closely at the examples given. Now select one of the language clusters for which you just identified goals and objectives, and design or select a week's worth of adult-directed activities for the children in that cluster. Try to use materials that come from the children's culture and environment as frequently as you can in your planning. Remember, the activities you design should be relatively short (ten to fifteen minutes in length). They can be done in any area of the classroom or outside on a community walk. They should involve the children's direct and active participation, and they should take into account the children's level of development. The activities may draw upon special talents of parents or other community resources.

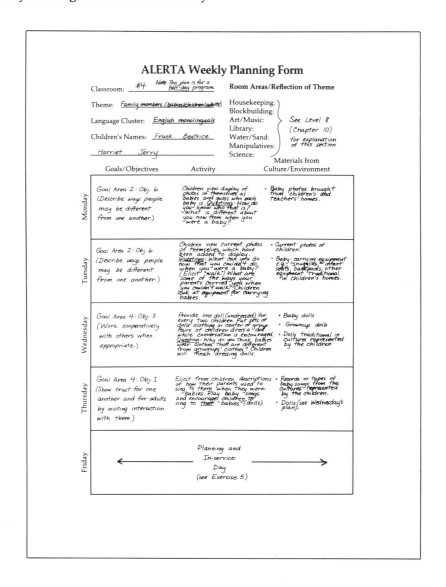

ALERTA Weekly Planning Form

Classroom: #4   *Note: This plan is for a half-day program.*

Room Areas/Reflection of Theme

Theme: *Family members (babies/children/adults)*

Language Cluster: *English monolinguals*

Children's Names: *Frank   Beatrice*

Harriet   Jerry

Housekeeping:
Blockbuilding:
Art/Music:
Library:
Water/Sand:
Manipulatives:
Science:

See Level 8 (Chapter 10) for explanation of this section

	Goals/Objectives	Activity	Materials from Culture/Environment
Monday	Goal Area 2: Obj. 6 (Describe ways people may be different from one another.)	Children view display of photos of themselves as babies and guess who each baby is. Questions: How do you know who that is? What is different about you now from when you were a baby?	• Baby photos brought from children's and teachers' homes.
Tuesday	Goal Area 2: Obj. 6 (Describe ways people may be different from one another.)	Children view current photos of themselves, which have been added to display. Questions: What can you do now that you couldn't do when you were a baby? (Elicit "walk.") What are some of the ways your parents carried you when you couldn't walk? Children look at equipment for carrying babies.	• Current photos of children. • Baby-carrying equipment e.g., "snuglies," infant seats, backpacks, other equipment traditional in children's homes.
Wednesday	Goal Area 4: Obj. 3 (Work cooperatively with others when appropriate.)	Provide one doll (undressed) for every two children. Put sets of dolls' clothing in center of group. Pairs of children dress a "doll" while conversation is encouraged. Question: Why do you think babies wear clothes that are different from grownups' clothes? Children will finish dressing dolls.	• Baby dolls • Grownup dolls • Dolls traditional in cultures represented by the children
Thursday	Goal Area 4: Obj. 1 (Show trust for one another and for adults by inviting interaction with them.)	Elicit from children descriptions of how their parents used to sing to them when they were babies. Play baby "songs" and encourage children to sing to their "babies" (dolls).	• Records or tapes of baby songs from the cultures represented by the children. • Dolls (see Wednesday's plan).
Friday		Planning and In-service Day (see Exercise 5) ⟵———⟶	

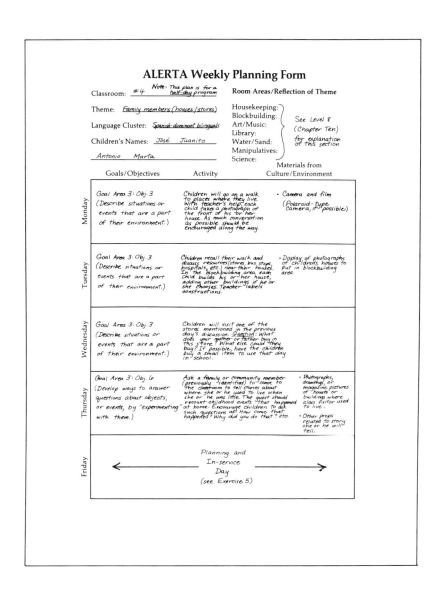

ALERTA Weekly Planning Form

Classroom: #4 *Note: This plan is for a half-day program*

Theme: *Family members (houses/stores)*

Language Cluster: *Spanish-dominant bilinguals*

Children's Names: *José Juanito*

Antonio Marta

Room Areas/Reflection of Theme

Housekeeping:
Blockbuilding:
Art/Music:
Library:
Water/Sand:
Manipulatives:
Science:

See Level 8 (Chapter Ten) for explanation of this section

	Goals/Objectives	Activity	Materials from Culture/Environment
Monday	Goal Area 3: Obj. 3 (Describe situations or events that are a part of their environment.)	Children will go on a walk to places where they live. With teacher's help, each child takes a photograph of the front of his or her house. As much conversation as possible should be encouraged along the way.	• Camera and film (Polaroid-type camera, if possible)
Tuesday	Goal Area 3: Obj. 3 (Describe situations or events that are a part of their environment.)	Children recall their walk and discuss resources (stores, bus stops, hospitals, etc.) near their houses. In the blockbuilding area, each child builds his or her house, adding other buildings if he or she chooses. Teacher labels constructions.	• Display of photographs of children's houses to put in blockbuilding area.
Wednesday	Goal Area 3: Obj. 3 (Describe situations or events that are a part of their environment.)	Children will visit one of the stores mentioned in the previous day's discussion. Question: What does your mother or father buy in this store? What else could they buy? If possible, have the children buy a small item to use that day in school.	
Thursday	Goal Area 3: Obj. 6 (Develop ways to answer questions about objects, or events, by "experimenting" with them.)	Ask a family or community member (previously identified) to come to the classroom to tell stories about where she or he used to live when she or he was little. The guest should recount childhood events "that happened" at home. Encourage children to ask such questions as: How come that happened? Why did you do that? etc.	• Photographs, drawings, or magazine pictures of houses or buildings where class visitor used to live. • Other props related to story she or he will tell.
Friday	⟵ Planning and In-service Day (see Exercise 5) ⟶		

ALERTA Weekly Planning Form

Classroom: _____

Theme: _____

Language Cluster: _____

Children's Names: _____

_____

Room Areas/Reflection of Theme

Housekeeping:
Blockbuilding:
Art/Music:
Library:
Water/Sand·
Manipulatives:
Science:

	Goals/Objectives	Activity	Materials from Culture/Environment
Monday			
Tuesday			
Wednesday			
Thursday			
Friday			

Now take a careful look at the week's worth of activities you have designed or selected for one of your clusters. You need to assess whether *each* of your activities is appropriate for the children for whom it was intended. Although such assessment is especially important when you have chosen to use commercially produced materials that may have been designed for another purpose, it is also a good idea to take a fresh look at activities of your own creation to see if they meet the criteria you had in mind. To conclude this exercise, use the following guide to double-check each of the learning activities you have planned.

Is This Learning Activity Appropriate?

1. Does this activity build on interests of children in the cluster? Yes ☐   No ☐

2. Is this activity appropriate for the developmental levels of the children in this cluster? Yes ☐   No ☐

3. Will this activity help the children in my group meet a specific objective (chosen ahead of time) of the ALERTA Program? Yes ☐   No ☐

4. Does the activity allow the children to be actively and directly involved in their learning? Will the children be able to manipulate materials or otherwise use their bodies during the course of the activity? Yes ☐   No ☐

5. Will this activity make use of material coming from the children's environment and/or cultures (if that is appropriate to the objective chosen)? Yes ☐   No ☐

6. Does this activity make use of learning materials that we already have in the classroom or center or that we could make? Yes ☐   No ☐

7. Will this activity work with the group or cluster size I am planning it for? Yes ☐ No ☐

EXERCISE 5

Weekly and Daily Planning Procedures

Time for planning is fundamental to your success in using ALERTA. As a responsible teacher you need time to reflect upon your observations of the children in your classroom and select or create learning activities that complement and extend the children's knowledge, skills, and attitudes.

ALERTA recommends that persons using the program have a prearranged period each week when they can sit down together to discuss the children's progress, exchange ideas, design activities, make needed learning materials, or receive specialized in-service training to deepen their knowledge of the children's cultures.

Many public school districts and the national Head Start office have encouraged their early childhood programs to consider scheduling to allow blocks of time for team planning and preparation. Some programs, for example, have the children come four days a week. The fifth day (usually a Monday or Friday) is used to keep records, plan activities, make materials, or receive in-service training. Other programs use Wednesday afternoons for these activities so that the children are at the center or school four and one-half rather than five days a week. If staff members at your center or school are contemplating such a change, it is very important that the proposed change be discussed with your school board or funding agency and the parents and that all parties be in agreement with the change before it is implemented.

In addition, it is very helpful if teachers have at least an hour each day to discuss the work of individual children in that day's activities and put the finishing touches on the activities planned for the next day. In schools or centers when the children go home between 2:00 and 3:00, this time for planning is easily fitted into the last hour of the workday, after the children have left. When an early childhood center or a school has double sessions, (one three-hour session in the morning and another in the afternoon), it may not be possible to plan until later in the day. The planning session should not be omitted, however. It might be possible to have another adult cover the class for the last hour of the program so that the classroom staff (and participating parents) can meet for planning.

As a final consideration of Level 6, assess the amount of time that you and your partners have available for planning. If you do have a block of time available each week, discuss with your supervisors and/or administrators ways that block can be used to support your work in ALERTA. If no such block of time is available to you, discuss with your supervisors and/or administrators ways that it might be arranged. Follow the same procedure for establishing your daily planning period.

In Level 7 you will be introduced to the strategies for continuing development of your children's first language and promoting their acquisition of a second language. These strategies will become an important part of your planning and refining of each day's learning activities.

CHAPTER NINE

Level 7: Integrating Strategies for Language Learning throughout the Program

The child-centered planning process described in Level 6 will give you consistent contact with each of your four clusters of children and will provide a variety of settings in which you can continue to observe their growth and development. Early in the year you clustered the children according to their degree of proficiency in the use of English and in the use of a second language. Part of your observation of the children's work from that time on included notes on the children's continued growth in English and in Spanish (or in the other language spoken). In Level 7 you will have the opportunity to use the information you have been collecting on the children's language use in order to refine both your design of learning activities and your observation of their effects on children in each of the four language clusters.

You remember that earlier in this source book we said that language is never taught separately in ALERTA. ALERTA teachers understand that language is very closely tied to the children's development in all domains (the socioemotional, cognitive, and psychomotor areas) and that language must represent observed or direct experience in order to be meaningful to young children. For that reason, ALERTA teachers weave strategies for language learning throughout the program—in the activities planned for each of the four clusters of children, in activities done with the whole group, and in their informal interactions with children during child-initiated portions of the day.

When ALERTA teachers are using only the child-centered and multicultural components of the program, all their attention to language development is focused on the children's continued growth in the use of English. When the teachers are using ALERTA's bilingual component, however, they must carefully plan for both the children's continued growth in their home language and their acquisition of a second language. ALERTA developers strongly believe that in bilingual circumstances, not only should speakers of other languages learn English but English speakers should also learn the other language being spoken in their classroom and community. In this way the gift of bilingualism is shared and can be used to further promote the goals of self-acceptance and acceptance of others that are a vital part of the program.

In bilingual ALERTA programs, then, two additional goal areas are addressed on a daily basis: continued development in the children's first language and the children's steady acquisition of a second language.[1] The latter goal requires that children not only learn the language in their classroom but also have many opportunities to use the second language in their everyday life outside the classroom.

In general, Spanish-speaking and English-speaking children come to the classroom in

---

[1] The examples that follow will use English and Spanish as examples of the two languages taught. You should substitute for Spanish whatever second language your program is using as you read the explanations in this chapter.

the United States with two different types of language experiences. Many Hispanic families use Spanish in their homes, but as soon as they leave their homes or their immediate community they hear English all around them. They also hear English on the radio and T.V. every day. The English speakers, on the other hand, speak English in their homes; they hear it on the radio and T.V. and anywhere they go in their community. If they hear any Spanish at all, it is only for brief periods of time in special circumstances, as when they shop in Hispanic stores or are invited to the homes of Spanish-speaking friends. The difference in amount of exposure of the children to the two languages outside of school has consequences for what any program in preschool can be expected to accomplish.

Difference in language experience can also come about as a result of the internal environment of the early childhood center or school. In some programs there are substantially more Spanish-speaking children in a single classroom than there are English speakers; as a result, the English speakers may in fact be immersed in Spanish during child-initiated portions of the day. In other classrooms just the reverse is true, with the Spanish speakers immersed in English in most free-play situations. Whether the bilingual member of the teaching team is Spanish-dominant or English-dominant may also make a difference in the amount of Spanish or English that children from both groups hear spoken in the classroom.

Another factor that can produce different results is the length of time the children are in the program. Many of the children in the center for which this curriculum was originally developed are in the program for two years. They come into the program at age three and leave as they are turning five. Some children, however, are in the program for only one year. Clearly, not as much can be accomplished in one year as can be accomplished in two.

In spite of the variations that exist in the circumstances noted above, it is important that each teacher or teaching team understand that *at least* an equal level of effort must be present in the teaching of both Spanish as a second language to English speakers and English as a second language to Spanish speakers. Equal time must be set aside for concentration on each of the two languages for both groups of children. Planning for the presentation of Spanish to English speakers must be as carefully done as that for the presentation of English to Spanish speakers. During child-initiated portions of the day the bilingual members of the teaching teams must use Spanish whenever possible with English speakers to strengthen and encourage the learning of Spanish vocabulary and language structures that has already been achieved during the adult-directed activities. In the same manner the English-speaking members of the team should use English to build upon the learnings in that language achieved by the Spanish speakers.

In ideal circumstances (in which there is sufficient opportunity for practice outside of the classroom and in which there has been consistency in adult-directed language portions of the day), it is the expectation of the ALERTA plan for language learning that:

1. The Spanish-speaking children who are in the program for two years will leave the program understanding and speaking English at or close to the same level as they understand and speak Spanish.

2. The English-speaking children who are in the program for two years will leave the program understanding and speaking Spanish at or close to the same level as they understand and speak English. *Note: When the only Spanish heard by the English monolingual speakers is that used in the classroom, it is reasonable to amend this second expectation in the following way:* The English-speaking children who are in the program for two years will

leave the program understanding Spanish (i.e., a basic vocabulary and basic structure). They may or may not speak Spanish, depending on the degree of their exposure to the language outside of the classroom.

3. Children who are in the program for less than two years will follow the same pattern as above, but at a lower level of proficiency.

4. Both groups of children will display an attitude of acceptance toward speaking a second language and toward people who speak a language other than their own.

This chapter looks at ways of organizing your daily schedule so you will be able to include on a regular basis both activities that extend the children's first language and activities that introduce and develop the children's second language. These activities are for the most part teacher-directed (although some examples will be given of instances in which you can build upon the children's language learning during child-initiated portions of the day). They are also generally short (ten to fifteen minutes each) and can be done in any setting (inside the classroom, in a gym, outside on a community walk, etc.). They are the *same* activities done with clusters of children that were presented in Level 6. The only difference is that now in your planning you will also be taking into account the strategies for language teaching and learning (that is, the *ways* you as a teacher will conduct any given activity in order to extend the children's first language or develop their second language).

Other exercises in this chapter will give you a chance to look closely at what each strategy entails. You will not be conducting an activity in the children's first language in the same way you will be conducting an activity in the children's second language. How you conduct the activity will depend on the degree to which the children have acquired the second language. More is said about these differences in the exercises that follow. Finally, this chapter illustrates how language strategies are incorporated into your daily planning procedures so that records are kept of the language approaches used with each of your four clusters.

EXERCISE 1

Preparing a Daily Schedule for an ALERTA Classroom

In preparing a daily schedule for an ALERTA preschool program, you should keep in mind two considerations: (1) the standards for scheduling set by your licensing agency or public school board and (2) the need in an ALERTA program for blocks of time devoted specifically to learning activities that incorporate strategies for development of the children's first language and acquisition of their second language.

Most early childhood programs (and

certainly the Head Start Program Performance Standards) stress the need for balance in the schedule of activities offered the children—balance among whole-group, cluster-, and individually-oriented activities; between active and quiet periods; and among the type of materials and activities made available. Children in a half-day program are expected to be in school for a minimum of three hours each day. Children in a full-day program are usually expected to be in school for a minimum of six and one-half hours each day. In either case balance must be shown in the allotted time.

In a multicultural classroom you must also provide balance in the use of material drawn from the cultures represented at the center so that one or more groups of children are not neglected. It is important that all the children find content with which they can identify in the activities; no child should be made to feel left out or unimportant. You need to plan carefully and keep track of which cultures you are using for source materials and when you are using them.

As has already been noted, a bilingual ALERTA program requires that there be blocks of time for adult-directed activities that incorporate first language development and second language acquisition. This portion of the day must occur without schedule changes in order to insure that all the children participate in both types of adult-directed language learning at least every other day. Some observations of language learning indicate that children are likely to concentrate on language use most readily in the morning, when they are alert and fresh. We recommend, therefore, that in full-day programs the cluster activities making use of specific strategies for promotion of first language development be held in the morning.

With these considerations in mind, a daily schedule for a full-day (six and one-half hours) preschool program might look something like this:

8:30–9:00 A.M. Teaching team prepares the classroom.

9:00–9:20 A.M. Children arrive and are greeted individually. Large-group meeting to talk about the activities for the day. When appropriate, children may make choices of an activity they wish to do that morning. (English or Spanish is used according to the nature of the activity chosen)[2]

2 More is said about this in Chapter Ten (Level 8).

9:20–9:30 A.M. Informal snack, with conversation. Discussion could continue to center on the activities of the day or could focus on interests of one child. (English or Spanish is used according to the language used by the child in his or her remarks).

9:30–10:00 A.M. Combination session: adult-directed activities/free-choice period.

9:30–9:45 Spanish-speaking or bilingual teacher works with cluster of five or six Spanish monolingual children in Spanish (development of children's first language) while English-speaking teacher circulates among the rest of the children working in different areas of the room.

9:45–10:00 Spanish-speaking or bilingual teacher works with cluster of five or six Spanish-dominant bilingual children in Spanish (development of children's first language) while English-speaking teacher circulates among the rest of the children working in different areas of the room.

10:00–10:30 A.M. Combination session: adult-directed activities/free-choice period.

10:00–10:15 English-speaking teacher works with cluster of five or six English monolingual children in English (development of children's first language) while Spanish-speaking or bilingual teacher circulates among the rest of the children working in different areas of the room.

10:15–10:30 English-speaking teacher works with cluster of five or six English-dominant bilingual children in English (development of the children's first language) while Spanish-speaking or bilingual teacher circulates among the rest of the children working in different areas of the room.

10:30–10:45 A.M. Clean up and put classroom in order, with children's help.

10:45–11:00 A.M. Preparation for going outdoors or to gym.[3]

11:00–12:00 noon Outdoor activities or (on rainy days) indoor active games or gym.

12:00–12:15 P.M. Return to classroom and wash up for lunch.

12:15–12:45 P.M. Lunch (served family style).

12:45–1:00 P.M. Bathroom, handwashing, toothbrushing, and preparation for rest.

1:00–2:00 P.M. Rest time and break period for teaching team.

2:00–2:10 P.M. Wake up, clear room of cots or mats, with children's help.

2:10–2:30 P.M. Combination session: adult-directed activities/free-choice period.

2:10–2:20 English - speaking teacher works with cluster of five or six Spanish monolingual children in English (second language acquisition) while Spanish-speaking or bilingual teacher circulates among the rest of the children working in different areas of the room.

2:20–2:30 English - speaking teacher works with cluster of five or six Spanish-dominant bilingual children in English (second language acquisition) while Spanish-speaking or bilingual teacher circulates among the rest of the children working in different areas of the room.

2:30–2:50 P.M. Combination sessions: adult-directed activities/free-choice period.

2:30–2:40 Spanish-speaking or bilingual teacher works with cluster of five or six English monolingual children in Spanish (second language acquisition) while English-speaking teacher circulates among the rest of the children working in different areas of the room.

2:40–2:50 Spanish-speaking or bilingual teacher works with cluster of five or six English-dominant bilingual children in Spanish (second language acquisition) while English-speaking teacher circulates among the rest of the children working in different areas of the room.

2:50–3:00 P.M. Clean up and put classroom in order, with children's help.

3:00–3:15 P.M. Large-group meeting or circle time to review the day's activities.

3:15–3:30 P.M. Snack and preparation for departure.

3:30–4:30 P.M. Classroom teaching teams meet for evaluation of day, assessment of progress of individual children, and planning of next day's learning activities.

You will notice that this schedule assumes there will be two adults in the classroom, which is the case in many early childhood programs. The usual pattern in programs promoting bilingualism is that one member of the teaching team is bilingual, and the other member is often a monolingual English speaker. Some classrooms do have the fortunate circumstance of having two bilingual teachers. In that case, the person who is most proficient in English would take the part of the "English-speaking teacher" in the schedule, and the person who is most proficient in Spanish (or in the other language being used in the program) would take the part of the "Spanish-speaking teacher."

Some early childhood classrooms have only one adult present. In this circumstance you would need to adjust the suggested schedule so that you work with only two of the four clusters each day. You can work with the other clusters on alternate days. Of course, to successfully carry out the bilingual component of ALERTA while working alone you must be fully bilingual.

Another variation on the suggested schedule may be made for early childhood programs that meet for only three hours a day (half-day programs). Half-

---

[3] Toileting of children may be done in small groups or individually at various points throughout the day, according to a program's preference.

day programs would have only one combination session each day. The person responsible for English language development would conduct activities in English with the Spanish monolingual cluster (second language) and with the English-dominant bilingual cluster (first language) on Monday, for example. During the same day, the person responsible for Spanish language development would conduct activities in Spanish with the English monolingual cluster (second language) and with the Spanish-dominant bilingual cluster (first language). On Tuesday, the two teachers would exchange clusters so that by the end of two days all children would have received both a first and a second language experience.

An important part of using ALERTA's Level 7 is for you to evaluate the daily schedule you have been using to see that it meets ALERTA's requirement for balance among the learning opportunities offered. You should also evaluate your schedule for consistent use of blocks of time throughout the day that integrate strategies for language teaching and learning. You will want to write down your daily schedule and make any adjustments necessary to achieve ALERTA's program goals.

Daily Schedule for My Classroom

EXERCISE 2

Strategies for First Language Development and Second Language Acquisition

Language learning is a part of almost everything a young child does. When children are very young, they start to think without the use of language. As they begin to develop speech their thinking becomes increasingly linked with language. The exact connection between thought and language is unknown; it has been shown, however, that there is a relationship between a child's ability to use language and his or her later achievement in school. That is one of the reasons the ALERTA Program is concerned with language learning in young children.

The bilingual component of ALERTA is specifically designed for early childhood classes in which 50 percent or more of the children speak Spanish[4] as their first language and in which another large percentage (30 to 50 percent) speak English as their first language. ALERTA accepts the position that the early learning of a second language encourages flexibility in children's thought processes, giving bilingual children an advantage over children speaking only one language. One aspect of this advantage may be that bilingual children are better able to cope

---

[4] Or another language widely used in the community.

with new situations. Furthermore, learning a second language while young is much easier for people than learning it when they are older. What for many children is a necessary skill becomes also a pleasant, natural experience that gives them alternatives for interpreting their world.

It was already stated that language learning is part of almost everything a young child does. It is an ongoing event. During school time teachers can help children make efficient use of their time by integrating strategies for language learning into all parts of the program. In this exercise we will take a close look at the strategies for language learning that should appear in the teacher-directed activities that you plan for the four clusters of children each day. The following is a summary of the basic elements of the strategies used to promote first language development, second language acquisition in monolingual speakers, and further development of a second language in bilingual children. Each of these sets of strategies is discussed individually in the material that follows.

The ALERTA Program
Strategies for Language Teaching and Learning

For Development of the Children's First Language (English or Spanish*)

1. Plan stimulating activities.
2. Provide many opportunities for children to speak.
3. Use a conversational style.
4. Use a full range of language repertoire.
5. Introduce new concepts.
6. Use open-ended questions as much as possible.

For Acquisition of a Second Language by Monolingual Speakers

1. Work on those concepts children already know in their first language.
2. Introduce a limited amount of new vocabulary at one time.
3. Imbed new vocabulary in a natural context.
4. Use "action" activities.
5. Use objects familiar to the children.
6. Allow children to manipulate and explore the objects.
7. Provide opportunities for natural repetition. Do *not* use drill.
8. Use songs and games as frequently as possible.

*Substitute another language, when appropriate.

Further Development of a Second Language in Bilingual Children

1. Plan stimulating activities.
2. Provide many opportunities for children to speak.
3. Introduce new concepts in the dominant language.
4. Imbed new vocabulary in a natural context.
5. Use open-ended questions as much as possible.
6. Use concrete objects in the activities.
7. Allow children to manipulate and explore the objects.
8. Provide opportunities for natural repetition. Do *not* use drill.
9. Use songs and games as frequently as possible.
10. Listen *carefully* for gaps in language and for stages of language learning.

Strategies for Development of the Children's First Language (English or Spanish)[5]

There are two purposes of ALERTA's bilingual component. The first is to help children develop their first language as fully as possible at their developmental levels. For this purpose, teachers encourage the children to use the language they bring with them to school and expand it to include new ideas and concepts they encounter in school. This activity is usually known as *language development* and/or *concept development*. It is very important that a child's first language is encouraged to develop, as it is the foundation on which many other types of learning may be built. There is evidence that learning basic concepts in the dominant or first language makes learning a second language easier for children. This premise is an underlying theme in the ALERTA approach to language learning.

In planning learning activities that will present opportunities for expansion of the children's first language, there is one important principle to remember. The activity planned should have a connection (easily recognized by the children) with activities that precede it, with current interests of the children, and with something that has meaning for them from their cultural backgrounds. Activities are most effective when there is a combination of child interest and bridges to former experience.

In group situations the children must *want* to use language and expand it to include vocabulary and concepts new to them. They will not want to do so unless the activity presented is enticing enough and related enough to their present understandings of the world that they respond to it. There is no point in doing an activity on tree frogs (*coquíes*), for exam-

ple, unless some children have mentioned them, a number of children in the classroom have lived in areas where tree frogs are common, or the teacher makes a connection between tree frogs and the common variety of frogs that the children recognize. Activities done over a period of time should show links to one another, like pieces of a puzzle.

This principle of child-centered planning was discussed fully in Level 6. It is raised again here because effective use of the ALERTA strategies for first language development depends on the power of the learning activities planned to generate connections in the children's minds. That is to say, the strategies count on the fact that the children will see the links between what they are doing in the activity and other experiences that they have had at school or outside of the classroom so that they will be able to talk about what they are doing with understanding.

In order for children to *want* to talk, then, activities must be stimulating and provide many opportunities for the children to speak. It is very important that the children speak more than the teacher in any given activity. Although it may seem obvious that children should be speaking in activities intended to promote language development, it is not uncommon in some early childhood classrooms to hear teachers' voices dominate an activity.[6] It is also critical to use a natural, conversational style. You are acting as a language model for children. If you use stilted, unnatural constructions, the children may imitate you and develop unnatural language patterns.

You should also use the full range

---

[5] If appropriate, substitute another language for Spanish.

[6] Recent research on teaching has shown that some early childhood teachers tend to use 80 to 90 percent of available time in speaking during an activity, leaving only 10 to 20 percent of available time for the children to speak. A better ratio might be 30 to 40 percent teacher speaking and 60 to 70 percent children speaking.

of your language repertoire (such as questions, complex sentences, exclamations, and so on). Linguists tell us that three-year-old children already have the underlying language structures necessary to understand adult speech, even though they themselves may not yet be speaking in such complex ways. Do not simplify the way you speak into any sort of "babytalk." That would only be a disservice to the children. If the children do not understand a word you have used, you should explain what the word means, which can be done as a continuation of your natural conversation.

All concepts new to the children should be taught to them in their first language. Part of your work in observing children's reactions to activities you have planned is to note which concepts (for example, those found under Goal Area 3 in the list of ALERTA's goals and objectives) the children have or have not yet acquired. As you discover what the children do not yet know, you will be able to design more activities that use the children's interests specifically to teach those concepts. Such activities should always be conducted in the children's first language so that the children do not have to learn both the concept and the expression of that concept in another language at the same time. Learning will be more efficient and long lasting if the concept is

---

Questions to Consider in Reviewing Audiotapes of Activities Incorporating Strategies for Promotion of the Children's First or Dominant Language

1. Were the children very interested in the activity? Did the activity stimulate a lot of spontaneous language? What were some of the comments that revealed the children's interest?

_____

_____

2. How frequently did you initiate a comment or explanation? (Tally the number of times you spoke during the activity. Time the length of your comments to see how long your speaking took.)

_____

How frequently did individual children comment, ask a question, or otherwise speak during the activity? (Tally the number of times the individual children spoke, and time the length of their speaking.)

_____

_____

3. Were you using a conversational style throughout the activity? What is an example of that style?

_____

4. Did you use variety in the language structures you employed? What are some examples?

_____

_____

5. Did your activity introduce the children to any new concepts? If so, what were those concepts?

_____

6. What are some examples of open-ended questions that you wove through the activity?

_____

_____

first acquired in the language of the children's home.

Finally you should try as much as possible to use open-ended questions in activities you conduct in the children's first language. Open-ended questions are those for which there is more than one answer and that require several phrases or sentences to answer. Examples of open-ended questions are: How can we build a garage here in the classroom? How can we prevent the blocks we use for our building from toppling over? What do you think is the reason people started building garages in the block corner?

Although reminders such as those discussed may be helpful to teachers wishing to promote children's first language development, nothing will refine your own work in that area more than conscious practice of the strategies. A good technique for practice is to audiotape yourself as you are conducting a learning activity that incorporates the strategies discussed. Position the tape recorder so that it can pick up both your voice and the voices of the children in your cluster, but so that it will not be noticed by the children. At the conclusion of the day play back the tape and listen carefully for the distinguishing characteristics of the strategy. Answer the questions on the worksheet regarding your success in using each of the techniques. This is an exercise that you should do many times. If you have a partner, the two of you may eventually want to assist one another by listening to each other's tapes and offering suggestions for improvement of technique or for individualizing your approach to the needs of particular children.

Strategies to Promote Second Language Acquisition in Monolingual Speakers

Encouraging young children to learn a language with which they are unfamiliar requires a very different set of teaching strategies from those previously presented. If children have been observed to speak and understand only their home language (that is, if they are monolingual), then you must build the children's knowledge of the second language from scratch. You must assume that the children will understand *nothing* in the second language, even the simplest request or direction. In order to convey meaning to the children as you are speaking, you will need to use as much body language as possible (gestures, facial expressions, and so on) and constantly act out what is required of children in a given activity.

As with any planned activity it is important that those making use of strategies for second language acquisition capture the children's interest. If the activity is appealing and enjoyable, the children will want to do it in spite of the fact that they do not yet understand what you are saying to them. The second thing to keep in mind as you are planning such an activity is that you should build it around concepts the children have already learned in their first language. For example, if the children have had a great deal of practice in using the concepts of *skip* and *hop* in their first language, it would be appropriate to introduce those concepts in the second language. Please note, though, that you should *not* use the same activity or materials you used previously to teach the concept in the first language. If you used a community walk through the park to review those concepts in the first language, you might use something like a variation of the "Duck, Duck, Goose" game to teach the vocabulary for *skip* and *hop* in the second language.

It is also very important that you introduce a limited amount of new vocabulary (perhaps only two or three words that will be stressed in the activity) at one time. This does not mean that you will be using only those words but that you will repeat those words often in the context of what you and the children are doing in the activity. For example, if you and the children are making cookies and you have decided to introduce the vocabulary words *spoon* and *stir* in that activity, you might be saying something like this while the children are mixing the dough:

"Has everyone got a spoon*? (Show spoon as you speak.) We are going to* stir *this batter now. (Show the children what you mean.) Mario, do you need a* spoon*? Jorge, would you please hand Mario that* spoon*? (Show the action that you intend.) Alicia, you* stir *so well!)*

During the first month or so of the school year, the children may not understand much of the rest of what you are saying, but they will hear the words being used in a natural context and will soon pick up whole phrases. You will want to encourage the children to say their new words as much as possible in the activity. Using words will not be difficult for the children if at first you teach vocabulary

---

Questions to Consider in Reviewing Audiotapes of Activities Incorporating Strategies for Promotion of a Second Language in Monolingual Children

1. Did you build on a concept the children already learned in their first language? Did you use a different activity from one you had used to teach the concept in the children's first language?

_____

2. Did you introduce a limited amount of vocabulary at one time? How many words did you introduce in this activity?

_____

3. Did you imbed the new vocabulary words in a natural context? What context?

_____

_____

4. Did you use an activity with a lot of action? What actions did the children do?

_____

5. Did you use objects familiar to the children in the activity? What objects were they?

_____

6. Did you allow the children to manipulate and explore the objects? How did the children do this?

_____

_____

7. How did you provide opportunities for natural repetition of the vocabulary to be learned?

_____

_____

8. Was it appropriate to use a song or game in this activity? If so, what song or game did you use?

_____

that names objects the children can manipulate (nouns, such as *spoon*) or describes actions the children can easily imitate (verbs, such as *stir*). Language becomes alive and meaningful for children when they associate it with familiar objects and events in their lives.

Providing such opportunities for natural repetition of vocabulary during the course of a learning activity is not the same as doing a language drill. In drills, children may repeat words again and again without associating those words with an event they have actually experienced. In the ALERTA approach, such drill is not helpful to children's acquisition of meaning. Natural repetition is easily promoted by the use of songs and games that feature the vocabulary being taught. If traditional games using particular words do not exist, teachers and parents can always adapt verses or make up games centering on the children's experiences that incorporate the vocabulary to be learned.

After reviewing the strategies for the promotion of a second language in young children, you should be ready to practice the teaching skills they require. Once again, audiotape yourself as you conduct an activity that incorporates the second language strategies for one of your clusters. Listen to your tape alone or with a partner to see which of the questions on page 000 you are able to answer affirmatively.

Strategies for Further Development of a Second Language in Bilingual Children

Unlike monolingual children, bilingual children come to the learning situation with an ability to speak or at least understand a second language. The degree to which the second language has been acquired will vary from child to child, and your observations will be very important in the process of deciding whether particular children should be placed in an English-dominant bilingual cluster or a Spanish-dominant bilingual cluster for adult-directed activities. In either case, the children's second language may be quite well developed. They may be able to understand ordinary conversations very well in the second language and demonstrate an ability to carry on (to a certain extent) such conversations themselves.

Here you have quite a different set of circumstances than you have with monolingual speakers who are being introduced to a second language for the first time, and your way of using the second language in learning activities must also be different from what we previously described. In certain respects, the strategies for promoting a second language in bilingual speakers are the same as those used to foster first language development. Once again you need to plan attractive activities that connect with the children's experience, make use of natural conversational style, provide ample opportunities for the children to speak, and incorporate open-ended questions. Certain elements from the second language teaching strategies should also be employed. You should draw upon concepts previously learned in the first language (using different materials or activities from those used originally to teach the concept), pay attention to the amount of new vocabulary being introduced at any one time, and, as much as possible, tie the new vocabulary to familiar objects and events.

Additionally, you need to be very sensitive to possible gaps in the children's knowledge of their second language, observing where they may be code switching because they do not know the word or phrase required in the second language. When you hear such a gap, do not tell a child that he or she is wrong. Instead, model the word or phrase that the child did not know. The following exchange is an example of vocabulary modeling.

Child: *"Yo vi un 'movie' bueno en la T.V."* (*"I saw a good movie on T.V."*)

Teacher: *"¿Y de que era esa película?"* (*"And what was that movie about?"*)

You notice that in responding the teacher substituted a Spanish word for *movie* so that the child could learn it without feeling corrected. This modeling procedure maintains a positive attitude while extending the children's facility with their second language.

It should be noted that not only in this category of language teaching (that is, in extending the second language of bilingual children) but also in all language used throughout the total program, developers of ALERTA recommend that the teaching adults try to avoid code switching. It is perfectly normal and natural for bilingual adults living in a society in which both languages are spoken to start a sentence in one language and finish it in another or insert words from one language here and there into the other

---

Questions to Consider in Reviewing Audiotapes of Activities Incorporating Strategies for Promotion of a Second Language in Bilingual Children

1. Were the children very interested in the activity? Did the activity stimulate a lot of spontaneous language? What were some of the comments that revealed the children's interest?

_____

_____

_____

2. How frequently did you initiate a comment or explanation? (Tally the number of times you spoke during the activity. Time the length of your comments to see how long your speaking took.)

_____

_____

How frequently did individual children comment, ask a question, or otherwise speak during the activity? (Tally the number of times the individual children spoke, and time the length of their speaking.)

_____

_____

3. Were you using a conversational style throughout the activity? What is an example of that style?

_____

_____

_____

4. Did you use variety in the language structures you employed? What are some examples?

_____

_____

_____

---

5. What are some examples of open-ended questions that you wove through the activity?

_____

_____

6. Did you build on a concept the children already had learned in their first language? Did you use a different activity from one you had used to teach the concept in the children's first language?

_____

_____

_____

7. Did you use an activity with a lot of action? What actions did the children do?

_____

_____

8. Did you use objects familiar to the children in the activity? What objects were they?

_____

_____

9. Did you allow the children to manipulate and explore the objects? How did the children do this?

_____

_____

10. How did you provide opportunities for natural repetition of the vocabulary to be learned?

_____

_____

11. What gaps were evident in the children's use of their second language? How did you help the children learn the appropriate word or phrase they lacked?

_____

_____

_____

language. This does not cause a problem for us as adults because we know which language is which. Young children, however, may not yet be fully distinguishing between the two languages and need to hear each language spoken without such mixing so they can continue to develop a sense that one way of speaking is "English" and another way of speaking is "Spanish."

As with the other strategies described in this chapter, audiotapes will allow you to hear your own patterns of modeling new vocabulary and language structures for the children. Tape record activities that you conduct in the second language of bilingual children, and listen to hear if in fact you incorporated many of the strategies presented. Use the questions on these pages to make notes.

Daily Planning to Refine Use of Language Strategies in Learning Activities for Each Cluster of Children

In Level 6 you were introduced to a procedure for the *weekly* planning of teacher-directed activities for each of your four clusters. At that time you designed or selected a series of learning activities and assessed the appropriateness of their use with the children for whom they were intended. With the knowledge and skills you have gained through the exercise just completed, you will now be able to refine your weekly activity plans with attention to the language strategies you use each day. The following chart shows an example of a typical day that has been expanded from weekly plans for each language cluster.[7] You will notice that there is space for notes on the language strategies to be used. There are also opportunities to make day-to-day adjustments of themes, goals and objectives, and activities as you see from your work of the previous day that such adjustments are necessary.

After looking closely at the example, take the set of activity plans you intend to use in the coming week in the clusters and expand your plans for one day using the blank form provided in the appendix. Every person who actually teaches in the clusters should take part in this planning process so that all staff and volunteering parents will be thoroughly familiar with

the language approach to be used in the activities for which they are responsible.

As you follow this planning procedure from day to day and from week to week you will begin to see that your activity plans will provide a kind of road map that will allow you to sharpen your focus in connecting the children's learning experiences to one another. Your weekly plans for each language cluster should show a sequence of activities connected to the developing interests and expanding skills of the children in each group. Whereas the weekly plans show you graphically the connections of the activities *within* each cluster, the daily plans should show such connections *across* the four clusters. Over time, both types of plans should show a balance in the developmental domains tapped (socio-emotional, cognitive/linguistic, and psychomotor), in the goal areas drawn upon, and in the cultural and community content incorporated. The culture of one group should not be emphasized at the expense of that of other children in the classroom. All children present should be well represented so that they too can experience the pleasure of sharing what they know of their traditions and present lives.

Extending the Use of the Language Strategies throughout the Program

The greater part of this chapter has concentrated on presenting the various language strategies used during the teacher-directed clusters conducted for a short

---

[7] Remember, these examples were done on the basis of collected child observations, which the ALERTA Program recommends for all planning.

ALERTA Daily Individualized Planning Form

Classroom: __#4__   Note: This plan is for a half-day program.   Date: __February 7 (Monday)__

Language Cluster	Spanish Monolingual	English Monolingual	Spanish-dominant Bilingual	English-dominant Bilingual
		MEMBERS — FAMILY		
Theme	Family composition / activities	Babies / children / adults	Houses / stores	Family travel
Goals/ Objectives	Goal Area 4: Obj. 2 (Work cooperatively with others when appropriate.)	Goal Area 2: Obj. 6 (Describe ways people may be different from one another.)	Goal Area 3: Obj. 3 (Describe situations or events that are a part of their environment.)	Goal Area 2: Obj. 1 (Describe some of their favorite family customs.)
Activity	Prepare raw vegetable salad, using vegetables like those grown in Roberto's uncle's garden	View and discuss baby photos.	Photograph fronts of children's houses.	Discuss family travel. Begin to construct cars and boats from large cardboard boxes.
Language Strategies	1st language	1st language	1st language (Spanish) • Many opportunities for children to speak • Conversational style • Full range of language repertoire • Open-ended questions • Introduce new concepts	1st language (English) • Many opportunities for children to speak • Conversational style • Full range of language repertoire • Open-ended questions • Introduce new concepts
	2nd language (English) • Use of known concepts • Limited amount of new vocabulary: wash, cut, lettuce, carrots • Natural context • Opportunities for repetition (NO DRILL)	2nd language (Spanish) • Limited amount of new vocabulary: la foto, el bebé, ¿Quién es? • Natural context • Use of familiar objects	2nd language	2nd language
Large-Group Activities		See Level 8 (Chapter Ten) for explanation of this section		
Notes on Resources to Be Used		of the daily activity plan.		

ALERTA Daily Individualized Planning Form

Classroom: **# 4** Note: This plan is for a half-day program. Date: **February 8 (Tuesday)**

Language Cluster	Spanish Monolingual	English Monolingual	Spanish-dominant Bilingual	English-dominant Bilingual
		FAMILY	MEMBERS	
Theme	Family composition / activities	Babies / children / adults	Houses / stores	Family travel
Goals/ Objectives	Goal Area 3 : Obj. 4 (Describe processes in which they participate.)	Goal Area 2 : Obj. 6 (Describe ways people may be different from one another.)	Goal Area 3 : Obj. 3 (Describe situations or events that are a part of their environment.)	Goal Area 4 : Obj. 2 (Work cooperatively with others when appropriate.)
Activity	Prepare and cook carrots. Discuss who does the cooking in their homes. Lead into other activities.	Compare and explore different equipment for carrying babies.	Recall walk to photograph houses, and recreate houses in blockbuilding area.	Paint cardboard vehicles.
Language Strategies	1st language (Spanish) • Many opportunities for children to speak • Full range of language repertoire • Introduce new concepts • Open-ended questions — 2nd language	1st language (English) • Many opportunities for children to speak • Full range of language repertoire • Introduce new concepts • Open-ended questions — 2nd language	1st language — 2nd language (English) • Many opportunities for children to speak • Use known concepts • New vocabulary in natural contexts • Listen for language gaps	1st language — 2nd language (Spanish) • Stimulating activity • New vocabulary in natural contexts • Concrete objects in activity • Opportunities for natural repetition (NO DRILL)
Large-Group Activities	See Level 8 (Chapter Ten) for explanation of this section of the daily activity plan.			
Notes on Resources to Be Used				

ALERTA Daily Individualized Planning Form

Classroom: _____   Date: _____

Language Cluster	Spanish Monolingual	English Monolingual	Spanish-dominant Bilingual	English-dominant Bilingual
Theme				
Goals/Objectives				
Activity				
Language Strategies — 1st language				
Language Strategies — 2nd language				
Large-Group Activities				
Notes on Resources to Be Used				

portion of each day. You should be aware, however, that because language is used throughout the day in an ALERTA classroom, these strategies actually are woven throughout the daily plan. This means that you must be conscious of how you use language when you are working with the whole class at once (as in many music and movement activities) or when you are interacting with individual children during the child-initiated portions of the day. You must also be conscious of your use of language during meal and snack times and during other routines such as transition periods. Chapter Ten (Level 8) looks at how all the parts of the ALERTA process fit together into a harmonious whole to promote children's socioemotional, cognitive, linguistic, and psychomotor growth—use of partnerships; awareness of culture and community; preparation of the classroom; and observation of children for the design of cluster activities, whole group activities, and opportunities for child-initiated work.

CHAPTER TEN

Level 8: Designing Opportunities for Learning

As you have moved through ALERTA's process, you have seen how each successive level of program use builds upon what has gone before it. It has been important to move from level to level slowly so that each piece of the puzzle could be fitted into place in your classroom. Now in Level 8 you will have the opportunity to look at the whole picture to see how each portion of the total program reflects other parts of its operation and how all teaching and learning in ALERTA mirrors the growing capacities of the children it serves.

In Level 7 we presented a chart to show the connections in your collected observations of the children, derivation of themes, choice of goals and objectives, and the design or selection of learning activities for each language cluster. The following is an extension of that chart that includes not only the planning process fundamental to the use of ALERTA (represented by the solid lines) but also the broader range of activity for which the adults in the classroom are responsible (represented by the broken lines).

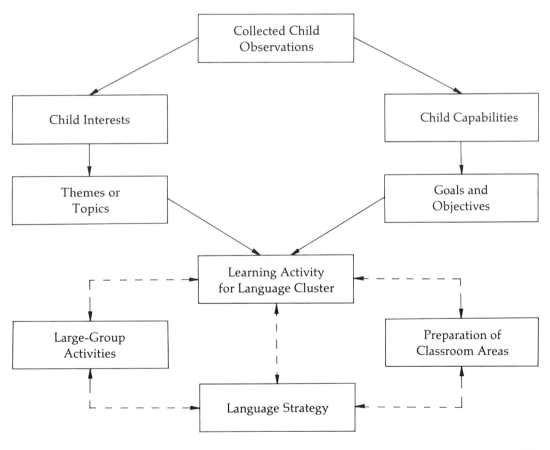

All planning that you and your partner do affects all other components of the program. For example, planning for cluster work usually involves use of specific materials, some of which will eventually be placed in various areas of the classroom. Introduction of new materials into the learning environment will invite more child-initiated activity and suggest use of particular language strategies. These strategies may affect what you introduce into large-group activities. ALERTA teachers need to pay attention to all these connections and their implications.

This chapter is divided into several parts to explain in greater detail (1) how to plan activities for large groups (the whole class), (2) how to support and promote child-initiated work to achieve the program's goals and objectives, (3) how to revitalize areas of the classroom to sustain children's interest and reflect ongoing themes, and (4) how to muster human and material resources for the continual enrichment of your program.

EXERCISE 1

Planning Activities for the Whole Class

ALERTA recommends that the largest part of each day be spent in the promotion of child-initiated work within the prepared environment and in the teachers' working with small clusters of children in activities tailored to those children's interests and emerging capabilities. Sometimes you will want to work with the whole class, perhaps to open and/or close the day or during especially active periods (dance, movement, game, song, or gym times).

For young children it is often best to limit open and closing talks or discussions (when children are expected to be quiet and attentive) to a short period, approximately ten minutes in length. Content for such periods must be very carefully chosen for its high interest to the children and for its connection to the theme incorporated into that week's activities. This is a good setting for songs and fingerplays that make use of concepts and vocabulary being learned in other contexts. Puppets, flannelboards, and short dramatizations may also be good devices for providing the group as a whole with review of vocabulary and concepts. Lengthy stories read to the

whole class are *not* recommended by ALERTA. Instead, it is suggested that stories be read in cluster activities.

When working with a class that ranges in language proficiency from monolingual English-speaking to monolingual speakers of another language (with all degrees of bilingualism in between), it is inevitable that some children will not at first understand everything you are saying during large-group time. Awareness of the strategies for working with monolingual and bilingual children in the promotion of a second language will help you remember to act out your meaning as much as possible as you conduct the activity. Try *not* to switch back and forth between languages. As much as possible, stay with one language for the duration of the large-group period. You may alternate using English and the second language in the whole-group setting every other day or every other week, as seems best for the children. Remember to give the two languages equal time over a two-week period so that one language is not suppressed in favor of another.

The following is an example of a daily activity plan originally presented in

ALERTA Daily Individualized Planning Form

Classroom: __#4__ Note: This plan is for a half-day program. Date: __February 7 (Monday)__

Language Cluster	Spanish Monolingual	English Monolingual	Spanish-dominant Bilingual	English-dominant Bilingual
Theme	Family composition/activities	Babies/children/adults	Houses/stores	Family travel
Goals/Objectives	Goal Area 4: Obj. 2 (Work cooperatively with others when appropriate.)	Goal Area 2: Obj. 6 (Describe ways people may be different from one another.)	Goal Area 3: Obj. 3 (Describe situations or events that are a part of their environment.)	Goal Area 2: Obj. 1 (Describe some of their favorite family customs.)
Activity	Prepare raw vegetable salad, using vegetables like those grown in Roberto's uncle's garden.	View and discuss baby photos.	Photograph fronts of children's houses.	Discuss family travel. Begin to construct cars and boats from large cardboard boxes.
Language Strategies	1st language 2nd language (English) • Use of known concepts • Limited amount of new vocabulary: wash, cut, lettuce, carrots • Natural context • Opportunities for repetition (NO DRILL)	1st language 2nd language (Spanish) • Limited amount of new vocabulary: la foto, el bebé, ¿Quién es? • Natural context • Use of familiar objects	1st language (Spanish) • Many opportunities for children to speak • Conversational style • Full range of language repertoire • Open-ended questions • Introduce new concepts 2nd language	1st language (English) • Many opportunities for children to speak • Conversational style • Full range of language repertoire • Open-ended questions • Introduce new concepts 2nd language
Large-Group Activities	Opening meeting: Discussion of places children went on the weekend (who they went with, how they went, what they did). Closing meeting: Childhood song typical of one of the cultures represented by the children (family theme).			
Notes on Resources to Be Used				

FAMILY   MEMBERS

Level 7. Notice how the section entitled "Large-Group Activities" has been filled out. A wide sampling of such plans would show a variety of activities to reflect whatever themes and concepts were incorporated into the cluster work for that week.

Take several of your recent daily plans and fill in the "Large-Group" space using the criteria just discussed. If you have already recorded whole-group experiences that you have done, review those plans to see if they met ALERTA's intent. If they did not meet the criteria, revise them to show how they would have. Continue to plan in this fashion on your upcoming daily activity forms.

EXERCISE 2

Supporting and Promoting Child-Initiated Work

The classroom environment discussed in Chapter Six is the "stage" on which children and adults function in an early childhood center. The suggested daily schedule in Chapter Nine shows that activities in such settings may be adult-directed, child-initiated, or a combination of both. This exercise is devoted to discussion of how you (and parents working with you) can encourage the children to reach the program's learning goals and objectives during free-play time each day.

Two important aspects of child-initiated activity are explored here—use of two languages during informal periods of the day and the learnings that can come from the children's interaction with the classroom environment. As an example of such learning we will discuss in detail the children's possible achievement of the objectives in goal area 1 (See Chapter Eight) through their work in classroom settings that embody those objectives and through informal interactions with adults and other children.

Use of the Language Strategies in Child-Initiated Work

In earlier chapters we talked about the importance of continued development of the children's first language and promotion of their second language in the adult-directed cluster work. Equally important, however, is the learning that comes from the children's natural use of language in the context of their child-initiated work in various areas of the classroom. It is here that children have the chance to experiment with language and apply what they have learned to new situations and events as they arise.

Your role as a promoter of the children's efforts in these areas requires that you be a careful observer of when individual children begin to try out new vocabulary and phrases. Whenever appro-

priate you should engage the children in conversation using that vocabulary in reference to what they are doing. We stress that this should be a *natural* exchange, however, and not a forced or artificial one.

If you are bilingual yourself, the general rule of thumb is for you to respond to children's invitation of conversation in the language they have used in addressing you. You might speak in a child's second language if you see that he or she is attempting to use the new vocabulary. If you are not bilingual, you might direct the child to the adult in the classroom who is, or ask a child who is bilingual to interpret for you. The following is a summary of the major points for you to

Major Points for You to Keep in Mind About Language Use During Free-Choice Periods and Other Child-Initiated Portions of the Day

1. The children bring to school a developed system of language use matching that which is usual in their homes and communities. Their use of language may not be the same as yours.

2. You must be open to and accepting of the variations in vocabulary or grammar that the children present.

3. A bilingual setting actively encourages the use of both English and the second language. One language is not suppressed in order to foster the other.

4. Concept development is continued in the children's first language to provide them with a growing foundation for significant communication.

5. Introduction of vocabulary in the second language should not occur until concepts relating to that vocabulary have been developed in the first language.

6. Development of both the first and the second languages should occur throughout the day in the many types of informal learning situations that occur constantly in the classroom.

7. You can act as a linguistic role model for the children by providing examples of "standard" communication (in English and/or the second language) and by presenting them with alternatives when regional variations in vocabulary are brought up.

8. When a child addresses you in a particular language (e.g., Spanish or English) during child-initiated portions of the day, you should respond in that language if you can. If you do not speak the language, you can ask a bilingual child or bilingual staff member to help with the communication.

The Structure for Language Learning
in the ALERTA Program

Point 1 Understanding and acceptance of ALERTA's definition of *bilingual education* as children from two linguistic groups learning each other's language while continuing to grow in their own first language.

Point 2 Careful observation of the children's language use to determine:

–*Which* language is being used.
–*To whom* a certain language is being addressed.
–*When* a certain language is being used.
–*Where* a certain language is being used.

Point 3 Formation of language clusters for small-group, adult-directed learning activities and use of particular strategies for language learning with the children in each of the clusters.

Spanish* Monolingual Spanish-dominant* Bilingual	1. Continued growth in Spanish as a first language. 2. Acquisition and expansion of English.	A. Goals and objectives from three domains of the child's development are selected on the basis of observations.
English-dominant Bilingual English Monolingual	1. Continued growth in English as a first language. 2. Acquisition and expansion of Spanish.	B. Culturally and/or environmentally appropriate content is chosen on the basis of observations of child interests.

Point 4 Encouragement of child-initiated activities.

1. Extension of first language through natural conversations.
2. Acquisition of second language through picking up on a child's spontaneous use of a word or phrase newly learned.

Total center reflects children's cultures and living environments.

*Substitute another language for Spanish as appropriate.

keep in mind about language use during free-choice periods. There is also a chart showing the complete structure for language learning in ALERTA and how child-initiated work fits into that structure.

Encouraging Development in Child-Initiated Work without "Taking Over"

The children's development can be encouraged not only by direct interaction with them but also by the way each area of the classroom is prepared and arranged. Classroom areas should incorporate culturally appropriate materials, and they should also present abundant opportunities for the children to achieve the program objectives on their own. In other words, possibilities for achievement of the objectives should be built into each classroom area. The following discussion illustrates how the objectives in Goal Area 1 (appreciation of self as a person capable of a wide variety of intellectual and physical activities) can be met in a well-prepared learning environment.

Growing awareness and knowledge of self cannot be separated from the child's pursuit of knowledge of the world about him or her, for the latter is the context for definition and meaning. Therefore, "What can I do?" is also connected with "What do others do?"; "Who am I?" also implies the "who" and "what" of mommy, daddy, friends, siblings, teachers, storekeepers, television characters, and all the other people—near and far—who are part of the child's world.

In attempting to define *self* along with the world of *people* and *things,* the child makes full use of the senses—hearing, touching, tasting, seeing, and smelling. Information coming in must be sorted, connected, altered, and modified. A curriculum must offer children varied opportunities in which they may raise their questions and have means by which to find answers for their questions.

In the classroom areas to be discussed we will explore some of the opportunities in activities initiated by the children for developing an understanding of self. We will also make some suggestions for parts you might play in the process without taking over the activity.

Housekeeping
In the housekeeping area there should be a continuity of experiences reflective of the home situation. The children's dramatizations within an area such as this are expressions of self and promote self-awareness.

One example of such dramatization is the use of a play telephone in the housekeeping area. Telephones allow children to engage in conversations with friends or family members. Children can discuss things that are unique about themselves such as, "I have a new puppy whose name is Silky," or "I went to see my friend Sandy, who has a brother younger than me." As a facilitator of these activities you might ask the children, upon completion of the conversation, "Can you tell me something about your friend?"

Blockbuilding
Perhaps the most immediate dilemma for three- to five-year-old builders within the blockbuilding area is that of defining a working space. Ways to help resolve this possible difficulty and promote individual self-awareness could be implicit in the arrangement of the curriculum area; that is, your organization of the area could give the children clues about what space can contain their physical bodies as well as their constructions.

Among the possibilities for the discovery and extension of the self is that of the child's realization that in a limited space "I can use my body in certain ways and not infringe upon the space of others. I can stand, kneel, squat, or sit while building. Given this space, I cannot lie on the floor and build. When there are only three people working in the area, I can use my body more freely than when there are more people."

There are many opportunities in block work for children to learn about physical laws—equilibrium, balance, gravity, and cause and effect. That block work offers these opportunities does not mean you are to use the area for these laws but rather that work in the area offers the experience of the concepts. For example, an unsteady (unbalanced) building will topple. If a child is repeatedly having such an experience, you might ask her or him, "I wonder why your building keeps falling over? Maybe you can do something to make it more steady." While you are engaged in conversation with the child and observing the child's activities, opportunities are presented for focusing the child's attention, sharpening observation skills, noting relationships, and providing labels that give form to experience.

The children may be building a garage or gas station where cars stop to get gas, but there may be no visible pumps. You might ask, "Where do the cars get gas?" If it becomes apparent that the children do not have clear information in that they are not making connections or finding the details of reality, you may take the children out on a trip where they can have the opportunity to directly observe, question, and discover.

Sand
Sand is a natural material; it is real, soothing, and malleable. Your role in this area is to provide natural materials with pleasing visual and tactile qualities. The materials are to be manipulated and controlled by the children so they can individually experience and extend their awareness. Discoveries and comparisons

about themselves can be made through the children's use of sand. They can handle the materials according to their own needs and judgments.

Wet sand is sensitive to imprint. The children can make handprints or footprints and then compare and notice differences. You can point out that no two are alike. Imaginary play can also take place at the sand area. On their own, children can practice working with each other cooperatively. Using objects to stand for other things may encourage verbal interaction. A stick can become a tree or a bridge. By working together and sharing materials children can dig holes, make hills, and even create small communities of their own.

Water
Water is another natural material that children enjoy playing with from the time they are infants. Water offers the opportunity for self-awareness through exploration and experimentation. By freely engaging in these activities, children begin to see that their actions bring results. They can launch boats, sink objects, and blow waves or bubbles. Children begin to see that as they add objects to a pan of water, the level rises. It takes longer to empty a pan of water when a small container is used and a shorter time when a larger one is used. You may interact with the children at some point by posing such questions as, "What floats?" or "What happens when you blow on the water?"

Art
With the activities in this area—painting, clay molding, drawing, and collage making—children have a variety of media and ample opportunities to express their knowledge and feelings about the world and themselves. With clay, paints, and crayons, children give form to the many elements—objects, situations, people— that make up their lives. For example, by touching and seeing a variety of leaves,

children begin to create some knowledge of form and texture. Variety, and characteristics that make an object or feeling distinctive come together, becoming connected and related as the children translate images, perceptions, and sensations into an art form. The process and the accomplishments reveal to the children what they are feeling; and in the doing, the children gain a knowledge of self that becomes tangible and that can be shared with others.

You should also encourage dialogue about the children's activities, noting any interesting use of color, the appearance of form, and the feel of various textures in the work. Such conversations should not focus on "What is this?," which gives to the children the message that they must create a product. Instead, the children (who at this age are more interested in process) are offered greater possibilities with a comment such as, "Tell me about your painting (or clay, drawing, or collage)." Or you might initiate a conversation with statements such as, "Those are interesting colors!" or "I see this time you have made some circles in your drawing."

You should be aware, too, that in addition to self-expression as a means toward self-awareness, children also experience a sense of mastery in the continued and refined use of materials. For that reason, children need ample opportunities and time for development and refinement. For example, four-year-olds are particularly interested in creating new colors and various shades of colors, which is why it is suggested that you provide primary colors (and, with time, black and white paint) so that children may create their own shades of purple, green, pink, and brown by mixing the paints in empty jars.

Table Materials
Self-awareness and self-esteem are reinforced through many table game activities in that the children have oppor-

tunities to see immediately what they are capable of doing. A child takes a puzzle apart and then puts it together, mixes a new color, creates a design with pegs on a board, and identifies and matches cards on a lotto board. In performing these activities children can see themselves as capable, masterful, and adequate to the task at hand; it is not necessary, in many instances, to seek another's confirmation. Success is self-evident, and the children actually observe their own knowledge.

Working with materials such as puzzles, pegs, rods, and many other games mentioned in the environment section provides a framework wherein the child may exercise and refine necessary classification and sorting skills and the other abilities noted earlier in a situation that is concrete and tangible. For the activities to be meaningful to the child, materials that utilize photographs and drawings should have content that is familiar to the child and that is culturally meaningful.

Music and Movement
Children move to music in a variety of ways as an expression of self. They can do many things with their bodies, such as pretending to be an object, an animal, or another person. You should provide various props that will help the children to act out roles or dramatizations spontaneously. Children may work out such feelings as anger, happiness, sadness, or uncertainty through movement. On their own, children can experience spatial awareness and awareness of how their bodies move; they will experience space in relation to their bodies. Curling up to make themselves round as a ball and then stretching to use more space are opportunities for both body and spatial awareness.

Group improvisations are also possible. The children can become involved in a story in which the characters create their own roles as you set the scene. Another possibility is for the children to develop their own original story.

If presented with the opportunity, children can take the initiative in exploring instruments, listening to nature, or singing. They can be offered the chance to express their ideas or feelings through music in a natural manner. Doing so will in turn foster self-confidence. The children can create or compose their own music and lyrics. When they do, you can provide them with the chance to record their voices. Later on each child can play the recording back and conclude that no one has a voice like hers or his.

Science

Keeping in mind that in this curriculum science is considered to be an approach that permeates the entire curriculum, how do you think the children's activity in this area might foster their awareness of self?

It may be helpful for you to illustrate what is meant by *an approach* by reviewing fairly typical activities in various curriculum areas. As mentioned in Chapter Six, considerable emphasis is placed on the scientific method—steps of observing, questioning, exploring, hypothesizing, experimenting, and validating. Essentially this means that children will be encouraged to express their curiosity by questioning the world surrounding them. They must be given opportunities to observe carefully and give form to their observations. Further, they should be encouraged to seek relationships and find connections.

In looking at the approach you might want to do the following: With your partner take turns observing and recording each other as you function in an area, during a group story time, or in a discussion. Together look over the notes so that you may have an opportunity to review your own functioning. Do you tend to make statements or ask questions? What kinds of questions do you ask? Do they lead to yes/no responses only? Do your questions lead the children to immediate, brief responses, or must they evaluate

and think about the questions by reflecting upon their own experiences?

You could also set up a simple "experiment" based on a question. For example, ask a small group of children, "How do you make scrambled eggs?" Write down each child's response. Follow up the activity by repeating the children's instructions. From our experiences with three- to five-year-olds we have had responses such as, "Put the egg in a pan," "Shake the egg," etc. In following up the above responses, you would shake the egg and ask, "Do we have scrambled eggs?" The next step would be to put the egg in a pan as directed and ask the question again. It may take some time to get all the steps and the details of the process of (1) breaking egg, (2) beating egg, (3) placing grease in pan, (4) turning on stove, (5) placing pan on stove, (6) melting grease, (7) pouring beaten egg in pan. The child here will have to attend to detail, connections, relationships, and cause and effect. Of course, the scientific approach in this instance also may lead to a tasty lunch prepared by the children.

As for the content of science, the sample activities suggest several activities with cooking and planting. The sand and water areas are rich in science learnings. The reconstituting of clay and cleaning up after using it is still another example of science learning.

Clay is a natural product. Exposed to air it will begin to lose its water content and dry. As children use clay on a tabletop the clay begins leaving traces on the table; as the traces dry, they adhere to the table. Scraped with a tongue depressor, the traces create a fine powder. The process of evaporation causes a profound change in the appearance of clay, from the soft, moist, malleable ball of clay to the powdery clay on the table.

Reconstituting the dry clay will help children increase their understanding. Dried clay objects may be placed in a plastic tub or bucket and covered with water. As some of the water evaporates and the hardened clay mixes with the water, something like a clay mush will be created. As more water evaporates, the clay will come closer to its original usable state. It can be made into ball shapes and left on a tray to continue to air dry. Prior to use as an art material the clay must be worked through by hand in order to remove any trapped air bubbles.

Children note these changes, but they may not give form or expression to their observations. You might ask the children to describe the changed state of the clay, and then ask them to hypothesize about the causes for the change. (What made it get hard?) Or consideration could be given to what is the "best" way to wash the table. (Using a sponge? pouring water on it? scraping the clay off? What are the various possibilities?) Try various methods; note what happens; discuss it together. Help children make connections between what may seem to be isolated acts, but do so without taking over the activity.

When we talk about science, emphasis is placed on cognitive functioning, but this is not to be construed as a neglect of either the emotional aspects or social context of an experience. Emotion is addressed not only in the exploration of feeling but also in the fact that the children are pursuing their self-initiated interests and thus are learning more about themselves. Children are constantly exploring their world, discovering new things, and interpreting and synthesizing their experiences.

The following are ten situations for you to consider as you practice applying the principles we have just discussed. Put a checkmark beside all the instances that you feel reflect ALERTA's intent.

What Do You Think?

If you wanted to encourage the children's development during their free-choice time without taking over the activity, which of the following might you do? (Check all the answers that you feel reflect ALERTA's intent.)

☐ 1. Set up opportunities for learning in each of the classroom areas before the children come to school.

☐ 2. Go into the housekeeping area and say, "Who's going to make me dinner?"

☐ 3. Say to the children working in the blockbuilding area, "That's not the way a garage should look. How about making it like this. . . ."

☐ 4. Move from area to area of the room slowly, interacting with children who invite your comments.

☐ 5. Say to the children at the easels, "I'll give you some paper so you can draw your houses."

☐ 6. Give a box of costumes and masks to children who are acting out a parade they saw.

☐ 7. Point out the weighing scales to two children who are trying to decide whether a piece of wood is heavier than the magnet they have.

☐ 8. Say to children working with clay, "What sorts of things can be done with this clay?"

☐ 9. Put a story record on to play softly in the library corner where a child is looking at a book of the same story.

☐ 10. Get out an instrument and start playing and singing one of the children's favorite songs.

If you checked numbers 1, 4, 6, 7, 8, and 9, you *are* reflecting ALERTA's intent. The other choices represent instances of a teacher's taking over an activity, moving from child control of the work to teacher control.

Revitalizing Areas of the Classroom to Sustain Children's Interest and Reflect Ongoing Themes

Revitalizing Curriculum Areas

Just as the learning style of each child is different and individual, each curriculum area (housekeeping, blockbuilding, etc.) offers its own learning opportunities. In child-initiated situations your role is one of guidance and suggestion. Through observation you may recognize the direction of the activity and discern possibilities for offering materials, raising questions, and so forth. Your role is not directive, although you determine and select possibilities in creating the environment.

In the previous section suggestions were offered for teacher functioning, that is, teacher style in response to child-initiated activities. This brief section offers suggestions for revitalizing curriculum areas at those times when you may feel that the area "needs something" without a clear idea of what that may be. What you may be saying to yourself is that you sense the area needs to challenge the children further, that what may be happening seems routine, that there seems to be a lack of investment or involvement on the part of the children. What does a teacher do in such instances?

General Considerations:

1. Review the learning opportunities being offered in an area. Are they clear to you? Can you state them to yourself in your own words and with personal meaning? Can you think of examples to back up your statements? For example, it is frequently stated that blockbuilding helps children in spatial relations. Can you imagine what this means in detail, in the actual classroom activity of the children? Can you think of this idea in relation to a particular child in your group and pinpoint his or her development?

2. Think about what it is in the child's behavior that makes you feel that there is a lack of involvement or challenge. Think about the same child's activities in other areas. Are there similarities? Differences? Can you make sense out of these different observations? Are you up-to-date on the child's life outside of school?

3. Think about your expectations for any of the areas. Having reviewed the available learning opportunities and matching these with your understanding of a particular child or children, think about what else may be shaping your expectations for activities and/or behavior in an area. Is what you expect appropriate for the child's age level? Is it appropriate for this particular child as he or she is uniquely manifesting developmental stage characteristics? For example (within the context of blockbuilding), are you expecting three-year-olds to be making representational buildings that contain wooden people and animals and that are used realistically to depict a social scene? Are you expecting a small group of four-year-olds to plan their building together and then use it cooperatively If you are, in both these instances the expectations are higher than the activities and behaviors one usually finds for these ages. (Three-year-olds are still at the stage in which their main use of blocks is experimental—finding

out what blocks do, what happens when you pile one on top of another, what happens to the blocks when they fall, do they break, how do or don't different shapes fit together, etc.) Generally, review how you form your basic expectations.

On the whole, in each of the general considerations presented, what has been asked of the teacher is that he or she review the ideas that are the foundation for practice. Teaching is a "mindful" activity, requiring considerable reflection and review for it to be kept vital and responsive to the children with whom we work.

Reflecting Ongoing Themes

Just as the way you prepare the classroom environment can encourage the children's own achievement of basic program goals and objectives, the materials you provide in the various classroom areas from week to week can promote the children's further exploration of themes. As you do your weekly planning you will see opportunities for placing materials you have used in the cluster sessions in various areas of the classroom. Or instead you might make available other materials that clearly reflect the theme being used that week.

You remember that on the weekly planning form introduced in Chapter Eight (Level 6) there was a space for notes on preparation of the classroom environment. The completed examples that follow show how such notes would be made for the plans presented. To see the implications of your own activities for the preparation of your classroom, take your newest set of weekly plans and fill in the space under "Room Areas." Once more, it will be very helpful if you can discuss your thoughts on this with a partner so that you can exchange ideas and extend each other's thinking.

ALERTA Weekly Planning Form

Classroom: ___#4___ *Note: This plan is for a half-day program.*

Theme: _Family members (babies/children/adults)_

Language Cluster: _English monolinguals_

Children's Names: _Frank   Beatrice_

Harriet   Jerry

Room Areas/Reflection of Theme

Housekeeping: Dolls, baby clothing, baby oil and powder containers.
Blockbuilding: Pictures of different rooms in houses
Art/Music: Records of baby songs from cultures represented.
Library: Baby albums, baby books, books on families
Water/Sand: Baby bottles, baby toys
Manipulatives:
Science:

	Goals/Objectives	Activity	Materials from Culture/Environment
Monday	Goal Area 2: Obj. 6 (Describe ways people may be different from one another.)	Children view display of photos of themselves as babies and guess who each baby is. Questions: How do you know who that is? What is different about you now from when you were a baby?	• Baby photos brought from children's and teachers' homes.
Tuesday	Goal Area 2: Obj. 6 (Describe ways people may be different from one another.)	Children view current photos of themselves, which have been added to display. Questions: What can you do now that you couldn't do when you were a baby? (Elicit "walk.") What are some of the ways your parents carried you when you couldn't walk? Children look at equipment for carrying babies.	• Current photos of children. • Baby-carrying equipment e.g. "snugglies," infant seats, backpacks, other equipment traditional in children's homes.
Wednesday	Goal Area 4: Obj. 3 (Work cooperatively with others when appropriate.)	Provide one doll (undressed) for every two children. Put sets of doll clothing in center of group. Pairs of children dress a doll while conversation is encouraged. Question: Why do you think babies wear clothes that are different from grownups' clothes? Children will finish dressing dolls.	• Baby dolls • Grownup dolls • Dolls traditional in cultures represented by the children
Thursday	Goal Area 4: Obj. 1 (Show trust for one another and for adults by inviting interaction with them.)	Elicit from children descriptions of how their parents used to sing to them when they were babies. Play baby songs and encourage children to sing to their "babies" (dolls).	• Records or tapes of baby songs from the cultures represented by the children. • Dolls (see Wednesday's plan).
Friday		Planning and In-service Day (see Exercise 5)	

ALERTA Weekly Planning Form

Classroom: __#4__ *Note: This plan is for a half-day program*

Theme: __Family members (houses/stores)__

Language Cluster: __Spanish dominant bilinguals__

Children's Names: __José   Juanito__

__Antonio   Marta__

Room Areas/Reflection of Theme

Housekeeping: *"Store goods" to stock shelves*
Blockbuilding: *Photographs of children's houses*
Art/Music:
Library: *Books showing different styles of houses/stores*
Water/Sand:
Manipulatives: } *Puzzles made from photos of children's homes*
Science: } *Lotto games made from photos of local stores*

	Goals/Objectives	Activity	Materials from Culture/Environment
Monday	Goal Area 3: Obj. 3 (Describe situations or events that are a part of their environment.)	Children will go on a walk to places where they live. With teacher's help, each child takes a photograph of the front of his or her house. As much conversation as possible should be encouraged along the way.	• Camera and film (Polaroid-type camera, if possible)
Tuesday	Goal Area 3: Obj. 3 (Describe situations or events that are a part of their environment.)	Children recall their walk and discuss resources (stores, bus stops, hospitals, etc.) near their houses. In the blockbuilding area each child builds his or her house, adding other buildings if he or she chooses. Teacher labels constructions.	• Display of photographs of children's houses to put in blockbuilding area.
Wednesday	Goal Area 3: Obj. 3 (Describe situations or events that are a part of their environment.)	Children will visit one of the stores mentioned in the previous day's discussion. Question: What does your mother or father buy in this store? What else could they buy? If possible, have the children buy a small item to use that day in school.	
Thursday	Goal Area 3: Obj. 6 (Develop ways to answer questions about objects, or events, by "experimenting" with them.)	Ask a family or community member (previously identified) to come to the classroom to tell stories about where she or he used to live when she or he was little. The guest should recount childhood events that happened at home. Encourage children to ask such questions as: How come that happened? Why did you do that? etc.	• Photographs, drawings, or magazine pictures of houses or buildings where class visitor used to live. • Other props related to story she or he will tell.
Friday	Planning and In-service Day (see Exercise 5)	← →	

EXERCISE 4

Mustering Human and Material Resources

As you more fully understand the cultures represented by the children in your center or classroom you will come to appreciate the tremendous richness of detail that makes up each set of traditions and values. Moving beyond the first level of culture to recognition of a culture's other two levels (See Chapter Four) requires that you have access to reliable resources. These resources may be human or material, that is, they may be people from the community who can tell you or show you some of the less obvious aspects of their cultures, or they may be books or records in a staff development library that focus on the cultural groups participating in your program. This concern turns us once again to the idea of partnerships among administrators and teachers, teachers themselves, and teachers and parents as sources of information exchange and support for the program's continued growth and expansion.

Parents are especially important. In order to provide the best educational environment and thus meaningful experiences for young children, both teachers and parents must work at understanding differences in cultural beliefs and behavior. This can be accomplished by a close communication network between the home and the center or school.

Many parents have clear ideas about what elements make up their cultures. Other parents seem not to know when they are first asked, but when they have the chance to explore ideas about culture informally with other parents or with classroom staff a wealth of ideas may emerge. These can be useful to you both in understanding certain aspects of the children's behavior and, as has been previously suggested, in providing content for activities you would like to try with the children. Parents may know songs, rhymes, verses, or stories that were part of their own childhood experiences. Parents may be able to explain to the children better than you the meaning of certain festivals (such as Chinese New Year) or tell you about customs that family members look forward to (such as a yearly trip to a family reunion). Once again, you could incorporate these insights into the activities you plan.

Although more reliable information about a culture may come from a member of the group than comes from books, there may be times when you need information quickly and no one around has the answer you need. Or you might want to find out more in general about a particular culture. Just as your school should have resources available to you on child development and possible learning activities, it should also have a collection of books or other source materials that deal with various aspects of the cultures represented in your classroom. There should be books for adults and for older children. The latter are often useful in providing teachers with details about a culture that can then be adapted and incorporated into learning activities for young children.

Building up such a resource library takes some thought and preparation on the part of administrators, teachers, and interested parents. Staff and parent-development materials must be selected carefully to insure that they mirror the intent of ALERTA so that users of the resources do not accidentally receive contradictory messages about program content or procedure.

In the appendix to this source book

there is a list of books collected for one such resource library. Not only commercially produced materials should be included, but also a variety of staff- and parent-development materials. Establishing a resource center in your own school or early childhood setting is an important way to help all participants continue to grow in the use of the program from year to year.

In your daily planning, resources you want to use can be noted in the space provided on the form, as shown in the following example. These notes can serve as reminders to you of books or materials that you want to check out of the resource center or of persons you may want to include in the presentation of the activity.

ALERTA Daily Individualized Planning Form

Classroom: #4   Note: This plan is for a half-day program.   Date: February 7 (Monday)

Language Cluster	Spanish Monolingual	English Monolingual	Spanish-dominant Bilingual	English-dominant Bilingual
		FAMILY MEMBERS		
Theme	Family composition/activities	Babies/children/adults	Houses/stores	Family travel
Goals/Objectives	Goal Area 4: Obj. 2 (Work cooperatively with others when appropriate.)	Goal Area 2: Obj. 6 (Describe ways people may be different from one another.)	Goal Area 3: Obj. 3 (Describe situations or events that are a part of their environment.)	Goal Area 2: Obj. 1 (Describe some of their favorite family customs.)
Activity	Prepare raw vegetable salad, using vegetables like those grown in Roberto's uncle's garden.	View and discuss baby photos.	Photograph fronts of children's houses.	Discuss family travel. Begin to construct cars and boats from large cardboard boxes.
Language Strategies	1st language 2nd language (English) • Use of known concepts • Limited amount of new vocabulary: wash, cut, lettuce, carrots • Natural context • Opportunities for repetition (NO DRILL)	1st language 2nd language (Spanish) • Limited amount of new vocabulary: la foto, el bebé, ¿Quién es? • Natural context • Use of familiar objects	1st language (Spanish) • Many opportunities for children to speak • Conversational style • Full range of language repertoire • Open-ended questions • Introduce new concepts 2nd language	1st language (English) • Many opportunities for children to speak • Conversational style • Full range of language repertoire • Open-ended questions • Introduce new concepts 2nd language
Large-Group Activities	Opening meeting: Discussion of places children went on the weekend (who they went with, how they went, what they did). Closing meeting: Childhood song typical of one of the cultures represented by the children (family theme).			
Notes on Resources to Be Used	Check with Roberto's family regarding salad ingredients.	Request baby photos from families ahead of time.	Camera/film from resource room.	Collect large cardboard boxes from grocery store.

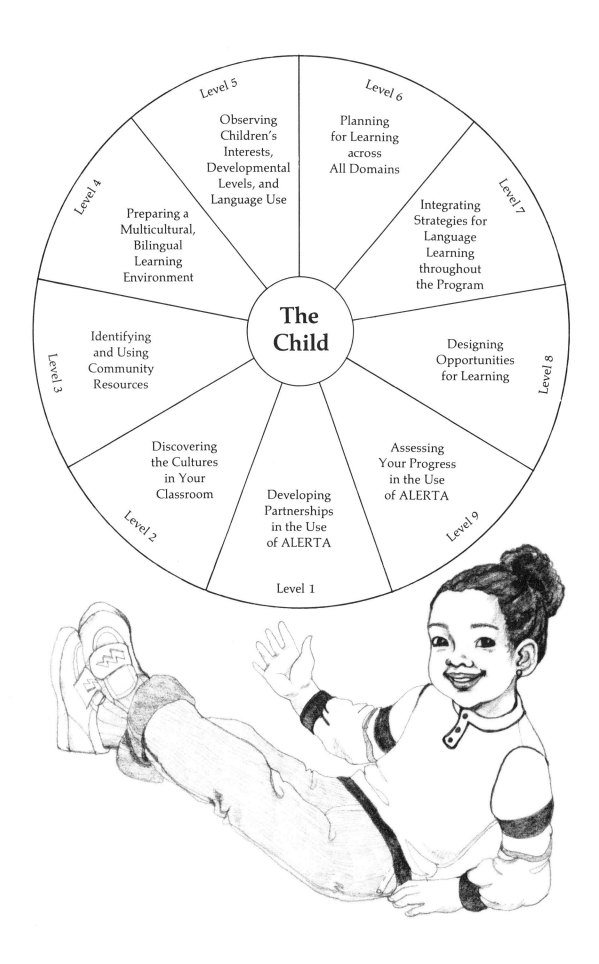

Level 5 — Observing Children's Interests, Developmental Levels, and Language Use

Level 6 — Planning for Learning across All Domains

Level 4 — Preparing a Multicultural, Bilingual Learning Environment

Level 7 — Integrating Strategies for Language Learning throughout the Program

Level 3 — Identifying and Using Community Resources

The Child

Designing Opportunities for Learning

Level 8

Discovering the Cultures in Your Classroom

Level 2

Assessing Your Progress in the Use of ALERTA

Level 9

Developing Partnerships in the Use of ALERTA

Level 1

CHAPTER ELEVEN

Level 9: Assessing Your Progress in the Use of ALERTA

ALERTA's Level 9 offers you the opportunity to review your work in setting the program in place and to assess the degree of your success at each point along the way. By now it is probably clear to you that ALERTA's levels are not so much like steps on a stairway as they are like points on the rim of a wheel.

At any time as you progress you are able to turn the wheel back to make adjustments in the work you have already done. In this way you are able to more and more closely match the developmental levels and promote the interests and skills of the children you serve.*

In Level 9 you are encouraged to take a long look backward over the past year's effort to identify those levels that need further concentration during the coming school year. By doing this you absorb more of ALERTA's process and are able to carry out an increasingly better, fine-tuned program. You, rather than an outside evaluator, have control over this process and are able to set priorities that accurately reflect all that has been accomplished to date. Four main indicators can be used to reveal your present degree of program implementation: (1) presence of the distinguishing characteristics of an ALERTA program, (2) results of a second survey of the learning environment, (3) patterns appearing in your collected child observations and activity plans, and (4) results of parent and administrator interviews. Each of these indicators is explained in the following exercises, and suggestions are given for expanding your program from year to year.

EXERCISE 1

The Distinguishing Characteristics of ALERTA

Use of a simple rating scale is often the best way to start a program assessment. The following is an example of such a rating scale that details distinctive features of ALERTA. To begin, review the list to see if you would add any items to it. Then, being as objective as you can, rate yourself on each of the items. You may wish to ask a colleague whom you respect also to rate your classroom on each of the items. This procedure allows you to compare perceptions and discuss the fine points involved in each aspect of program implementation. At the conclusion of your rating note the items where you have a 0, 1, or 2, and list your priorities accordingly for work in the coming year.

---

*We thank Deborah Maher, an ALERTA workshop leader, for devising this accurate image.

Indicators of Progress in the Use of ALERTA

Center/School _____   Teacher(s) _____

Classroom _____   Observer(s) _____

Directions: For each of the items below, rate the degree of program implementation that you have observed in this classroom.

Key: 0 = No implementation
        1 = Implementation begun
        2 = Consistent use (but not yet perfected)
        3 = Full implementation

1. Partnerships are evident in carrying out the program.   _____

2. Parents' input is encouraged and coordinated.   _____

3. Hallways, offices, kitchen, etc., reflect the cultures and interests of program participants.   _____

4. Materials in classroom areas reflect the community, cultures, interests, and developmental levels of the children.   _____

5. Daily teacher-directed activities make use of themes, goals and objectives, and content drawn from cultures and community.   _____

6. The teacher-directed activities (clusters) incorporate strategies for first language development and second language acquisition.   _____

7. Provision is made for a period of child-initiated work each day.   _____

8. Both languages addressed in the program are used throughout the day.   _____

9. Staff members do daily written child observations.   _____

10. Staff members make direct use of their child observations in daily and weekly planning.   _____

EXERCISE 2

Second Survey of the Learning Environment

Working alone or with a partner, do the survey of the classroom environment once again. (See appendix for a fresh copy of the form.) Compare your results at this point in time with the results of the first survey you conducted when you began ALERTA's Level 4. Note those classroom areas that still need additional preparation, and, as appropriate, make entries on your list of priorities for the coming year.

Review of Collected Child Observations and Activity Plans

Lay out before you the child observations (anecdotal records, observation guides on child interests, and observation guides on children's skills and attitudes) that you have done over the past program year. Scan each set in turn, and then answer the following questions. This is another exercise in which the opinion of a respected colleague may be especially valuable in providing insight into the patterns that appear. At the conclusion of your review consider the results and make notes as relevant on your list of priorities for the coming year.

Patterns Revealed in Reviewing Child Observations and Activity Plans

1. Do your collected observations of the skills and developmental levels of the children in each language cluster show steady attainment in each of the four major goal areas over the year? If not, describe patterns that appear.

---

2. Do your collected observations of the children's skills and developmental levels show balanced profiles of attainment over the four major goal areas for *individual* children? If not, describe patterns that appear.

---

3. Do your collected observations of child interests show heavy use of *all* the areas of your classroom? If not, describe patterns that appear.

---

4. Do your collected activity plans show regular use of themes drawn directly from the children's interests? If not, describe patterns that appear.

---

5. Do your collected activity plan show use of community and cultural content drawn from the traditions of *all* the families that participated in your program (rather than from the traditions of only one or two groups)? If not, describe patterns that appear.

---

6. Do your collected activity plans show connections of themes, goals and objectives, and cultural/community content in cluster work with the materials made available in the various classroom areas and with activities done with the class as a whole? If not, describe patterns that appear.

EXERCISE 4

Parent and Administrator Interviews

Still another type of insight is gained by asking parents and administrators who have worked closely with you to describe their perceptions of the program. The elements they emphasize in their responses may reveal areas to which you have given special attention or areas that need more work in the future.

To encourage frankness of approach in the respondents you may wish to have a colleague conduct the interviews in-stead of doing them yourself. It is recommended that at least two administrators or supervisors and five parents be invited for interviews. Interview questions are provided that are designed to tap parents' and administrators' opinions and understanding of ALERTA.

Interviews with either parents or administrators should not be conducted as if they were a test of how much people know. Instead they should be like infor-

---

Parent/Administrator Interview

1. After working with ALERTA for a year, do you feel there is something you have learned from the program that you would like to talk about?

_____

_____

_____

_____

2. Do you think that using ALERTA in our school (or center) was helpful to the children? to the parents? Would you explain your answers?

_____

_____

_____

_____

3. How far along do you feel we are in using the program? (Are we just beginning? still learning? using it the way it was designed to be used?) How did you come to your conclusion? (How do you know?)

_____

_____

_____

_____

4. What things about ALERTA do you think worked particularly well this year?

_____

_____

5. What things do you feel did not work so well as you had hoped they would?

_____

_____

6. What could we do to improve those areas?

_____

_____

mal conversations. That way you will learn much more about how people think and what they feel. You can introduce the conversation by saying that you would really like to know what people are thinking about the use of ALERTA in the school and that you are hoping to gather suggestions for improving the work of the program. If the interviewees indicate they are willing to talk with you, you can move easily into the questions just as you would in any conversation. It is often better not to write in front of the person who is talking with you. Instead make your notes right after the conversation, when the person has left. Review all the responses you receive and consider them in light of the priorities you have already identified for the coming year's work.

Suggestions for Expanding Your Program from Year to Year

Once you have gathered information from several sources (such as the previous exercises) on the degree of success you have experienced in using the program, you will be in a good position to confirm your priorities in continuing ALERTA's process. When your new children arrive next fall, you and your partners will be repeating the nine levels of program use. But this time you will have the wonderful advantage of your cumulative efforts of the year before. Using materials previously made and procedures now established in your classroom, you will be able to move ahead rapidly to refine the less developed areas and pursue particular interests that you have. In successive years you might want to experiment with designing and presenting your own ALERTA workshops for parents and other teachers; making slide shows or videotapes of your program; developing completely new types of learning materials; or setting up a multicultural, bilingual resource center for your school. The possibilities will continue to expand with your vision of them and your desire to make them happen.

CHAPTER TWELVE

Adapting ALERTA for Use
with Other Populations

In its present form, ALERTA is designed for use with three- to five-year-old children who are developing normally. The program can be used with any cultural or linguistic group living in any region of the country. The only requirement for regional adaptations is that you and those working with you consistently incorporate aspects of the local cultures and community as vehicles for promoting the children's learning within the nine-level ALERTA Program.

It is also possible to use ALERTA with older children or with mildly handicapped preschool populations, provided that appropriate adaptations are made in the learning environment preparation, goal setting, and language-teaching strategies. In concluding this source book, each of those three program areas is discussed in relation to both older and exceptional populations. It is hoped that the issues raised will provide useful guidelines for those considering extending the program upwards or shaping it for children with special needs.

Preparing an ALERTA Learning Environment

The descriptions for preparation of the classroom (and the center or school as a whole) provided in Chapter Six concentrate on those interest areas most related to young children's learning. Many elementary schools today continue the tradition of open classrooms with a similar arrangement of learning areas. A major difference from what has been described here, of course, is that the centers in the primary grades tend to be organized around the acquisition of academic skills: reading, writing, mathematical computation, experimentation in science, social studies, and so on. The basic principles in preparing these centers is the same as described earlier: you choose or create learning materials for each of your selected areas to reflect the community and the cultures represented by the children in your program.

Traditionally organized classrooms can also incorporate aspects of the community and local cultures in the learning materials and activities selected by the teacher. Although the children in that case would not be using interest areas, they could have projects that draw upon their increasing knowledge of the cultural diversity that characterizes their society as ways of refining their academic knowledge and skills.

In preparing an ALERTA learning environment for children with mildly handicapping conditions, teachers must work toward providing the least restrictive environment for the children in the program. This means that attention must be given to removing any obstacles to the children's progress and to making the children's learning as much like that of their normally developing peers as possible. For instance, if children are confined to wheelchairs, the room must be arranged so that they can move about easily from area to area. If children are visually impaired, the materials and furniture must remain in set locations so that the children can orient themselves easily and be as independent as possible in their efforts. If children have developmental delays (are mildly retarded), materials need to be especially well selected to suit their developmental characteristics. All such adaptations can be made while still following ALERTA's basic intent.

Goal Setting

In Chapter Eight a procedure was presented for tailoring learning goals to the children in your program. Although the setting of appropriate goals and objectives is always important in ALERTA, the procedure must be given even more attention in situations in which you are adapting the program to older or developmentally different children. It is critical that your goals match children's emerging capabilities so that the children will be neither bored by work that is too easy for them nor frustrated by work that is too difficult.

Work with children in the elementary grades requires systematic incorporation of all the subject areas required by local school districts and state curriculum plans. Following ALERTA's process, these subject areas should be addressed in an integrated way, because they relate to one another and to the cultural and linguistic experiences that the children bring with them to the classroom. For example, children in the fourth grade might be studying the river on which their town or community is located. During their project they might observe the river ecology (the patterns of interaction among the plants and animals that the river supports), an activity that would be a lesson in science. They might also study the length, depth, and volume of the river (mathematics), the role of the river in the current life of their town (social studies), the former uses of the river (history), and any literature that features that river or others like it (reading and language arts). In this case the learning goals for the class would reflect both the developmental levels of the children and the subject areas to be addressed.

Work with children who have handicapping conditions will also require attention to the particularities of the situation. Goals will need to be set that take into account the special skills training those children may require to enable them to develop in all domains (socioemotional, cognitive/linguistic, and psychomotor) to the best of their abilities. For example, children who are hearing impaired will need to have lipreading and signing as part of their program. These survival skills would be integrated into all aspects of an ALERTA program for the hearing-impaired as another aspect of the children's development and culture.

It is expected that ALERTA teachers working with exceptional populations would have training in special education as well as training for teaching at a particular grade level. Teachers without such preparation who are receiving "mainstreamed" children may find ALERTA's processes of child observation and child-centered planning helpful in their learning about each child's characteristics.

Language-Teaching Strategies

In working with children in the elementary grades, the ALERTA Program recommends basically the same strategies for continued extension of the first language and second language acquisition as are used with younger children. One difference would be in the pacing and complexity of the children's various learning activities. As children mature, of course, they are more and more able to attend to a task for longer periods and to manage several aspects of an activity within a short period of time (such as observation of an animal in the classroom, looking up information about it in the library, and writing a report or story on it).

It is also true that once children's underlying structures in their first language become fully developed (at approximately age eight), they are in an especially good position for concentrating on the acquisition of a second language. At this point, children usually adapt well to an increased amount of time spent on learning activities conducted in the second language, provided that the first language as a medium for learning is not abandoned. Through this strategy, the children continue to build upon the structures of their first language for fuller elaboration of the second.

With children who are experiencing developmental delays or specific language disabilities, the issue of the acquisition of a second language becomes problematical. These children may be having difficulty forming the underlying structures and using the rules of their first language, and adding a second language to their learning task may be very confusing for them. Many speech and language therapists recommend that teachers do *not* use a bilingual approach with children experiencing this difficulty. Instead they urge that teachers work with the children only in the language of the home. The child-centered and multicultural aspects of ALERTA could still be effectively used with the children, however. Introduction to a second language might be added at a later point, when individual children have demonstrated mastery of their home language. The same consideration would hold for children who are hearing-impaired. (Of course, one could consider the learning of sign language as the children's second language in this case.)

Some Concluding Thoughts

Adaptation of the ALERTA program to older or exceptional populations should not be considered a procedure different from the process described in this source book. The essence of ALERTA's approach to teaching is recognition of individual differences in the context of group (cultural) experience, and using that experience to help children more effectively cope with today's rapidly shrinking and changing world. Learning is most long lasting when it is intimately connected with the objects and events that have personal meaning for us as children and as adults. Such connections are constructed, in turn, through our interaction with people and environments that respond to and extend our collected knowledge, skills, and attitudes. The total, reciprocal process leads us again to the most fundamental goal of this educational program—promotion of greater competence through a learning environment responsive to all.

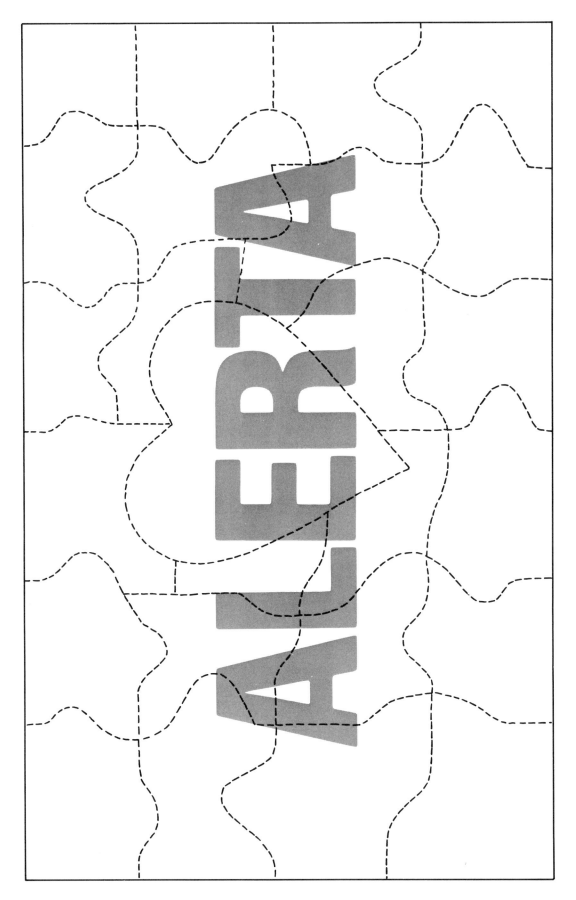

ALERTA

Questionnaire on Preferences and Capabilities

Directions: Answer each of the questions below quickly, using the first thoughts that come to mind as you read each one.

1. People who know me think I am _____

   _____

   _____

2. I love to 1. _____

   2. _____

   3. _____

3. I can _____ very well.

4. At my job I don't like to _____,

5. and I like to _____.

6. Professionally in the future I would like to _____

   _____

   _____

7. Personally in the future I would like to _____

   _____

   _____

Cultural Group: _____

What?	How?	Why?

Gathering Information from Parents/Caregivers

1. _____ was born in _____
          Child's name   City/place of birth

*2. _____ was born in _____
          Mother's name   City/place of birth

*3. _____ was born in _____
          Father's name   City/place of birth

*4. _____ was born in _____
          Caregiver   City/place of birth

5. The family lives at: _____

   _____

6. They have lived there for _____
                                           Length of time

7. There are _____ family members living together.

8. The family members living together are: (List and give relationship to child)

   _____

   _____

   _____

   _____

   _____

   _____

   _____

*Omit if not applicable.

9. _____ has traveled to (List city/cities, country)
   Child's name

   _____

   _____

   _____

   _____

10. by (Means of transportation) _____

    _____

    _____

    _____

11. At home _____ is/are spoken.
    Language(s)

12. _____ usually plays (Location; e.g., playground, home, etc.)
    Child's name

    _____

    _____

    _____

Questions to Ask Yourself When Examining Learning Materials for Evidence of Stereotypes

Portrayal of Racial/Ethnic/Cultural Groups

1. Do the materials contain negative messages about a particular group?

_____

_____

2. Are illustrations of the physical characteristics of characters in the materials unreal or unnatural (for example, Asians portrayed as yellow, Blacks having "white" facial features, Native Americans having red skin)?

_____

_____

3. In books, is there evidence of condescension in the treatment of a minority group character?

_____

_____

4. Are the lifestyles of minority group members depicted as inferior to the lifestyle of the majority group?

_____

_____

5. Do particular words used to describe a minority group present negative images of the group?

_____

Portrayal of Women

1. Are women appearing in the materials always portrayed in traditional sex roles (for example, teacher, nurse, secretary, housewife)?

_____

2. In books, do women have passive roles and men have active roles in the story?

_____

3. Are high-status occupations (such as being a doctor or holding a decision-making position) associated only with men in the story?

_____

4. Are women depicted as defenseless and/or dependent?

_____

_____

5. Is the success of a woman based on her good looks and physical attributes or on her initiative and intelligence?

_____

_____

Questions to Ask Yourself

1. How would you describe this community to someone who has never visited it?

    _____

    _____

2. What do you see when you come to work in the morning? Go home from work in the afternoon?

    _____

    _____

3. What do you think the children notice as they come to school?

    _____

    _____

4. Who lives in this neighborhood? How do the people spend their time? (What kinds of work do they do? What kinds of recreation do they enjoy?)

    _____

    _____

5. What do the children do when they are not in school?

    _____

    _____

6. What do you think is special (interesting) about the neighborhood where the center is located? What makes this neighborhood a little different from other neighborhoods in the city or town?

    _____

    _____

    _____

    _____

    _____

Guide for Community Observations

1. What sorts of buildings make up the neighborhood? (Tall, narrow buildings? Low, wide buildings? Apartments? Single-family dwellings?) Of what types of material are the buildings made?

_____

_____

2. What types of industry or agriculture are found in your community? What do they produce?

_____

_____

3. What types of goods are sold in the stores? Do some of the stores show an orientation toward particular cultural groups? If so, how?

_____

_____

4. What special service agencies are found nearby? (Hospital? Community center? Post office? Farmers' exchange?)

_____

_____

5. What easily recognizable occupations are in evidence in the neighborhood? (Doctors or nurses? firefighters? construction workers? farmers?)

_____

_____

6. What types of vehicles are seen in the neighborhood? (Buses? subways? cabs of different kinds? trucks?)

_____

_____

7. What special machinery is in evidence? (Streetcleaners? cranes or other construction units? tractors? road graders?)

_____

8. What is the topography of the neighborhood? (Hilly? flat? straight streets? crooked streets?)

_____

9. What sorts of recreational facilities are available? (Movies? penny arcades? parks? swimming pools? basketball courts?)

_____

10. If there are parks, what kinds of plants and trees grow there? Are there any animals around? (Squirrels? dogs? cats?)

_____

_____

11. What kinds of games do children play in the streets?

_____

_____

12. What styles of clothing are popular?

_____

_____

13. What sorts of special events go on in the neighborhood? (Feast days? art carnivals? street fairs? block parties?)

_____

_____

14. What sounds can be heard in the neighborhood?

_____

_____

15. What colors are frequently used in building decoration?

_____

_____

16. What are common signs or symbols seen in the neighborhood?

_____

_____

Things to Note *Before* and *After* a Home Visit

1. What language(s) is (are) spoken at home?

    _____

2. Is a regional variation of the language used in the home? What are some of its characteristics?

    _____

3. What is the general composition of the family? (How many children are in the family? Do grandparents or other relatives live in the same home?)

    _____

    _____

4. Does the family travel a lot with the children? Where do they go? How often? What experiences have the children had as a result of traveling?

    _____

    _____

5. What types of toys and games are used in the home?

    _____

6. Do any of the activities at the center go against the parents' values or beliefs?

    _____

    _____

7. What approval or disapproval of certain types of behavior in children is given? What behaviors are particularly singled out for comment? What style of discipline is used at home?

    _____

    _____

8. What expectations are held for the children? Do the expectations differ according to sex, position in order of birth, etc.?

    _____

    _____

Your Suggestions for Learning Materials
Using Photographs or Audiotapes

_____

_____

_____

_____

_____

_____

_____

_____

_____

_____

_____

_____

_____

_____

_____

_____

_____

_____

_____

_____

_____

The ALERTA Program

Survey of the Classroom Environment

1. Housekeeping Area or Family Corner

Is the space large enough for several children to move around in easily?
Yes ☐   No ☐

Is it located near the blockbuilding area, which may serve to stimulate the dramatic play in each of the areas? Yes ☐   No ☐

In addition to the usual furniture, dishes, pots, pans, and cutlery, does the area include many of the following? (Check the articles that do appear.)

☐ "Grownup" clothing commonly worn (every day and for festivals or holidays) by people of the cultures represented in the program.

☐ Boy and girl dolls that have the skin color, hairstyles, facial features, and varieties of clothing of the cultural groups represented in the program.

☐ Puppets that have the skin color, hairstyles, and facial features of the people, and varieties of clothing of the cultural groups represented in the program.

☐ Food packages (cans, boxes, etc.) that have labels in the children's native language as well as those that have labels in English (e.g., popular brands found in local supermarkets or grocery stores).

☐ Additional kitchen utensils commonly used in the kitchens of people from the cultures represented in your program.

☐ Furniture typical or distinctive of the cultures of the families in your program.

☐ Materials that show men and women in nurturing roles and in various types of family structures (e.g., photographs or illustrations of men feeding children; single-parent families; families including grandparents, etc.).

☐ Decoration reflecting colors, patterns, and family scenes common in the cultures represented in your center.

2. Blockbuilding Area

Is this area large enough for five or six children to use it at one time?
Yes ☐   No ☐

Is the area located as far as possible away from the quiet area or library corner?
Yes ☐   No ☐

In addition to the usual building blocks, are there sets of scaled-down objects reflecting the place where your program is located (trees, animals, etc.) to be used in fantasy play?
Yes ☐   No ☐

Are there scaled-down, multiracial figures of people? Yes ☐   No ☐

Do the figures avoid sex-role stereotyping? Yes ☐   No ☐

Is the area decorated with illustrations of typical building styles from your area, such as photographs of the children's homes or easily recognizable landmarks? Yes ☐ No ☐

3. Sand Area

Is this area easily accessible to the children? Yes ☐   No ☐

Are a variety of materials for digging and filling provided (e.g., spoons, shells, cans, pie pans, funnels, sieves, etc.)?
Yes ☐   No ☐

Is there any setup in the area that makes use of the role of sand or earth within the children's cultural traditions? Yes ☐   No ☐

4. Water Area

Is this area easily accessible to the children? Yes ☐   No ☐

Are a variety of materials for measuring, filling, and pouring provided (e.g., "squirty" bottles, tubing, pitchers, food coloring, bubble pipe, measuring cups, etc.)?
Yes ☐   No ☐

Is there any setup in the area that makes use of the role of water within the children's cultural traditions? Yes ☐   No ☐

5. Art Area

Is this area set up near a source of water (faucets or tubs of water)? Yes ☐   No ☐

Is the area well lit by natural light? Yes ☐   No ☐

In addition to paints, crayons, collage material, and clay, are any designs or motifs displayed that are part of the cultures represented? Yes ☐   No ☐

In the area are children exposed to crafts (e.g., weaving, pottery, basketry, beadwork, metalwork, woodworking, etc.) common in the cultures of their families?
Yes ☐   No ☐

6. Table Materials/Manipulatives

Are there materials that allow the small muscles to be used in several different ways?
Yes ☐   No ☐

Are there at least three different types of materials for each of the learning opportunities listed below?

Classify objects Yes ☐   No ☐

Classify pictures Yes ☐   No ☐

Put objects in a series (e.g., by length) Yes ☐   No ☐

Put pictures of objects in a series Yes ☐   No ☐

Sequence or form patterns Yes ☐   No ☐

Experiment with spatial orientations Yes ☐   No ☐

Try out their memory Yes ☐   No ☐

Do many illustrations on the materials reflect the children's environment (urban, suburban, or rural)? Yes ☐   No ☐

Do many illustrations on the materials reflect the various racial/cultural groups represented in the center? Yes ☐   No ☐

Are any words appearing on the materials written in the two languages used in your program? Yes ☐   No ☐

Do the collected materials have several levels of complexity so that children will still find some of the materials challenging even after they have developed skill with others? Yes ☐   No ☐

Are the materials displayed in a way that makes the choice evident to the children (clearly visible and easily reached)? Yes ☐   No ☐

7. Music and Movement Area

Are there records of the various types of music common in the cultures represented? List the types that do appear:

_____   _____

_____   _____

_____   _____

Are there records that use culturally distinctive instruments? Yes ☐   No ☐

Is there a variety of culturally appropriate instruments for the children's use?
Yes ☐   No ☐

Are dances distinctive of all the cultures represented taught at some time?
Yes ☐   No ☐

Are games (including rhythmic and/or musical games) taught that are distinctive of the various cultures represented? Yes ☐   No ☐

8. Library Area

Is this area placed in a quiet spot, out of the mainstream of activity? Yes ☐   No ☐

Is the area soft, cozy, and inviting? Yes ☐   No ☐

Do the bookshelves allow the books to be broadly displayed at the children's eye level? Yes ☐   No ☐

Does each classroom have available at least two books for every child, although they may not all be displayed at once? Yes ☐   No ☐

How many of the books are bilingual (written in both languages used in the program)? _____

How many of the books are written in English? _____

How many of the books are written in the second language used? _____

Do the illustrations in at least half of the books reflect the children's environment (e.g., urban, suburban, or rural)? Yes ☐   No ☐

Do the illustrations in many of the books reflect the various cultures and races represented in the center? Yes ☐   No ☐

Does the content of many of the books represent the children's life experiences (cultural and environmental)? Yes ☐   No ☐

Do the books give positive messages about particular cultural groups and about the roles of women? Yes ☐   No ☐

If the answer to the above question is *no,* make notes about the books in question.

9. Large-muscle Area

Is space available for the children to play games that require use of their large muscles? Yes ☐   No ☐

If *Yes,* is the space indoors ☐? Outdoors ☐?

Are games taught that are distinctive of the various cultures represented by the children in your program? Yes ☐   No ☐

What games are played by the children?

_____   _____

_____   _____

_____   _____

What equipment is available for those games?

_____   _____

_____   _____

_____   _____

10. Woodworking Area

Is there room enough in the area for two or three children to use it at one time? Yes ☐ No ☐

Is there a woodworking table available? Yes ☐   No ☐

Which of the following tools are available for the children's use?

☐ vise attached to workbench   ☐ sandpaper (various grains)

☐ hammers   ☐ assortment of nails

☐ saws   ☐ supply of soft wood

☐ c-clamps

Have rules for use of the area been posted in picture form where the children can easily see them? Yes ☐   No ☐

Is the area decorated with wooden objects or pictures of wooden objects distinctive of the cultures represented in your program? Yes ☐   No ☐

11. Science

Are special opportunities and activities made available in most or all of the areas named above that allow the children to experiment, hypothesize, solve problems, try out various possibilities for action, etc.? Yes ☐   No ☐

Do the opportunities available make use of a variety of materials drawn from the children's natural environment (such as leaves, twigs, pebbles, seashells, etc.)? Yes ☐   No ☐

List the opportunities and activities especially set up for these purposes today.

_____   _____

_____   _____

_____   _____

_____   _____

_____   _____

12. Rotating Point of Interest

Is the children's work displayed in a way that they can easily see it? Yes ☐   No ☐

Are the work displays changed frequently? Yes ☐   No ☐

Is there any picture of an event that has special significance to the children in your program? Yes ☐   No ☐

Are such displays or pictures used in story times or discussions? Yes ☐   No ☐

Is there a space somewhere in your school or center especially devoted to the interests and cultural backgrounds of the *parents* of the children in your program? Yes ☐   No ☐

Do menus available reflect foods common in each of the cultures represented? Yes ☐   No ☐

Planning for the Housekeeping Area

Review the materials suggested for the two sample groups. Now think of the children in *your* program and note materials other than those you already have in the housekeeping area that would reflect the children's cultural and community experiences.

1. Commercial materials: _____

_____

_____

_____

_____

2. Teacher- and/or parent-made materials: _____

_____

_____

_____

_____

3. Food products or packages: _____

_____

_____

_____

_____

4. Additional kitchen utensils (besides the usual pots and pans):

_____

_____

_____

_____

_____

Planning for the Blockbuilding Area

Review the materials suggested for the two sample groups. Now think of the children in *your* program and note materials other than those you already have in the blockbuilding area that would reflect the children's cultural and community experiences.

1. Additional wooden unit blocks needed: _____

_____

_____

_____

_____

_____

2. Supplemental building materials to reflect the children's environment:

_____

_____

_____

_____

_____

3. Photographs of landmarks or buildings well known to the children:

_____

_____

_____

_____

_____

Planning for the Sand Area

Review the materials suggested for the two sample groups. Now think of the children in *your* program and note materials other than those you already have in the sand area that would reflect the children's cultural and community experiences.

1. Basic sand materials needed: _____

_____

_____

_____

_____

_____

_____

_____

2. Materials for possible special setups: _____

_____

_____

_____

_____

_____

_____

_____

_____

Planning for the Water Area

Review the suggested materials. Now think of the children in *your* program and note materials other than those you already have in the water area that would reflect the children's cultural and community experiences.

1. Basic water materials needed: _____

    _____

    _____

    _____

    _____

    _____

    _____

    _____

    _____

2. Materials for possible special setups: _____

    _____

    _____

    _____

    _____

    _____

    _____

    _____

    _____

    _____

Planning for the Art Area

Review the suggested materials and techniques. Now think of the children in *your* program and note materials other than those you already have in the art area that would reflect the children's cultural and community experiences.

1. Basic art materials needed: _____

   _____

   _____

   _____

   _____

   _____

2. Materials from the children's environment for use in art: _____

   _____

   _____

   _____

   _____

   _____

   _____

3. Decorations for the area drawn from the community: _____

   _____

   _____

   _____

   _____

   _____

Planning for the Table Materials/ Manipulatives Area

Review the suggested materials and techniques. Now think of the children in *your* program and note materials other than those you already have in the table materials/manipulatives area that would reflect the children's cultural and community experiences.

1. Manipulatives with illustrations representative of the local community:

_____

_____

_____

_____

_____

2. Manipulatives made from local materials: _____

_____

_____

_____

_____

3. Manipulatives that offer a wider range of opportunity to the children for developing their skills:

_____

_____

_____

_____

Planning for the Music and Movement Area

Review the materials suggested for the two sample groups. Now think of the children in *your* program and note materials other than those you already have in the music and movement area that would reflect the children's cultural and community experiences.

1. Music for listening: _____

_____

_____

_____

_____

_____

_____

_____

2. Instruments for creation of music: _____

_____

_____

_____

_____

_____

_____

_____

_____

_____

Planning for the Library Area

Review the suggestions for the library area. Now think of the children in *your* program and note types of books or other materials you need to acquire in order to reflect the children's cultural and community experiences.

1. Books positively representing the children's cultural and racial groups:

_____

_____

_____

2. Books positively representing the setting where your program is located (urban, suburban, rural):

_____

_____

_____

3. Books written in the second language used in your program: _____

_____

_____

_____

4. Books made by children, parents, or teachers of events in the children's lives:

_____

_____

_____

5. Tapes of stories from the oral traditions of families in the program:

_____

_____

_____

Planning for the Large-Muscle Area

Review the materials and techniques suggested for the children's large-muscle development. Now think of the children in *your* program and note materials other than those you already have available for large-muscle development that would reflect the children's cultural and community experiences.

1. Special equipment needed: _____

_____

_____

_____

_____

_____

_____

_____

_____

2. Boundaries or game outlines needed: _____

_____

_____

_____

_____

_____

_____

_____

_____

_____

Planning for the Woodworking Area

Review the suggested materials. Now think of the children in *your* program and note materials other than those you already have in the woodworking area that would reflect the children's cultural and community experiences.

1. Basic woodworking materials needed: _____

    _____

    _____

    _____

    _____

    _____

    _____

    _____

    _____

    _____

2. Materials reflecting the children's cultural or environmental experiences with wood:

    _____

    _____

    _____

    _____

    _____

    _____

    _____

    _____

    _____

    _____

Planning for Science

Review the techniques suggested for incorporating science into the various areas of the classroom. Now think of the children in *your* program and note materials drawn from the local environment that would foster the children's problem-solving abilities in each area below.

1. Housekeeping: _____

_____

_____

_____

2. Blockbuilding: _____

_____

_____

_____

3. Sand: _____

_____

_____

_____

4. Water: _____

_____

_____

_____

5. Art: _____

_____

_____

_____

6. Table materials: _____

_____

_____

_____

7. Music and movement: _____

_____

_____

_____

8. Library: _____

_____

_____

_____

9. Large-muscle area: _____

_____

_____

_____

10. Woodworking: _____

_____

_____

_____

Assessing the Appropriateness of a Material's Use in Your ALERTA Program

1. Will this material help the children meet one of ALERTA's goals?

_____

_____

_____

_____

2. Does this material reflect some aspect of my children's direct (cultural/community/environmental) experience?

_____

_____

_____

_____

3. Is this material accurate and nonstereotypic in its portrayal of cultural groups or geographic settings?

_____

_____

_____

_____

4. Is this material developmentally appropriate for the children in my program?

_____

_____

_____

_____

Placing an Order

Check your material budget with your director or principal. Determine your budget allowance, and prepare a list of materials to be ordered.

Item Name	Company Producing Material	Number of Items	Price per Item	Total Price

Preparation for Materials-Making Workshops

Type of Item	Materials to Be Collected Ahead of Time

Planning for Change

1. What are your priorities in materials making? (What type of materials do you want to make first, next, and so on?)

_____

2. How do you plan to make the materials that you need for the various areas of the classroom? (Parent/teacher workshops? use of resource people? individual work after class?)

_____

3. Who has special expertise that might be able to help you with each type of materials construction?

_____

4. What dates have you identified for materials-making sessions?

_____

5. What printed resources might you draw upon for materials making? (Idea books, commercial materials that might be adapted to meet ALERTA's goals, stories and traditions collected from parents, etc?)

_____

_____

6. What procedures do you need to follow to insure that needed materials are ordered according to school or center policy?

_____

_____

7. When will specific changes in your classroom be made?

_____

8. Who will help you do any needed rearranging of your classroom?

_____

Observations of Child Interests Over a Week

Observer(s) _____   Dates _____

Center/School _____   Classroom _____

	Tally of Times Children Used Area for Extended Work	Materials Selected by Children for Frequent Use	Topics Raised in Children's Spontaneous Conversations
Housekeeping/ Family			
Blockbuilding			
Art/Music			
Library			
Water/Sand			
Manipulatives/ Table Toys			
Other:			
Community Walks/ Field Trips	Not applicable	Not applicable	

Psychomotor Development

Control of the Body within a Defined Space

Control of the Body While Moving through Space

Independent Use of the Limbs within a Defined Space

Independent Use of the Limbs While Moving the Body through Space

Control of the Body as a Whole While Surroundings Are Moving

The ALERTA Program

Guide for Clustering Children for Combination (Adult-Directed) Sessions

Child's Name _____   Observer _____

Classroom/Center _____   Date _____

Directions: Place either number 1 or 2 in each category below that applies to your observations of this child. 1 = understands the language. 2 = speaks and understands the language. Total each column as you finish it; then combine your totals. Use the totals to select an appropriate language cluster for adult-directed work with the child.

Languages Child Uses at Home:	English	Spanish	Other
with mother	_____	_____	_____
with father	_____	_____	_____
with brothers/sisters	_____	_____	_____
with grandparents	_____	_____	_____
with aunts/uncles	_____	_____	_____
with others	_____	_____	_____
Totals	_____	_____	_____

Child's Use of Language with Others in Classroom:

with _____
  (Teacher's name)
while he/she is speaking _____   _____ _____ _____
  (Language)
with _____
  (Teacher's name)
while he/she is speaking _____   _____ _____ _____
  (Language)
with _____
  (Peer's name)
while he/she is speaking _____   _____ _____ _____
  (Language)
with _____
  (Peer's name)
while he/she is speaking _____   _____ _____ _____
  (Language)

Totals   _____ _____ _____

ALERTA

Child's Use of Language According to Classroom Setting:

	English	Spanish	Other
Blockbuilding	_____	_____	_____
Art	_____	_____	_____
Science	_____	_____	_____
Library	_____	_____	_____
Housekeeping/Dramatic Arts	_____	_____	_____
Sand/Water	_____	_____	_____
Music	_____	_____	_____
Manipulatives	_____	_____	_____
Outdoors	_____	_____	_____
Snacks/Meals/Routines	_____	_____	_____
Totals	_____	_____	_____

Complexity of Child's Use of Language in Classroom:
(NOTE: Here circle the number that *best* represents how the child uses each language. Count only circled numbers in totals.)

	English	Spanish	Other
Single words	1	1	1
Phrases/sentences	3	3	3
Full conversations	5	5	5
Totals	_____	_____	_____

The combined totals are: _____ _____ _____

The **combined totals** indicate that this child should *initially* be placed in an:

☐ English monolingual cluster   ☐ English-dominant bilingual cluster

☐ Spanish monolingual cluster   ☐ Spanish-dominant bilingual cluster

☐ _____ monolingual cluster   ☐ _____-dominant bilingual cluster

A Plan for Ongoing Child Observations:
Continuous Use of ALERTA's Level 5

Weeks	Observers	Circle Only Observations of Child Interests	Underline Only Observations of Skills/ Developmental Levels	Circle Observations of Interests and Underline Skills/Developmental Levels	Observations of Language Proficiency

[3]After week 12, teachers continue observing the children's interests, skills, and developmental levels throughout the year. Language proficiency observations can be incorporated into the ongoing anecdotal observations.

Collected Child Interests

English Monolingual Cluster	English-dominant Bilingual Cluster

Spanish-dominant Bilingual Cluster*	Spanish Monolingual Cluster*

*Substitute as appropriate the second language used in your program.

Individualizing a Theme

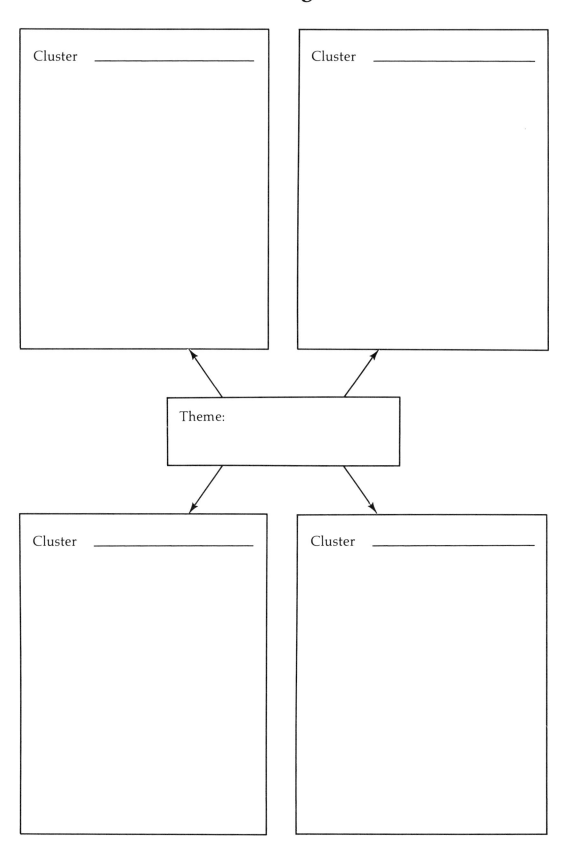

Cluster _____

Cluster _____

Theme:

Cluster _____

Cluster _____

Procedure for Adapting and/or Revising the Learning Goals and Objectives

Talk with other people working in the classroom(s) at your school or center.

1. Do the children in your classroom appear to be at the same developmental level as the children for whom these goals and objectives were designed? Yes ☐   No ☐

2. Write the names of all of the children in your class on slips of paper and put the paper slips into a bag. Without looking at the names, draw out ten of the slips. Using the list of goals and objectives from the source book, discuss which objectives have already been achieved by each of the ten children you picked out.

_____

_____

3. On the basis of what you have found about the achievements of a sample of children in your program, how should you change the objectives listed in the chapter to better fit the developmental levels of your children?

_____

_____

Talk with the parents of the children in your classroom.

1. Give the parents copies of the goals and objectives. (You might want to spread this activity out over several meetings so that people will not have too much to react to at once.)

2. Discuss the goals and objectives with the parents, asking which ones they would change and what their reasoning is for the change.

Goals and objectives to be changed: ———————————————————————

_____

Reasons for suggested changes: _____

_____

3. Ask the parents for suggestions of other goals and objectives to be added.

Goals and objectives to be added: _____

_____

_____

Talk with your administrators and/or advisory board.

1. Give your administrators and/or advisory board copies of the goals and objectives. (Again, the board might prefer to read them section by section.)

2. Do the administrators or board members see any special needs of the children or circumstances in their community that are not reflected in the goals and objectives?

Suggestions: _____

_____

_____

_____

3. Do the administrators and/or board members have in mind specific changes for goals and objectives?

Changes suggested: _____

_____

Reasons for suggested changes: _____

_____

Put it all together.

1. One person from your school or center should take notes from all three types of meetings and put the suggestions together on a master copy of the goals and objectives.

2. The revised version of the listing should be typed up and given to each member of the staff. The revised listing should also be made available to the parents and members of the advisory board.

3. Space is provided below for the staff member who is putting all the suggestions together to make notes.

_____

_____

_____

_____

_____

_____

Use an additional piece of paper to complete any of these items.

Summary of Goals and Objectives to Use in Activity Planning over the Next Week

English Monolingual Cluster

Goal Area: _____   Objective _____

Goal Area: _____   Objective _____

Goal Area: _____   Objective _____

English-dominant Bilingual Cluster

Goal Area: _____   Objective _____

Goal Area: _____   Objective _____

Goal Area: _____   Objective _____

Spanish-dominant Bilingual Cluster

Goal Area: _____   Objective _____

Goal Area: _____   Objective _____

Goal Area: _____   Objective _____

Spanish Monolingual Cluster

Goal Area: _____   Objective _____

Goal Area: _____   Objective _____

Goal Area: _____   Objective _____

ALERTA Weekly Planning Form

Classroom: _____

Theme: _____

Language Cluster: _____

Children's Names: _____

_____

Room Areas/Reflection of Theme

Housekeeping:
Blockbuilding:
Art/Music:
Library:
Water/Sand:
Manipulatives:
Science:

	Goals/Objectives	Activity	Materials from Culture/Environment
Monday			
Tuesday			
Wednesday			
Thursday			
Friday			

Is This Learning Activity Appropriate?

1. Does this activity build on interests of children in the cluster? Yes ☐   No ☐

2. Is this activity appropriate for the developmental levels of the children in this cluster? Yes ☐   No ☐

3. Will this activity help the children in my group meet a specific objective (chosen ahead of time) of the ALERTA Program? Yes ☐   No ☐

4. Does the activity allow the children to be actively and directly involved in their learning? Will the children be able to manipulate materials or otherwise use their bodies during the course of the activity? Yes ☐   No ☐

5. Will this activity make use of material coming from the children's environment and/or cultures (if that is appropriate to the objective chosen)? Yes ☐   No ☐

6. Does this activity make use of learning materials that we already have in the classroom or center or that we could make? Yes ☐   No ☐

7. Will this activity work with the group or cluster size I am planning it for?
Yes ☐   No ☐

Daily Schedule for My Classroom

ALERTA

Questions to Consider in Reviewing Audiotapes of Activities Incorporating Strategies for Promotion of the Children's First or Dominant Language

1. Were the children very interested in the activity? Did the activity stimulate a lot of spontaneous language? What were some of the comments that revealed the children's interest?

_____

_____

2. How frequently did you initiate a comment or explanation? (Tally the number of times you spoke during the activity. Time the length of your comments to see how long your speaking took.)

_____

How frequently did individual children comment, ask a question, or otherwise speak during the activity? (Tally the number of times the individual children spoke, and time the length of their speaking.)

_____

_____

3. Were you using a conversational style throughout the activity? What is an example of that style?

_____

4. Did you use variety in the language structures you employed? What are some examples?

_____

_____

5. Did your activity introduce the children to any new concepts? If so, what were those concepts?

_____

6. What are some examples of open-ended questions that you wove through the activity?

_____

_____

Questions to Consider in Reviewing Audiotapes of Activities Incorporating Strategies for Promotion of a Second Language in Monolingual Children

1. Did you build on a concept the children already learned in their first language? Did you use a different activity from one you had used to teach the concept in the children's first language?

2. Did you introduce a limited amount of vocabulary at one time? How many words did you introduce in this activity?

3. Did you imbed the new vocabulary words in a natural context? What context?

4. Did you use an activity with a lot of action? What actions did the children do?

5. Did you use objects familiar to the children in the activity? What objects were they?

6. Did you allow the children to manipulate and explore the objects? How did the children do this?

7. How did you provide opportunities for natural repetition of the vocabulary to be learned?

8. Was it appropriate to use a song or game in this activity? If so, what song or game did you use?

Questions to Consider in Reviewing Audiotapes of Activities Incorporating Strategies for Promotion of a Second Language in Bilingual Children

1. Were the children very interested in the activity? Did the activity stimulate a lot of spontaneous language? What were some of the comments that revealed the children's interest?

_____

_____

_____

2. How frequently did you initiate a comment or explanation? (Tally the number of times you spoke during the activity. Time the length of your comments to see how long your speaking took.)

_____

_____

How frequently did individual children comment, ask a question, or otherwise speak during the activity? (Tally the number of times the individual children spoke, and time the length of their speaking.)

_____

_____

_____

3. Were you using a conversational style throughout the activity? What is an example of that style?

_____

_____

_____

4. Did you use variety in the language structures you employed? What are some examples?

_____

_____

_____

5. What are some examples of open-ended questions that you wove through the activity?

_____

_____

6. Did you build on a concept the children already had learned in their first language? Did you use a different activity from one you had used to teach the concept in the children's first language?

_____

_____

_____

7. Did you use an activity with a lot of action? What actions did the children do?

_____

_____

8. Did you use objects familiar to the children in the activity? What objects were they?

_____

_____

9. Did you allow the children to manipulate and explore the objects? How did the children do this?

_____

_____

10. How did you provide opportunities for natural repetition of the vocabulary to be learned?

_____

_____

11. What gaps were evident in the children's use of their second language? How did you help the children learn the appropriate word or phrase they lacked?

_____

_____

_____

ALERTA Daily Individualized Planning Form

Classroom: _____   Date: _____

Language Cluster	Spanish Monolingual	English Monolingual	Spanish-dominant Bilingual	English-dominant Bilingual		
Theme						
Goals/ Objectives						
Activity						
Language Strategies	1st language	1st language	1st language	1st language		
	2nd language	2nd language	2nd language	2nd language		
Large-Group Activities						
Notes on Resources to Be Used						

What Do You Think?

If you wanted to encourage the children's development during their free-choice time without taking over the activity, which of the following might you do? (Check all the answers that you feel reflect ALERTA's intent.)

- [ ] 1. Set up opportunities for learning in each of the classroom areas before the children come to school.

- [ ] 2. Go into the housekeeping area and say, "Who's going to make me dinner?"

- [ ] 3. Say to the children working in the blockbuilding area, "That's not the way a garage should look. How about making it like this. . . ."

- [ ] 4. Move from area to area of the room slowly, interacting with children who invite your comments.

- [ ] 5. Say to the children at the easels, "I'll give you some paper so you can draw your houses."

- [ ] 6. Give a box of costumes and masks to children who are acting out a parade they saw.

- [ ] 7. Point out the weighing scales to two children who are trying to decide whether a piece of wood is heavier than the magnet they have.

- [ ] 8. Say to children working with clay, "What sorts of things can be done with this clay?"

- [ ] 9. Put a story record on to play softly in the library corner where a child is looking at a book of the same story.

- [ ] 10. Get out an instrument and start playing and singing one of the children's favorite songs.

Indicators of Progress in the Use of ALERTA

Center/School _____   Teacher(s) _____

Classroom _____   Observer(s) _____

Directions: For each of the items below, rate the degree of program implementation that you have observed in this classroom.

Key: 0 = No implementation
      1 = Implementation begun
      2 = Consistent use (but not yet perfected)
      3 = Full implementation

1. Partnerships are evident in carrying out the program.   _____

2. Parents' input is encouraged and coordinated.   _____

3. Hallways, offices, kitchen, etc., reflect the cultures and interests of program participants.   _____

4. Materials in classroom areas reflect the community, cultures, interests, and developmental levels of the children.   _____

5. Daily teacher-directed activities make use of themes, goals and objectives, and content drawn from cultures and community.   _____

6. The teacher-directed activities (clusters) incorporate strategies for first language development and second language acquisition.   _____

7. Provision is made for a period of child-initiated work each day.   _____

8. Both languages addressed in the program are used throughout the day.   _____

9. Staff members do daily written child observations.   _____

10. Staff members make direct use of their child observations in daily and weekly planning.   _____

Patterns Revealed in Reviewing
Child Observations and Activity Plans

1. Do your collected observations of the skills and developmental levels of the children in each language cluster show steady attainment in each of the four major goal areas over the year? If not, describe patterns that appear.

_____

_____

2. Do your collected observations of the children's skills and developmental levels show balanced profiles of attainment over the four major goal areas for _individual_ children? If not, describe patterns that appear.

_____

_____

3. Do your collected observations of child interests show heavy use of _all_ the areas of your classroom? If not, describe patterns that appear.

_____

_____

4. Do your collected activity plans show regular use of themes drawn directly from the children's interests? If not, describe patterns that appear.

_____

_____

5. Do your collected activity plans show use of community and cultural content drawn from the traditions of _all_ the families that participated in your program (rather than from the traditions of only one or two groups)? If not, describe patterns that appear.

_____

_____

6. Do your collected activity plans show connections of themes, goals and objectives, and cultural/community content in cluster work with the materials made available in the various classroom areas and with activities done with the class as a whole? If not, describe patterns that appear.

_____

_____

Parent/Administrator Interview

1. After working with ALERTA for a year, do you feel there is something you have learned from the program that you would like to talk about?

_____

_____

2. Do you think that using ALERTA in our school (or center) was helpful to the children? to the parents? Would you explain your answers?

_____

_____

3. How far along do you feel we are in using the program? (Are we just beginning? still learning? using it the way it was designed to be used?) How did you come to your conclusion? (How do you know?)

_____

_____

4. What things about ALERTA do you think worked particularly well this year?

_____

_____

5. What things do you feel did not work so well as you had hoped they would?

_____

_____

6. What could we do to improve those areas?

_____

_____

Guide for Observing
Children's Present Skills/Attitudes

Child's Name _____   Date of Birth _____

School/Classroom _____   Teacher(s) _____

Date Observations Begin _____   Date Observations End _____

Goal Area One: Appreciation of Self as Capable of a Wide Variety of Intellectual and Physical Activities

1.   The child shows willingness to try new activities.

Dates Observed: Specific instances:

_____   _____

_____   _____

_____   _____

_____   _____

2.   The child communicates to others the belief that he/she can do the new activity.

Dates Observed: Specific instances:

_____   _____

_____   _____

_____   _____

_____   _____

3. The child shows pride in work completed.

Dates Observed: Specific instances:

_____   _____

_____   _____

_____   _____

_____   _____

4. The child describes things he/she likes to do.

Dates Observed: Specific instances:

_____   _____

_____   _____

_____   _____

_____   _____

5. The child defines a space in which he/she can work without interfering with the work of others.

Dates Observed: Specific instances:

_____   _____

_____   _____

_____   _____

_____   _____

6. The child initiates and calls a halt to activities.

Dates Observed: Specific instances:

_____   _____

_____   _____

_____   _____

_____   _____

7. The child participates in both quiet and active experiences.

Dates Observed: Specific instances:

_____   _____

_____   _____

_____   _____

8. The child works in all areas of the classroom.

Dates Observed: Specific instances:

_____   _____

_____   _____

_____   _____

_____   _____

Goal Area Two: Positive Recognition of the Ways People from Various Groups Are the Same/Different

1. The child describes some of his/her family customs.

Dates Observed: Specific instances:

_____   _____

_____   _____

_____   _____

2. The child associates himself/herself and his/her family with a particular cultural group (or groups).

Dates Observed: Specific instances:

_____   _____

_____   _____

_____   _____

3. The child describes characteristics of himself/herself and members of his/her family.

Dates Observed: Specific instances:

_____   _____

_____   _____

_____   _____

_____   _____

4. The child describes ways in which people are alike (for instance, all have names, all can feel happy or sad, all live somewhere, and so on).

Dates Observed: Specific instances:

_____   _____

_____   _____

_____   _____

_____   _____

5. The child identifies something unique about himself/herself.

Dates Observed: Specific instances:

_____   _____

_____   _____

_____   _____

_____   _____

6. The child describes ways in which people may be different from one another (for instance, differences in height or coloring; differences associated with infancy, childhood, or maturity; differences in ways of doing things at home).

Dates Observed: Specific instances:

_____   _____

_____   _____

_____   _____

_____   _____

7. The child associates friends with particular cultural groups, events, or customs.

Dates Observed: Specific instances:

_____   _____

_____   _____

_____   _____

_____   _____

8. The child associates objects, events, or customs new to him/her with particular cultural groups.

Dates Observed: Specific instances:

_____   _____

_____   _____

_____   _____

_____   _____

Goal Area Three: Communication and Problem Solving

1. The child is able to describe the uses of most of the common objects found in his/her classroom and in his/her home.

Dates Observed: Specific instances:

_____   _____

_____   _____

_____   _____

_____   _____

2. The child is able to describe the common attributes of objects.

Dates Observed:

_____   a. Color

_____   b. Shape

_____   c. Size

_____   d. Weight

_____   e. Texture

_____   f. Taste

_____   g. Smell

_____   Others:

3. The child is able to describe situations or events that are a part of his/her environment (e.g., workers repairing the street).

Dates Observed: Specific instances:

_____   _____

_____   _____

_____   _____

_____   _____

4. The child is able to describe processes in which he/she participates (e.g., how he/she helped feed the baby).

Dates Observed: Specific instances:

_____   _____

_____   _____

_____   _____

_____   _____

5. The child is able to create and/or carry out a role play in which he/she uses non-verbal communication to represent various characters.

_____ a. Works alone

_____ b. Interacts with peers

_____ c. Interacts with adults

6. The child develops ways to answer his/her questions about objects by "experimenting" with them (e.g., finding out which objects are heavier than others by weighing them).

Dates Observed: Specific instances:

_____   _____

_____   _____

_____   _____

_____   _____

7. The child is able to group objects in various ways.

_____ a. Color

_____ b. Size

_____ c. Shape

_____ d. Texture

_____ e. Function

_____ f. Association

8. The child is able to arrange objects in an identifiable sequence.

_____ a. Tallest to shortest

_____ b. Thickest to thinnest

_____ c. Largest to smallest

_____ d. Heaviest to lightest

                    Others:

9. The child demonstrates his/her understanding of and ability to use comparative and superlative terms.

_____ a. Big, bigger, biggest

_____ b. Small, smaller, smallest

_____ c. Thin, thinner, thinnest

_____ d. Fat, fatter, fattest

_____ e. Heavy, heavier, heaviest

_____ f. Light, lighter, lightest

_____ g. Tall, taller, tallest

_____ h. Short, shorter, shortest

_____ Others:

10. The child demonstrates his/her ability to use terms which show spatial relationships.

_____ a. In front of

_____ b. In back of

_____ c. Over

_____ d. Under

_____ e. Around

_____ f. In

_____ Others:

11. The child demonstrates his/her ability to use terms which show a relationship to time.

_____ a. Now

_____ b. Before

_____ c. After

_____ d. First, next, last

_____ Others:

12. The child demonstrates a one-to-one correspondence between common objects (for example, providing a full set of clothing for each doll).

Dates Observed: Specific instances:

_____   _____

_____   _____

_____   _____

_____   _____

13. The child demonstrates his/her understanding of the concepts "more than," "less than"/"fewer than," and "the same as"/"as many as," in relation to weight, volume, and number of objects, when the arrangement of the objects or the containers holding the objects are identical.

Dates Observed: Specific instances:

_____   _____

_____   _____

_____   _____

_____   _____

14. The child follows as many as three simple directions in sequence (for example, "Henry, please pick up the books and take them to the library corner, and place them on the top shelf.").

Dates Observed: Specific instances:

_____   _____

_____   _____

_____   _____

_____   _____

15. The child uses language as part of the problem-solving process (to predict, hypothesize, etc.) when they are faced with objects or events that they do not presently understand (for example, "I think that . . .", "What will happen is . . .", "Maybe next week . . .").

Dates Observed: Specific instances:

_____   _____

_____   _____

_____   _____

_____   _____

16. The child gives directions to another in order to assist in solving a problem (for example, "You need a ramp to make the road smooth.").

Dates Observed: Specific instances:

_____   _____

_____   _____

_____   _____

_____   _____

17. The child moves from use of simple materials to use of materials of increasing complexity.

Dates Observed: Specific instances:

_____   _____

_____   _____

_____   _____

_____   _____

18. The child uses materials symbolically as well as literally (for instance, using a block as a "truck," as well as using it to build a structure).

Dates Observed: Specific instances:

_____   _____

_____   _____

_____   _____

_____   _____

Goal Area Four: Acquisition of Specific Attitudes and Skills for Success in School within a Culturally Plural Society

1. The child shows trust for other children and for adults by inviting interaction with them.

Dates Observed: Specific instances:

_____   _____

_____   _____

_____   _____

_____   _____

2. The child works cooperatively with others when appropriate.

Dates Observed: Specific instances:

_____   _____

_____   _____

_____   _____

_____   _____

3. The child works independently when appropriate.

Dates Observed: Specific instances:

_____   _____

_____   _____

_____   _____

_____   _____

4. The child shows and talks about his/her feelings.

Dates Observed: Specific instances:

_____   _____

_____   _____

_____   _____

_____   _____

5. The child describes how another child may be feeling in a given situation.

Dates Observed: Specific instances:

_____   _____

_____   _____

_____   _____

_____   _____

6. The child accepts that he/she might not have objects or experiences that are unsafe or otherwise inappropriate in a given situation.

Dates Observed: Specific instances:

_____   _____

_____   _____

_____   _____

_____   _____

7. The child uses language to work out difficulties arising between himself/herself and other children.

Dates Observed: Specific instances:

_____   _____

_____   _____

_____   _____

_____   _____

8. The child invites other children different from himself/herself to play or work with him/her.

Dates Observed: Specific instances:

_____   _____

_____   _____

_____   _____

_____   _____

9. The child attends to his/her own hygiene (such as toileting, toothbrushing, handwashing).

Dates Observed: Specific instances:

_____   _____

_____   _____

_____   _____

_____

10. The child puts on or takes off outside clothing with a minimum of adult assistance.

Dates Observed: Specific instances:

_____   _____

_____   _____

_____   _____

_____

11. The child serves self at snack or lunch without spilling food or drink.

Dates Observed: Specific instances:

_____   _____

_____   _____

_____   _____

_____

12. The child gets out materials to work with and puts them away when finished.

Dates Observed: Specific instances:

_____   _____

_____   _____

_____   _____

_____   _____

ALERTA

13. The child shows respect for his/her environment by keeping it clean and by taking care of the animals and plants within it.

Dates Observed: Specific instances:

_____   _____

_____   _____

_____   _____

_____   _____

14. The child uses materials that require coordination of the fingers.

Dates Observed: Specific instances:

_____   _____

_____   _____

_____   _____

_____   _____

15. The child uses materials that require use of the whole body.

Dates Observed: Specific instances:

_____   _____

_____   _____

_____   _____

_____   _____

16. The child reproduces and creates body movements that go together in a particular sequence (as in a dance or a game).

Dates Observed: Specific instances:

_____   _____

_____   _____

_____   _____

_____   _____

17. The child reproduces and creates sound patterns (as in repeating songs or rhymes and in making up sounds to accompany a story).

Dates Observed: Specific instances:

_____   _____

_____   _____

_____   _____

_____   _____

18. The child reproduces and creates visual patterns (as in doing puzzles, weaving a mat, or stringing beads in a particular order).

Dates Observed: Specific instances:

_____   _____

_____   _____

_____   _____

_____   _____

Resource List

This resource list has been compiled to aid teachers in developing materials and activities that reflect the specific cultures, experiences, developmental levels, and interests of the children in their classrooms. Some of the books contain descriptions of elements of particular cultures and may provide information new to teachers who are working with children from those groups. It should be understood that the perspectives represented in these books vary. Inclusion of the book on the list does not imply that the material it contains is noncontrovertible. Instead, these books are seen as possible points of departure which may inspire teachers to add to their own ideas or create new ones for the effective teaching of the children they serve.

Multicultural Strategies/Approaches/Information

Baker, G.C. *Planning and Organizing for Multicultural Education.* Menlo Park, CA: Addison-Wesley Publishing Company, 1982.

Banks, J. A. *Teaching Strategies for Ethnic Studies.* Boston: Allyn and Bacon, 1975.

Cardona, L. A. *An Annotated Bibliography of Puerto Rican Materials.* Bethesda, MD: Carreta Press, 1983.

Chase, J. and L. Parth. *Multicultural Spoken Here: Discovering America's People through Language Arts and Library Skills.* Santa Monica, CA: Goodyear Publishing Company, Inc., 1979.

Dunfee, M. *Eliminating Ethnic Bias in Instructional Materials: Comment and Bibliography.* Washington, DC: Association for Supervision and Curriculum Development (1701 K Street, Suite 1100, Washington, DC, 20006), 1974.

García, E. E., I. Ortiz, and F. Lomeli. *Chicano Studies: A Multidisciplinary Approach.* New York: Teachers College Press, 1984.

Gold, M. J., C. A. Grant, and H. N. Rivlin, eds. *In Praise of Diversity: A Resource Book for Multicultural Education.* Washington, DC: Teacher Corps and the Association of Teacher Educators, 1977.

Gollnick, D. M. and P. C. Chin. *Multicultural Education in a Pluralistic Society.* St. Louis: The C. V. Mosby Company, 1983.

Griffin, L., compiler. *Multi-ethnic Books for Young Children.* Washington, DC: National Association for the Education of Young Children, 1970.

Guide to Implementing Multi-cultural, Non-sexist Curriculum Programs in Iowa Schools. State of Iowa Department of Public Instruction (Grimes State Office Building, Des Moines, IA, 50319), 1976.

Guidelines for Selecting Bias-free Textbooks and Storybooks. New York: Council on Interracial Books for Children (1841 Broadway, New York, NY, 10023), n.d.

Hale, J. *Black Children: Their Roots, Culture and Learning Style.* Provo, UT: Brigham Young University Press, 1984.

Hansen-Krening, N. *Language Experiences for All Students.* Menlo Park, CA: Addison-Wesley Publishing Company, 1982.

Interracial Books for Children Bulletin. New York: Council on Interracial Books for Children, 1966–present.

Kendall, F. E. *Diversity in the Classroom: A Multicultural Approach to the Education of Young Children.* New York: Teachers College Press, 1983.

King, E. W. *Teaching Ethnic Awareness: Methods and Materials.* Santa Monica, CA: Goodyear Publishing Company, 1980.

Lass-Woodfin, M. J. *Selected Books on American Indians.* Chicago: American Library Association, 1977.

Mills, J., ed. *The Black World in Literature for Children: A Bibliography of Print and Non-print Materials.* Atlanta: Atlanta University School of Library Science, 1975.

Perl, L. *Piñatas and Paper Flowers: Holidays of the Americas in English and Spanish.* New York: Clarion Books, 1983.

Saracho, O. N. and B. Spodek, eds. *Understanding the Multicultural Experience in Early Childhood Education.* Washington, DC: National Association for the Education of Young Children, 1983.

Stone, J. C. and D.P. DeNevi, eds. *Teaching Multi-cultural Populations: Five Heritages.* New York: D. Van Nostrand Company, 1971.

Tiedt, P. L. and I. M. Tiedt. *Multicultural Teaching: A Handbook of Activities, Information and Resources.* Boston: Allyn and Bacon, Inc., 1979.

Van Why, E. W., compiler. *Adoption Bibliography and Multi-ethnic Sourcebook.* West Hartland, CT: Open Door Society of Connecticut, 1977.

Wisconsin Department of Public Instruction. *Starting Out Right: Choosing Books about Black People for Young Children, Preschool through Third Grade.* Washington, DC: Day Care and Child Development Council of America, n.d.

Classroom Ideas/Materials Construction

Baratta-Lorton, M. *Workjobs.* Menlo Park, CA: Addison-Wesley Publishing Company, 1972.

Baratta-Lorton, M. *Workjobs II.* Menlo Park, CA: Addison-Wesley Publishing Company, 1979.

Bates, E. and R. Lowes. *Potpourri of Puppetry.* Belmont, CA: Fearon Publishers, Inc., 1976.

Burton, L. and W. Hughes. *MusicPlay.* Menlo Park, CA: Addison-Wesley Publishing Company, 1979.

Burton, L. and K. Kuroda. *ArtsPlay.* Menlo Park, CA: Addison-Wesley Publishing Company, 1981.

Cole, A., C. Hass, F. Bushnell, and B. Weinberger. *I Saw a Purple Cow.* Boston: Little, Brown and Company, 1972.

Davidson, T., et al. *The Learning Center Book: An Integrated Approach.* Pacific Palisades, CA: Goodyear Publishing Company, Inc., 1976.

Huff, V. *Let's Make Paper Dolls.* New York: Harper and Row, 1973.

Jenkins Kohl, J. and P. Macdonald. *Growing Up Equal.* Englewood Cliffs, NJ: Prentice-Hall, Inc., 1979.

Johnson, S. and L. Moolenaar. *Folk Toys of the Virgin Islands.* Project Introspection, Department of Education, Government of the United States, Virgin Islands, 1973.

Kohl, M. and F. Young. *Games for Children.* New York: Cornerstone Library, 1979.

Krevy, N. and P. Byrnes. *Southwestern Arts and Crafts Projects.* Santa Fe, NM: The Sunstone Press, 1979.

Marzollo, J. and J. Lloyd. *Learning through Play.* New York: Harper and Row, 1972.

Orlans, F. B. *Animal Care From Protozoa to Small Mammals.* Menlo Park, CA: Addison-Wesley Publishing Company, 1977.

Platts, M. E. *Create.* Stevensville, MI: Educational Service, Inc., 1977.

Rippy, R., ed. *Finding and Using Scrounge Materials.* New York: Teacher Corps at The Bank Street College of Education, 1975.

Seidelman, J. E. and G. Mintonye. *Shopping Cart Art.* New York: Collier Books, 1970.

Tarrow, N. B. and S. W. Lundsteen. *Activities and Resources for Guiding Young Children's Learning.* New York: McGraw-Hill, 1981.

Veitch, B. and T. Harms. *Cook and Learn.* Menlo Park, CA: Addison-Wesley Publishing Company, 1981.

A Sample Library Collection
for an ALERTA Classroom

The following list of children's books provides an example of the contents of the library area in one ALERTA classroom. The area has been designed for use by four- and five-year-old children living in an urban area. Approximately one third of the children are Black, coming from several parts of the United States and the Caribbean. Another third are Hispanic. Their families originate from the United States, Mexico, the Caribbean, and South America. A few children are recent immigrants from Vietnam. The remaining children are of a variety of European descents. The key to selection of books for the library is to provide the children with as many opportunities as possible to see themselves reflected in reading materials. In such cases, books with no particular cultural orientation (such as animal stories, fantasy works, and concept books) would be included in the collection, as they are in this example.

Alexander, M. *Nobody Asked Me if I Wanted a Baby Sister.* New York: Dial Press, 1971. (Feelings surrounding the arrival of a sibling)

Alexander, M. *The Story Grandmother Told.* New York: Dial Press, 1969. (African-American)

Anderson, L. *The Day the Hurricane Happened.* New York: Charles Scribner's Sons, 1974. (Caribbean Black)

Ayer, J. *Nu Dang and his Kite.* New York: Harcourt Brace Jovanvich, 1959. (Thai)

Baldwin, A. N. *Sunflowers for Tina.* New York: Four Winds Press, 1970 (African-American)

Belpré, Pura. *Santiago.* New York: Warne, 1968. (Puerto Rican)

Blue, R. *I am Here: Yo estoy aquí.* New York: Franklin Watts, Inc., 1971. (Hispanic)

Brenner, B. *Faces.* New York: E. P. Dutton and Company, Inc., 1970. (Concept of variety in the human face)

Burch, J. *Joey's Cat.* New York: Viking Press, Inc. 1969. (African-American)

Caines, J. F. *Window Wishing.* New York: Harper and Row, Publishers, 1980. (African-American)

Cameron, A. *The Seed.* New York: Pantheon Books, 1975. (Concept of growth and change)

Carter, D. S. *The Enchanted Orchard and Other Folktales of Central America.* New York: Harcourt Brace Jovanovich, 1973. (Hispanic)

Clifton, L. *The Boy Who Didn't Believe in Spring.* New York: E. P. Dutton and Company, Inc., 1973. (Urban environment)

Del Rosario, R., I. Freire de Matos, and A. Martorell. *A B C de Puerto Rico.* Sharon, CT: Troutman Press, 1968. (Puerto Rican)

De Paola, T. *Watch Out for the Chicken Feet in your Soup.* Englewood Cliffs, NJ: Prentice-Hall, Inc., 1974. (Italian-American)

Eichler, M. *Martin's Father.* New York: Lollipop Power, 1971. (Sex role reversal in parenting)

Ets, M. H. *Gilberto and the Wind.* New York: Viking Press, Inc., 1963. (Mexican-American)

Fujikawa, G. *Puppies, Pussy Cats and Other Friends.* Tokyo: Zokeisha Publications, 1975. (Animal story)

Greenfield, E. *Africa Dream.* New York: John Day, 1977. (African-American)

Grifalconi, A. *City Rhythms.* Indianapolis: Bobbs-Merrill Company, Inc., 1975. (Urban environment)

Guardarrama, E. *Un Sueño musical.* Bronx, NY: Canbbe Northeast, Northeast Regional Curriculum Adaptation Center, 1975. (Hispanic)

Hitte, K. *Mexicali Soup.* New York: Parents Magazine Press, 1970. (Chicano)

Hoban, T. *Count and See.* New York: MacMillan Company, 1972. (Concept of number)

Howell, R. R. *A Crack in the Pavement.* New York: Atheneum Publications, 1970. (Urban environment)

Lapp, E. *In the Morning Mist.* Chicago: Albert Whitman and Company, 1978. (European descent)

Leaf, M. and R. Lawson. *The Story of Ferdinand the Bull.* New York: Viking Press, 1964. (European descent)

McClosky, R. *Blueberries for Sal.* New York: Viking Press, 1948. (European descent)

McGovern, A. *Black is Beautiful.* New York: Scholastic Books Services, 1969. (African-American)

Maiorano, R. *Francisco.* New York: Macmillan Company, 1978. (Dominican)

Rosario, I. *Idalia's Project A B C: An Urban Alphabet Book in English and Spanish.* New York: Holt, Rinehart and Winston, Inc., 1981. (Urban environment)

Sendak, M. *Where the Wild Things Are.* New York: Harper and Row Publishers, 1963. (Fantasy)

Serra Deliz, W. *Poemas y colores.* Universidad de Puerto Rico: Editorial Edil, 1968. (Hispanic)

Shub, E. *Seeing is Believing.* New York: Greenwillow Books, 1979. (European descent)

Simon, N. *All Kinds of Families.* Chicago: Albert Whitman and Company, 1975. (Concept of variation in family composition)

Solbert, R. *I Wrote my Name on the Wall.* Boston: Little, Brown and Company, 1971. (Multiethnic urban environment)

Trần, V. D. and W. Gritter, eds. *Cô Tích Nhi Đồng: Folktales for Children.* Skokie, IL: National Textbook Company, 1982. (Vietnamese)

Vuong, L. D. *The Brocaded Slipper and Other Vietnamese Tales.* Reading, MA: Addison-Wesley, 1982. (Vietnamese)

Yarbrough, C. *Cornrows.* New York: Coward, McCann and Geoghegan, 1979. (African-American)

ALERTA